Mitteilungen der Vorderasiatischen Gesellschaft. 1905. 3.
Eingetragener Verein.

10. Jahrgang.

The Doctrine

of

Sin in the Babylonian Religion.

By

Julian Morgenstern.

THE BOOK TREE
SAN DIEGO, CALIFORNIA

Originally published 1905

ISBN 1-58509-204-5

Cover layout and design
Lee Berube

Printed on Acid-Free Paper
in the United States and United Kingdom
by LightningSource, Inc.

Published by
The Book Tree
P O Box 16476
San Diego, CA 92176

INTRODUCTION

This is an extremely rare and important book on religion, first published in Germany in 1905. When studied closely it reveals powerful and interesting aspects of the idea of sin and its origins. Most people believe that the concept of sin first arose in Christianity with Adam and Eve in the Garden of Eden. This may have been the first instance of sin, but Christianity was not around for another two thousand years (or more) to include it in their belief structure. In the meantime, those who recognized the concept of sin included the Babylonians, among others.

The recognition of sin and trying to avoid it in ancient Babylon is ironic because Christianity in general considers Babylonia to have been one of the most sinful and depraved societies to have ever existed. To this day the evil stigma remains strong toward this ancient culture. The reasoning behind this stems from the fact that Babylonians worshipped multiple gods, which is often seen as evil or misguided by Christians, who worship only one. Also is the fact that the first civilized culture to recognize sin would (and did) record many instances of it occurring—which would not go unnoticed by later religions.

The first page of this book clarifies what sin really was, in its original form. It is defined as having been anything done to anger the gods. With multiple gods present in this culture, the likelihood of angering any of them is magnified when compared to a monotheistic belief structure. This definition does not go against the Adam and Eve scenario, who angered God so much in the Garden of Eden that they were permanently banned from "paradise." Nor does it go against multiple gods being angered, since the word for God in the Old Testament is *elohim*—which is actually a plural word when translated properly.

Facts like this make this book an indispensable and vital source for early theological truths. It offers an outstanding rundown on the early gods, who they were and what they stood for. This book is jam-packed with information one will not find elsewhere concerning our origins, the source of evil, the gods themselves, and humankind's interactions with them.

Paul Tice

Table of contents.

		pp.
	Tahle of Contents	III
Chap. I.	The Babylonian Conception of Sin	1
Chap. II.	Evil Spirits	6
Chap. III.	Good Spirits	22
Chap. IV.	Removal of Evil Spirits	28
Chap. V.	The Gods of the *Āšipu*-Ritual	83
Chap. VI.	The Sin-Offering	101
Chap. VII.	Analyses	119
Chap. VIII.	Recapitulation	141
Chap. IX.	Purification-ceremonies in the *Bārū*-Ritual	146
	Conclusion	152
	General Index	154
	Index to Biblical Passages	157

Chap. I.

The Babylonian Conception of Sin.

As has been shown, religion was originally the relation existing between the gods and man. The duty of man to bring sacrifices and to please the gods in every possible way, that he might enjoy their favor — this was religion. The relation of man to man was entirely foreign to this. Not until late do religion and morals become one[1]).

Misfortune of all kinds was the result of the divine anger. The gods were the arbiters of destiny, the judges, who decreed good or evil as man deserved. If evil came, the god was angry. What could have caused this? Sin! This is one of the fundamental principles of the Babylonian religion, if not of all primitive religions — whatever incites the anger of the gods, is sin[2]).

And what could this sin have been; what could have so enraged the deity that he sent this evil? Perhaps the unfortunate

---

[1]) Cf. Tiele: "Elements of the Science of religion." I102 Relig. Sem. 53f.

[2]) Notice that this is the argument advanced by Bildad, Job 83—4 This principle is especially noticeable in the Babylonian "penitential psalms". There the afflicted man cries out in his anguish, "The sin I have committed, I do not know" (B. P. IV obv. 19—21, 42—45 cf. V R. 50a 33/34) His suffering proved that he must have sinned, although he could not tell wherein the sin lay. Often he would accuse himself of many sins (B. P. II rev. 3/4; IV obv. 36—41, rev. 45—48; VII obv. 18; B. M. S. VII 47), would regard himself as a sinner from childhood (Cr. II pl. 3 obv. 19—21). Sometimes he did not even know against what god he had sinned; who it was that was angry. (B. P. IV obv. 3—9). For this principle in the N. T. cf. John 9, 2.

man had violated the laws of justice; had wronged a neighbor, whose protecting god thus exacted vengeance. This answer is possible, and, as morals became more and more a part of religion, came indeed to be considered a valid cause of divine anger. But originally this lay nearer home. What could have aroused this anger, must have been some wrong offered the god himself. But since man was related to the gods only in a religious sense, only through sacrifice, sin must originally have been purely ritual. Either the man had neglected to offer his sacrifice, or else had not offered it properly[1].

For not everything was suitable for sacrifice. The gods partook of only the purest foods, offered in such a manner that no uncleanliness could come upon them. The least impurity, and the sacrifice was defiled[2]. And not every one could offer sacrifice or participate in the divine services[3]. Before the *bārū*-priest could perform his holy duties, he had to fulfill certain requirements, had to be of noble, priestly blood, a descendant of Enmeduranki; had to be of perfect bodily growth, and thoroughly acquainted with his priestly duties[4]. Without doubt similar conditions had to be met, not only by other priests, but by laymen as well[5]. Before the layman could bring sacrifice, he had to be ritually clean; otherwise it would not be accepted. Therefore, since it was man's duty to offer sacrifice, it was first of all his duty to keep himself ritually pure. Any neglect of these duties was sufficient cause for the gods' anger; was sin. Sin was thus originally merely the transgression of ritual laws, and as such appears throughout the Babylonian religious literature[6].

The usual method, by which the gods visited their anger upon man, was through sickness. Sickness was therefore an indication of sin. But more than this, it was also a state of

---

1) Cf. Relig. Sem. 163.

2) Cf. IV R. 19 No. 2 61/62; 26 No. 7 33/34; No. 5, 10ff.

3) Cf. Relig. Sem. 148, 151f.

4) Beitr. XXIV 23—24.

5) Cf. below.

6) In *Šurpu* alone were moral transgressions regarded as sin. No distinction was there made between them and ritual sin.

impurity, unfitting man for participation in religious services; was therefore, not only an indication of, but in itself, sin. Sickness was caused by evil spirits, the messengers of the gods' anger. They entered the doomed man's body, and firmly seated there, carried on their work of evil, undisturbed. Their presence was therefore synonymous with sickness and uncleanliness; consequently also with sin. In time the evil spirits ceased to be looked upon as messengers of the gods' anger; became independent of them; the inveterate enemies of their creature, man. Consequently, even more than before, was a sick man, one possessed by evil spirits, unclean and distasteful to the gods, *i. e.* a sinner.

Therefore in the Babylonian religious literature the expressions, sin, uncleanliness, sickness, possession by evil spirits, are pure synonyms. They denote an evil state of the body[1]), the result of the divine anger[2]). It unfitted man for participation in religious ceremonies; made him, for the time being, an outcast[3]).

Thus we read[4]): Mayest thou be freed from *aranka māmītka ḫiṭītka gillatka nīška muruṣka tānīḫka kišpu ruḫū rusū upšašu limnūti ša amelūti*, from thy sin, bann[5]), transgression, wickedness, curse, sickness sighing, witchcraft, spell, charm, evil machinations of men.

And again[6]):

maruštu imḫurannima dīna ana dān,
purussā ana parāsi maḫarka akmis;
dīni dīn purussa purus;
usuḫ murṣu limnu ša zumriia;
kuššid mimma limnu ša šērāniia u buānēia;
limuttu ša ina zumriia šērāniia u buānēia ibbašū
ina ūmi annē littaṣīma anāku nūra lūmur.

---

1) *Lumnu ša zumri.*

2) A common expression for "sin" was *šêrtu*. It also denoted "punishment" (for sin?) (cf. H. W. B. 636a). According to Jensen, (K. B. VI, I, 340), its original meaning was "anger" (of the gods?).

3) *Šurpu.* III, 115—125.

4) *Šurpu* VIII, 26—28.

5) *Māmītu* = "bann" = "uncleanliness;" cf. below.

6) Sm. 1371 + Sm. 1877 (= K. B. VI, I, 266—267).

Uncleanliness[1]) has come aginst me, to judge (my) cause,
To decide (my) decision, have I knelt down before thee;
Judge my cause, decide my dicision;
Tear out the evil sickness of my body;
Destroy all evil of my flesh and my sinews;
May the evil in my body, my flesh, and my sinews
On this day come forth, and may I see the light.

Again[2]), we find Ašurbanipal praying during an eclipse, which was also considered the work of the evil spirits:

ina lumun idāte pl. ittāte pl. limnēti pl. lā ṭābāte pl.
ša ina ekalliia u mātiia ibašā (-a)
aššum ūpiš limutti (-ti) murṣu lā ṭābu arni
qillat ḫiṭīti ša ina zumriia . . .
ekimmu limnu ša ittiia raksuma ušaḫ . . .
amḫurka ušapīka
nīš qātiia muḫur šimè taṣlīti
pušur kišpiia pusisi ḫiṭāteia
usuḫ (-uḫ) mimma limnu ša ana nakās napištiia illi-ka (-ka).

In the evil of the signs and portents, evil and not good,
Which are in my palace and my land;
Because of the evil magic, the disease that is not good, the iniquity,
The transgressions, the sin, that are in my body[3]) . . .
The evil specter that is bound to me and . . .
I have petitioned thee, have glorified thee!
The raising of my hand accept! Hearken to my prayer!
Free me from my bewitchment! Remove my sin!
Tear away whatever evil may come to cut off my life!

---

[1]) For this meaning of *maruštu*, cf. K. B. VI, I, 374f.

[2]) B. M. S. L., 15—23.

[3]) King reads here, „The transgression, the sin that is in my body, etc." He seems to refer the clause, *ša ina zumriia* to *ḫiṭīti* alone. However from analogy with other passages in the religious texts, where all the evils here enumerated, are located in the body, it is better to refer the clause to all these terms; cf. *mimma epēš limutti ša ina zumrišu bašū* (IV R. 20 No. 2, rev. 2); *nakma u nakimti ša zumriia* (IV R. 28 No. 3 obv. 11) *murṣu ša zumriia* (B. M. S. XXX, 12); and Sm. 1371 etc. (cited above).

Finally of the evil spirits it is said[1]):

asakka marṣa ina zumrišu iškunu;
māmīt limuttim ina zumrišu ibšū;
umunnā ina zumrišu iškunu;
namtāra limna ina zumrišu ibšū;
imta limutta ina zumrišu iškuni;
arrat limutta ina zumrišu ibšū;
limna arna ina zumrišu iškuni;
imta šērta elišu ibšū;
limutta iškunu;
amēlu limnu pāni limnu pū limnu lišānu limnu,
kišpi ruḫū rusū upšašē mimma limnu,
ša ina zumur marṣi iššak (?) -nu . . .

They put a woeful fever in his body;
A ban of evil hath settled in his body[2]);
An evil disease they have put in his body;
An evil plague hath settled in his body;
An evil venom they have put in his body;
An evil curse hath settled in his body;
Evil (and) sin they have put in his body;
Venom (and) iniquity have settled upon it;
They have worked evil;
The evil man, evil face, evil mouth, evil tongue,
Evil spell, witchcraft, sorcery,
Enchantment, and all evil,
Which have been put in the body of the sick man . . .

These, and many other passages[3]), prove that sin, evil, sickness, possession by evil spirits, witchcraft, and misfortune, are all one and the same thing in the Babylonian religion[4]); something material, that has entered the body of the

---

[1]) U. L. III, 40—54.

[2]) Or better, „they caused to settle;" cf. ll. 46—47 where *ibšū* is not only in parallelism with *iškuni*, but is also followed by an accusative.

[3]) Cf. IV R. 17 obv. 47—rev. 3; 57 (= B. M. S. XII) obv. 62ff.; B. M. S. I, 39—48; II, 32—39; XXVII, 15ff.

[4]) Exactly the same idea is found in the N. T. Math. 9, 2; Mark 2, 5; Luke 5, 20. Jesus says to the sick man, whom he has cured, „Go, thy sins are forgiven." Cf. John 9, 2; also Relig. Sem. 152f.

afflicted man. Consequently, the curing of sickness, the expulsion of evil spirits, and the expiation of sin, are identical, and must be so treated.

It is however necessary to first understand thoroughly the manner in which sin came upon the body, and man's means of defense against this. The following chapter will therefore treat of evil spirits.

Chap. II.
Evil Spirits.

As has been said, sickness was a manifestation of the divine anger. To the lively, picture-building, Semitic imagination, this was something more than a calamity sent by the gods; it became their actual messenger, carrying out their wrathful commands. And not alone sickness, but all evils, to which man is heir, were regarded in this light. And, as servants of the gods, they took on, to a certain extent, a divine nature; were, for all purposes, gods of inferior rank, fulfilling the destructive orders of their enraged superiors. However, so far they existed only as mediators of evil between the great gods and men [1]).

But gradually men began to see that evil comes at the most unexpected times; that apparently he who deserves it least, suffers most. And along with the conception of unknown sin [2]), came perhaps a faint presentiment, that the evil was not from the great gods at all; that their messengers had power to work evil according to their own wills. This view developed, until finally we have a host of gods, whose only aim is to work evil to mankind [3]). They are, as far as their acts are concerned, entirely independent of the great deities, who now in turn, become gods of good alone. In this relation, the two

---

[1]) Cf. Tiele: "Elements of the Science of Religion" I 89 ff.

[2]) Cf. p. 1 note 2.

[3]) For evil spirits in the European mythology, cf. Höfler: „Krankheits-Dämonen", Archiv für Religionswissenschaft, Bd. II.

hosts are mutually opposed, are actively hostile; but the good gods are the more powerful. In their presence the evil ones can not stand; at the very mention of their names, the latter tremble and disappear.

In time the pantheon of the gods of evil was systematized. The different members were distinguished, and names given to each. They were no longer misfortune itself, but mighty spirits of evil, bringing all calamities upon man. However not all attained this stage of development. Some remained mere demonifications of a particular sickness; were not its bringers, but sickness itself. Others again seem to have represented disease in general. Other calamities, such as destructive tempests, were demonified in the same way.

But although independent of, and hostile to, the evil spirits never entirely lost their original nature as servants, of the gods. And as such, according to the established theological system, they were regarded as of divine birth. Now they appear as children of Anu[1]); again as the offspring of Ea and Damkina[2]); and finally as the progeny of Bēl and Ereškigal[3]).

As gods of sickness, the cause of death, it was only natural to associate them with the underworld. That is their real home, from whence they go forth to work their evil upon man[4]). They are the servants of Ereškigal, queen of the underworld. When Nērgal is sent against her[5]), Ea gives him as attendants, fourteen spirits, the demonifications of different sicknesses. These Nērgal stations at the various gates of the underworld, while he himself boldly enters, overthrows Ereškigal, and associates himself with her in the government of the dead. It is significant, that Nērgal bears a twofold relation to the evil spirits[6]). On the one hand, he is, like the other gods, their enemy, who drives them forth from man; on the other hand, as ruler of the underworld, he is closely allied

---

[1]) U. L. V. Col. I ,1—4; IV R. 58 Col. II, 33; *Maqlū* IV, 45—46.
[2]) U. L. XV, 1—5.
[3]) Ibid. V Col. I, 5—8; IV R. 58 II, 34.
[4]) U. L. III, 25—27; V Col. I, 12/13, 22/23; Cun. Texts XVII pl. 25. II, 25.
[5]) K. B. VI, I, 76 ff.
[6]) Cf. below, Chap. V.

with him. As creatures of the underworld, they are associated with darkness, and therefore carry out their evil work chiefly at night.

But the home of the evil spirits was not confined to the underworld. They were as much the offspring of the deep[1]), of Ea and Damkina. These two conceptions are easily harmonized. The Babylonians regarded the deep, the apsū, as not merely surrounding, but also underneath the earth. In this sense then, the evil spirits were creatures of both the underworld and the deep.

And not only these, but any deserted, or awe-inspiring place was a favorite haunt of theirs. Thus ruins, cemeteries, mountains, and, above all, the desert, were full of evil spirits[2]), who, without warning, would sally forth and attack every hapless, belated wanderer.

But there were other evil spirits, besides those of sickness. First of all were the ghosts of the dead, especially those, whose deaths were associated with unusual circumstances. Thus[3]):

Whether thou art a ghost that hath come from out the earth,
Or *lilū*, that hath no couch,
Or a woman (that hath died) a virgin,
Or a man (that hath died) unmarried,
Or one that lieth dead in the desert,
Or one that lieth dead in the desert, uncovered with earth,
Or one that in the desert . . .
Or one that . . .
(Some lines wanting.)
Col. V. Or one that hath been torn from out a date-palm,
Or one that hath sunk[4]) in the water, from out a boat,
Or a ghost unburied,
Or a ghost with none to care for it,
Or a ghost with none to make offerings,

---

1) U. L. V Col. V, 28—35; XVI, 1—10.

2) Notice that this view was held by the Israelites and Arabs also.

3) U. L. IV Col. IV, 41—Col. V, 58; cf. V Col. I, 48—Col. II, 4 and A. S. K. T. XI Col. II, 6—16.

4) From טבא and not חבא, as Thompson translates.

Or a ghost with none to pour libations,
Or a ghost that hath no posterity [1]),
Or the *labartu*,
Or the *labaṣu*,
Or the *aḫḫazu*,
Or a harlot whose body was sick,
Or a woman (that hath died) in travail,
Or a weeping woman (that hath died) with a babe at the breast,
Or an evil man [2]),
Or an evil *utukku*
Or one that haunteth the neighborhood,
Or one that haunteth the vicinity,
Or one with whom I have on some day eaten,
Or with whom on some day I have drunk,
Or with whom on some day I have anointed myself,
Or with whom on some day I have clothed myself,
Or with whom I have entered and eaten,
Or with whom I have entered and drunk,
Or with whom I have entered and anointed myself,
Or with whom I have eaten when hungry,
Or with whom I have drunk when thirsty,
Or with whom I have anointed myself with oil, when sore,
Or with whom, when I was cold, I have clothed myself with the garments from his body [3]),
Until thou art removed,
Until thou departest from the body of the man, the son of his god, etc.

In this list those ghosts that had received proper burial rites, whose bodies had not been covered with earth, or whose

[1]) For the correctness of Thompson's translation of *zakar šumi* by "posterity" cf. A. S. K. T. XI Col. III, 50—60 where *zakrat šumi ša ilāni* stands in parallelism with *mārat (il) Anim*. Cf. also Col. II, 32—34.

[2]) Thompson's explanatory emendation, "or an evil man (that hath died)", is neither necessary nor correct. That *utukku limnu* follows, shows that this line refers to the evil spirit, *amēlu limnu*; cf. below, p. 10.

[3]) Thompson translates this line, "Or with whom, when I was cold I have clothed his nakedness with a garment". For the underlying meaning of this line, cf. Relig. Sem. 335 f.

relatives had not performed the usual sacrifices and libations for the dead, seem to play an especially important role.

Another class, that can hardly be called evil spirits, but rather, workers of evil, were the witches. Almost the entire *Maqlû*-series is devoted to them, their evil deeds, and incantations against them. They were both male and female, but the latter seem to have been more numerous. They possessed powers superior to the average man, which they used for his destruction. They too carried on their work chiefly at night. They brought all manner of evil, not only to individuals, but also to families and to whole communities. So great was their power that even the evil spirits were subject to their commands.

The conception of witches among the Babylonians probably arose from their innate belief in omens. Almost everything, certainly everything unusual, was for them a portent of good or evil. Therefore it was but natural that a man or woman, distinguished perhaps by unusual bodily characteristics, should be regarded as ominous of evil. And not that alone, but in time such a person came to be looked upon as the actual cause of evil. In the incantations references to the evil man are not infrequent. He is *limnu ša pāni limnu pū limnu lišānu limnu*, "an evil being, whose face is evil, whose mouth is evil, whose tongue is evil[1])". Through his evil mouth and tongue he bewitches men[2]); whoever approaches him may come under his spell.

However the evil spirits most feared, were those of the first class. They were real gods, the ones spoken of as the children of Anu, the offspring of Ea and Damkina. Chief among

---

[1]) Cf. above, p. 5, l. 52; also A. S. K. T. XI (= II R. 17) Col. I, 31—33:

pān limnūti īnu limuttu
pū limnu lišān limuttu
šaptu limuttu imtu limuttu.
The face of the evil ones, the evil eye,
The evil mouth, the evil tongue,
The evil lip, the evil venom.

[2]) U. L. tablet. C. 177/178. *Pū limnu lišānu limuttu mutamū.* Cf. V R. 50 a 67—72 and Cun. Texts XVII. pl. 32, 19/20.

them were "The Ṣeven". Really only six[1]) of these are ever mentioned by name[2]). Often they are said to be twice seven[3]).

The six are the *utukku, alû, ekimmu, gallû, ilu* and *rabiṣu*. To each the epithet *limnu* is generally applied. These six demons fall naturally into three groups, *utukku* and *ekimmu, alû* and *gallû, ilu* and *rabiṣu*.

Of these, the last group had its origin in the gods. *Ilu limnu* is nothing but the evil god, who brings calamity. *Rabiṣu* (MAŠKIM)[4]) is thought to denote, "The one who lies in wait"[5]), from the stem רבץ[6]). There was a good *rabiṣu*, as well as an evil. Thus the god, Ṣēru is called the *rabiṣ Ešarru*[7]), and Išum is the *rabiṣu ṣēru ša ilâni*[8]). An (*il*) *rabiṣu bîti* also occurs[9]). The work of these good spirits is *rabiṣûtu*, a synonym of *maṣṣartu*, "watch"[10]). Of the *ilu limnu* and *rabiṣu limnu* but little is known. As they appear in the religious texts, they have lost all trace of their divine origin, and become completely identified

---

[1]) Thompson seems to regard "The Seven" as a group, different from the six whose names are always mentioned together. ("Devils and Evil Spirits" I, Introd. pp. XXIV ff. and XLII ff.). However, U. L. V Col. III, 20—28, disproves this theory: —

sibit ilâni (pl.) limnûtum,
sibit labarti limnûtum,
sibit labartum li'bu limnûtum,
25. ina šamê sibit ina irṣitim sibitma.

UTUG-ḪUL A-LÁ-ḪUL GIDIM-ḪUL MULLA-ḪUL DINGIR-ḪUL MAŠKIM-ḪUL.'
Here "The Six" and "The Seven" are clearly identical.

[2]) With this may be compared how, in the Bible, although seven nations were driven out of Palestine by Israel, no more than six are ever mentioned together. Cf. below.

[3]) Cf. l. 25, above, and U. L. V Col. IV 60/61; V 56/57.

[4]) Brün. 5659.

[5]) Cf. HWB. 611; K. B. VI, I, 527.

[6]) Cf. Genesis 4, 7, also K. A. T.[3] 464, 3.

[7]) V R. 52 Col. I 20.

[8]) A. S. K. T. XI Col. IV, 47—48; U. L. tablet K. 178—180.

[9]) III R. 66 obv. Col. III 30.

[10]) K. 111 rev. I 28 (cf. *Maqlû.* notes, p. 127).

with the other evil spirits. And even as such it is doubtful if they were to the Babylonians more than mere names. Unlike the other evil spirits, they have no especial characteristics, and are seldom mentioned elsewhere than in the lists of the six[1]).

The *utukku limnu* and *ekimmu limnu* were originally ghosts, who, unable to rest, wandered about the earth, doing harm wherever possible. *Ekimmu* is the usual word for ghost[2]), while *utukku* is used once in that meaning[3]). The ideograms for these two words are almost identical. That for *ekimmu* is GIDIM (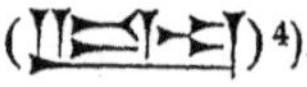)[4]), that for *utukku*, UTUG ()[5]), both compounds of  +  or . Delitzsch[6]) considers the first of these signs a compound of  (IŠ) and  (TAR). The last two signs denote respectively one third and two thirds.[7]). In the Babylonian astronomical-theological system, the goddess Ištar had the numerical value, fifteen. This would then give the *utukku* and *ekimmu* the values, ten and five respectively[8]). The *utukku* is mentioned far more than the *ekimmu*, oftener in fact than any of the evil spirits[9]). The Babylonians even went so far as to distinguish between *utukku's* of the plain, the mountain, the sea, the grave, the river, the forest and the street[10]). The spirit, *šēdu*, may also be designated by either

---

[1]) But cf. IV R. 58 Col. I 16—17, where the *labartu* is said to be surrounded by evil gods and evil *rabiṣu's* (*ilāni limnūti rabiṣē limnūti, šūt pāniki ša ina pāniki illaku*).

[2]) Cf. H. W. B. 57. In V R. 47 a, 46 a synonym for *ekimmu*, *šūlum*, a name derived from the practice of necromancy, is used. Cf. H. W. B. 66a, N. E. XII Col. III—IV (K. B. VI, 1, 262 ff.), and I Sam. 28, 11 ff.

[3]) N. E. XII Col. III 24, 28 (K. B. VI, I, 262—263).

[4]) Brün. 11307. Another ideogram for *ekimmu* is GUD (= *alpu*. cf. below); U. L. V Col. IV 14—16.

[5]) Brün: 11312.

[6]) H. W. B 57 b, 157 a.

[7]) Cf. Brün. 11221 and 11224, and H. W. B. 695 a and 655 a.

[8]) This hypothesis I owe to the kindness of Prof. Bezold.

[9]) Cf. the series *Utukkē limnūti*.

[10]) A. S. K. T. XI, Col. I 2—3 and Cun. Texts XVII pl. 16, 27—29.

of the above ideograms[1]), while UTUG is once used for *rabiṣu*[2]).

Finally, the last pair, the *alū* (= A—LÁ)[3]) and the *gallū* (= MULLA)[4]). The literal meaning of these ideograms is unknown, but that the last part of each is identical, shows perhaps that they are closely related. These are evil spirits proper; they have no other origin. They are apparently ugly apparitions, changing their forms at will, appearing now as some animal, and again as a distorted, terrifying human being. There are in the Babylonian literature three *alū's*, the heavenly steer (GUD-AN-NA), created by Anu to avenge Ištar on Gilgameš, a strom demon (GÁL-LU), and the *alū* above[5]). As Jensen has shown, these are merely three different forms of the same spirit. When we compare the reading of the ideogram with that for the *gallū*, and furthermore remember, that a favorite form, in which the latter visited mortals, was a raging bull[6]), we have further proof that the *alū* and the *gallū* were but different forms of one and the same demon[7]).

Another evil spirit often mentioned in connection with these six, and perhaps forming the unknown seventh of the group, is the *šēdu*[8]). But little is known of him. He has his counterpart in the *šēdu damqu*, the god spirit, that protects

---

[1]) Cf. Brün. 11308 and 11314. The note to the former is to be omitted, since in the second edition of IV. R. the ideogram is repeated, and also occurs twice in U. L. tablet G. col. I 14—17 and Cun. Texts, XVII pl. 5 35/36. However Brünnow's surmise for no. 11309 is proved correct by IV R.[2] and Cun. Texts, XVI. In II R. 17 Col. 19 and Col. II 60 UTUG is used for *ekimmu*. Haupt (A. S. K. T. pp. 82 and 90) has corrected the latter passage and placed an interrogation-mark after the former.

[2]) Cf. Brün. 11313.

[3]) Brün. 11638.

[4]) Ibid. 7732. MULLA is a compound of GÀL (MUL?) + LÁ. May not MULLA perhaps be read GALLA, and the word *gallū* be derived from it? Cf. below n. 7.

[5]) Cf. H. W. B. 60 and K. B. VI, I, 452 f.

[6]) Cf. U. L. V Col. IV, 14/15 and Cun. Texts. XVII pl. 21, 113/114.

[7]) It may be remarked here, that, with the exception of *ilu* and *rabiṣu*, these six names are of Sumerian origin.

[8]) Cf. *Maqlū*, notes, p. 127, and Cun. Texts. XVII pl. 2, 8—16; pl. 4, 9—11.

mankind. That he is closely related to "The Seven", is beyond doubt. In fact the term *šēdu* is used collectively for the entire group[1]).

That "The Seven" had originally nothing to do with sickness, is clear from the above description. That they were rather storm-demons may be inferred from the following[2]):

The evils gods are raging storms,
Ruthless spirits, created in the vault[3]) of heaven;
Workers of woe are they,
That each day raise their evil heads for evil[4]),
To wreak destruction . . .
Of these seven [the first] is the South Wind . . .
The second is a dragon with mouth agape,
That none can . . .
The third is a fierce leopard that carries off (?) young . . .
The fourth is a terrible serpent . . .
The fifth is a furious beast(?)[5]) after which no restraint? . . .
The sixth is a rampant . . . which against god and king . . .
The seventh is a cyclone, an evil windstorm which . . .
These seven are the messengers of Anu, the king,
Bearing gloom from city to city,
A tempest that furiously scours the heavens,
A dense cloud that brings gloom over the sky,
A rushing windgust, casting darkness over the bright day,
Forcing their way with the baneful windstorm.
The deluge of the Storm-God, mighty destroyers are they;
Stalking at the right hand of the Storm-God.

---

[1]) U. L. XVI, 3—4.

[2]) Ibid. 1—5; Cf. 227—276 and Cun. Texts. XVII pl. 37, 1—6; and K. A. T.[3] 459 f.

[3]) For a different rendering of *šupuk šamē* cf. K. B. VI, I, 467 f. However since the sun, moon and stars are located in it, and it is synonymous with *elat šamē*, and *kirib šamē*, and is the opposite of *aralū*, it seems rather to denote the whole vault of heaven. Cf. H. W. B. 679 f.

[4]) Since there was an evil spirit known as the *mukīl rēš limutti* (cf. Beitr. XLV Col. I 7 note), it is perhaps better to consider it used here collectively, for all the evil spirits, like *šēdu* in l. 5.

[5]) Cf. Thompson's note, p. 89.

45. In the foundation[1]) of heaven like lighting they flash,
To wreak destruction they lead they way;
50. In the broad heaven, the home of Anu, the king,
They take their stand for evil, and there is none to oppose.

So great is their power that they dare to attack the gods themselves[2]) and even by them are not easily repulsed. But in time, perhaps as the result of their relations with other evil spirits, they too became bringers of sickness. As such, they are the heralds of the plague-god Ura[3]), the messengers of the *namtāru*[4]), the throne-bearers of Ereškigal[5]).

The real spirits of sickness may be also divided into three classes; *labartu, labaṣu* and *aḫḫazu*; *lilû, lilītu* and *ardat lilē*; *namtāru, asakku* and sickness in general. Of these, each of the first two classes are internally closely related; the third represents a sort of "tailing off" process to the end of which we never come.

The close relationship of the *labartu, labaṣu* and *aḫḫazu* is shown by their ideograms, respectively *il* RAB-KAN-ME, *il* RAB-KAN-ME-A and *il* RAB-KAN-ME-KIL[6]). The reading of the first name is uncertain, *lamastu* being possible. The etymology of the word is of course unknown. *Labaṣu* is usually regarded as coming from the stem, לבץ, "to overthrow", "to

---

[1]) That Thompson's and Kugler's renderings of *išid šamē* as "the height of heaven" and "the milky way" respectively, are both incorrect, is almost self-evident. *Išid šamē* can mean only "the foundation of heaven", i. e. "the horizon". This is born out by IV R. 20 No. 2, obv. 1/2, where *išid šamē* is the place where the sun rises (cf. V. R. 50, 7/8 a.) K. 8531 (Hrozný. M. V. A. G. 103, 5 pp. 8—9) 13/14 speaks of *išid šamē* as the place where Ninib thunders, cf. N. E. XI, 104—106 (K. B. VI, I, 236—237 and note p. 496). In IV R. 28 No. 2 23/26 *išid šamē* is contrasted with *elat šamē* and seems also to be in parallelism with *irṣitum* while *elat šamē* is in parallelism with *šamē*. We must therefore conclude that *išid šamē* can mean only "the horizon", perhaps that point where the sun rises, and *elat šamē*, "the zenith". Delitzsch (H. W. B. 64 b) translates *elat šamē* by "the South", and *išid šamē* by "the North". This of course to be corrected.

[2]) U. L. XVI 70 ff.; K. 64/65.

[3]) Cf. K. B. VI, I, 58 ll. 7—11.

[4]) U. L. V Col. III 7/8.

[5]) Ibid. 9/10.

[6]) Brün. 4246—4248.

destroy". *Aḫḫazu* is probably derived from the stem, אחז "to seize". The last two demons are met with only in connection with the *labartu*, and as their ideograms show, were particular forms of that evil spirit. The *labartu* was a female demon, the daughter of Anu[1]). She seems also to have been in part identified with Ištar. She, together with her two companion-spirits, were closely related to *li'bu*, the fever-demon, and we may probably conclude that all three were demonifications of different kinds of fever[2]). The special prey of the *labartu* was children, but she also attacked grown persons and cattle. In one passage[3]) *labartu* is used as a collective term for "The Seven". This shows how completely the distinction between the different classes of evil spirits was in time lost sight of. In another passage[4]) *aḫḫazu* is mentioned as the name of a disease.

The next class consists likewise of three members, *lilū*, *lilītu*, and *ardat lilē*. That these two are internally closely related is shown by their ideograms, respectively, LIL-LÁ[5]), KI-EL-LIL-LÁ[6]) and KI-EL-UD-DA-KAR-RA[7]). The ideograms show that the first two were storm-demons[8]). LIL-LÁ is also equivalent to *šāru* and *zaqīqu*[9]). KI-EL-LIL-LÁ is therefore equivalent to "maid of the storm"[10]). KI-EL-UD-DA-KAR-RA on the contary means "the maid of him who oppresses the day"[11]); is therefore a demon of the night. The three however must have become related very early, since they are always met with together in the incantations. So close was this relationship, that

---

1) For a thorough treatment of the *labartu*, cf. Myhrman, in Z. A. XVI.

2) In IV R. No. 1 (Cun. Texts. XVII pl. 25) obv. 5 and 51/52, *labartu* is identified with *ṭi'u*, a sickness of the head.

3) U. L. V Col. III 21—24.

4) A. B. M. III Sp. IV 28 ff. Küchler suggests that this may be equivalent to yellow fever.

5) Brün. 5939.

6) Ibid. 9834.

7) Ibid. 7920.

8) Cf. KAT[3] 460, 7.

9) Brün. 5940—5941.

10) *Ardat zaqīqi* or even *ardat lilē.*

11) *Ardat mukarrē ūmi.*

the ideogram for *lilītu* was often used for *ardat lilē*[1]). Often the determinative, *amēlu*, stands before LIL-LÁ, but the feminine determinative never[2]) precedes the other two ideograms. Probably the first part of these, KI-EL, had the force of a determinative.

That the Babylonians regarded these three chiefly as storm-demons, is beyond question[3]). But it is just as certain that they connected them also with the night. This is no doubt due to the close resemblance of their names to the Assyrian word for evening, *lilātu*. The fact that all demons were supposed to carry on their work chiefly at night, must have furthered this idea. As a demon of the night *lilītu* passed into Jewish traditions, and then into the Syriac.

Of the actual workings of *lilū* and *lilītu* nothing is known. The *ardat lilē* however was more troublesome. Of her we read:

---

[1]) An interesting passage in this connection is U. L. III 197. The ideograms there are MULU-LIL-LÁ, KI-EL-LIL and KI-EL-LIL-DA-KAR-RA. It will be noticed in the first place, that the second ideogram lacks the usual LÁ To LIL of the third ideogram another tablet gives the expected variant, UD. This proves LIL to be a mistake. The scribe had begun to write KI-EL-LIL-LÁ, for *ardat lilē*, but, remembering that he had already used this for *lilītu*, changed it to the customary KI-EL-UD-DA-KAR-RA, forgetting however to substitute UD for LIL.

[2]) *Maqlū* I 138 reads: *amēl* LIL-LÁ *sinniš* KI-LIL-LÁ, KI-EL-LIL-LÁ. In the second ideogram the usual EL is wanting. In fact one of the duplicates of this text omits KI as well, and only *sinniš* LIL-LÁ remains. This is probably because the scribe, intending to use KI-EL-LIL-LÁ for *ardat lilē*, was forced to distinguish in some way between it and the ideogram for *lilītu*. But with EL or KI-EL omitted, it became necessary to distinguish between this ideogram and that for *lilū*. *sinniš* LIL-LÁ rendered into Assyrian, would be *lilītu*, while KI-EL-LIL-LÁ would be *ardat lilē* and not "the maid of him who oppresses the day". This is exactly the Babylonian conception of the two.

[3]) LIL-LÁ must have been originally a Sumerian storm-demon (cf. Cun. Texts, XVII pl. 37, 1—6, and KAT³ 460, 7). From the Sumerian name according to the usual process of lengthening the end vowel, the Assyrian *lilū* was derived, and from this the feminine *lilītu*. This became in turn equivalent to the Sumerian, "maid of the storm". The derivation of *lilū* from the Semitic stem ללה, "to be abundant", proposed by Martin ("Textes Religieuses" p. 25) and half way accepted by Thompson ("Devils and Evil Spirits" I p. XXXVII) is of course groundless. The usual ideogram for Bēl, *il*EN-LIL (-LÁ) probably points to him originally as a storm-god.

ardatu ša bīt zaqīqi ana ardatu ina apti itanūru ardat lilē ša ina apti bīti ana amēli işruru ardatu ša kīma sinništi ardu la ir-[— — — — —] 𒐖 *ša kīma sinništi ardu lā ikipuši* 𒐖 *ša ina sūn mūtiša kuzba lā ilputu* 𒐖 *ša ina sūn mūtiša şubātsa lā išhuṭu* 𒐖 *ša idlu damqu šillaša lā ipṭuru* 𒐖 *šā muššiša šizba lā ibšū* [1]). From this and other passages[2]) it is clear that the *ardat lilē* was a half-human, female spirit, that appeared chiefly to men, and excited their passions, but did not always gratify them[3]). Perhaps we may see in her the demonification of unpleasant sexual dreams[4]).

The final group of evil spirits, as has been said, "tails off" into sicknesses themselves. The chief members of this group are the *asakku*[5]) and the *namtāru*. With them is usually

[1]) W. B. 151.

[2]) *Maqlū*, notes p. 128.

[3]) V R. 50, 59—62a reads as follows:

ša ardat lilē iḫīrušu
idlu ša ardat lilē ikrimušu.

(One) whom the *ardat lilē* has looked upon (sexually),
a man whom the *ardat lilē* has cast to the ground.

It is possible with Thompson ("Devils and Evil Spirits" I pp. XXVII and XXXVIII) to translate the first line, "one whom the *ardat lilē* has married", but comparison with the next line seems to indicate that the *ardat lilē* has exerted violence upon the man. This coupled with the above quoted text and A. S. K. T. XI Col. II 30/31, *ardat (lilē) ša mutu lā išū*, "the *ardat lilē* that has no husband", and the expression, *ḫāru ša lilē*, "being looked upon by *lilū*", (II R. 62 Col. III, 9 f.) seems sufficient argument for the above conception. It is also noteworthy that A. S. K. T. XI 32/33 speaks of the *idlu lilē ša aššatu lā iḫzu*, "the man of *lilū* who has taken no wife". This was hardly *lilū* himself, but probably a fourth of this group, a male demon, artificially conceived of, to correspond to the *ardat lilē*.

The Lilith of Rabinic and Syriac tradition, who was the wife of Adam, previous to Eve, originated from this *ardat lilē* rather than from the storm-demon *lilītu*. The tradition recorded in Midrash Ber. Rab. XX and XXIV, that in the one hundred and thirty years after the expulsion from Eden, when Adam was separated from Eve, each had connection with evil demons of both sexes, resulting in various forms of offspring, all of course evil, may also go back to our *ardat lilē* and *idlu lilē* above. Cf. Conway: "Demonology and Devil-Lore", II pp. 88, 100.

[4]) Cf. U. L. tablet B. 18/19.

[5]) For the reading, *asakku*, instead of *ašakku*, cf. K. B. VI, I, 433 f.

mentioned the *murṣu lā ṭābu*, "the sickness not good", and sometimes the names of particular diseases [1]) or other calamities. Often either word, *asakku* or *namtāru*, is used to denote sickness or pestilence in general [2]).

Both names are derived from the Sumerian; *asakku* from AZÀG [3]), meaning, "the one who weakens the strength", and *namtāru* from NAM-TAR [4]), "the one who decides the fate". The *namtāru* was the son of Bēl and Ereškigal [5]), and the latter's messenger. When Nērgal was sent against her, the *namtāru* betrayed his mistress [6]), and thus became subject to Nērgal. As the messenger of Ereškigal the determinative for god stands before his name [7]). "The Seven" are once termed collectively, "the *namtāru*, the beloved son of Bēl and Ereškigal" [8]), and again, "the heralds of the *namtāru*, the throne-bearers of Ereškigal" [9]). In one text *namtāru* appears with the variant *gallū* [10]).

Of the *asakku* little can be said. Apparently the Babylonians dit not conceive of it otherwise than as a pest-demon, and so gave it no definite form nor attributes. In one passage [11]) the names of a long list of ghosts are summed up in the exorcism *asakku māmīt il Anunnaki utammēka*, "*O asakku*, I exorcise thee by the bann of the Anunnaki".

It will thus be seen that, no matter what the origin of the different evil spirits, the Babylonians ceased in time to

---

1) *Dimētu, li'bu, ṭi-u*, etc., cf. also K. B. VI, I, 76, 6—8 and Beitr. XLV Col. I and notes.

2) U. L. V Col. III 39/40. cf. 41/42. Ibid. III 164, the *namtāru* appears both as an evil spirit and as a sickness.

3) = ID ¦+ PA. Brün. 6592. Jensen (K. B. VI, I, 433 f.) connects *asakku* with the stem, חשך.

4) Brün. 2110. In U. L. V Col. III 7/8. LIL-LÁ-DA-RA = *namtāru*. Does this indicate a relation to *lilū*?

5) Ibid. Col. I 5—7.

6) K. B. VI, I, 76, 19—21 and note 393.

7) In the myth of Ištar's descent to Hell, this is invariably the case; in that of Nērgal and Ereškigal on the contrary, the determinative is always omitted.

8) U. L. V Col. I 5—8.

9) Ibid. Col. III 7—10.

10) B. M. S. I, 49.

11) U. L. V Col. II 3—10.

make any distinction between them. They were the bringers of all evil; they caused eclipses; were raging storms, that swept over the land; destroyed the family life; killed cattle; tore down buildings; they crawled through the cracks in the door and brought all manner of misfortune with them. But, as has been so often said, as demons of sickness, they did most of their evil work. All disease was caused by them entering a man's body. With proper care they might be kept away, but when once they had forced their way into the body, it was not so easy to expel them. To the Babylonian, an evil spirit was something material; not a spirit in the modern sense, but something that entered a man bodily, and had to be driven forth in the same way. And so real was this idea to him, that he came to regard the different parts of the human body as apportioned to the various evil spirits. This is clear from two texts both, alas, very fragmentary.

a-sak-ku ḫab-bi-lu ana qaq-qad [*amēli*]
nam-ta-ru- lim-nu ša a-na na-piš-ti [*amēli*]
ú-tuk-ku lim-nu ša a-na ki-šad [*amēli*]
a-lu-ú lim-nu ša ana ir-ti [*amēli*]
e-kim-mu lim-nu ša ana qab-li a[*mēli*]
gal-lu-ú lim-nu ša ana qa-ti [*amēli*]
ilu limnu [— — — — — — — — —] [1]).
The destructive *asakku* to the head of [the man],
The evil *namtāru*, which to the breath (?) [of the man],
The evil *utukku*, which to the neck of [the man],
The evil *alū*, which to the breast of the m[an],
The evil *ekimmu*, which to the waist of the m[an],
The evil *gallū*, which to the hand of [the man]
The evil god [— — — — — — —].

And.: [— — — —] *a-na ir-ti-* [*šu* — — —]
e-kim-mu lim-nu a-na qab-li-šu iṭ-ṭe-ḫi
gal-lu-ú lim-nu a-na qa-ti-su iṭ-ṭe-ḫi
ilu lim-nu a-na še-pi-šu iṭ-ṭe-ḫi
si-bit-ti-šu-nu išteniš (*-niš*) *iṣ-ṣab-tu-ni*
zu-mur-šu kīma i-ša-ti lum-mu-du-uš

---

[1]) IV R. 29 No. 2.

ki-ma e-peš limuttim (*-tim*) [— — — —] [1])
[— — — —] to [his] breast [— — — —]
The evil *ekimmu* approaches his waist;
The evil *gallū* approaches his hand;
The evil god approaches his foot;
"The Seven" together seize (him);
They lay hold of his body like fire;
Like the working of evil [— — — — —].

In each of these texts, the parts of the body assigned to the *ekimmu* and *gallū* are identical; and we may infer the same, not only for the *alū* and the *ilu limnu,* but for the rest of the evil spirits as well. However it is doubtful if this apportioning the body would hold good throughout the entire religious literature, since the evil spirits were not distinguished from one another by hard and fast lines.

Accordingly, to the Babylonian, sickness consisted in being possessed by evil spirits, who had entered the body of the afflicted man [2]). Could they be expelled, the man would recover; if not, he remained sick, possibly became worse, and perhaps died [3]).

But since the evil spirits were thus the enemies of man, and their attacks so dangerous, man had to have some means of defence against them; otherwise the whole human race would inevitably perish. What was this?

---

[1]) IV R. 18* No. 4.

[2]) It is possible that not all diseases were so considered. In A. B. M. evil spirits are but seldom mentioned in connection with sickness (cf. above p. 16, note 4). However many of the remedies prescribed in these texts were also used to drive out evil spirits. At any rate there need not be the slightest doubt, that dangerous sicknesses, and especially those but little understood, implied the presence of an evil spirit.

[3]) May we perhaps infer that a dead person was one over whom the evil spirits had acquired complete control, or one in whom an evil spirit was permanently located?

Chap. III.
Good Spirits.

Whether the Babylonians were aware of it or not, there is apparent in their theology a trace of dualism, a law of contrast as it were. Whether it may be called a law is uncertain, for the word implies consciousness of a principle, and nowhere, throughout the Babylonian literature, do we find the slightest indication of such a consciousness. But, as is the case with every Nature-religion, this principle does exist; may almost be said to form the very basis of the entire Babylonian theology.

They saw how, during the winter, vegetation was dead, only to be awakened to a new life with the spring. They saw the passage of the sun foreward and backward from north to south; the cycle of the moon's phases; the changes of the seasons, and the many other revolutions, that Nature works. And for them it was not a mere succession of phases, but a fixed motion back and forth; a motion from one end to the other. These ends were direct counterparts. From this went forth the whole doctrine of opposites. Heaven was the counterpart of the earth; the gods, the counterparts of men; winter, the counterpart of summer; death, the counterpart of life; evil, the counterpart of good. This was their solution of the great mystery of life. Life is a state of activity, of "somethingness"; death, on the contrary, passivity, nothingness. The ghosts of the dead retain their earthly forms, but they lie in the underworld inactive, and their food is dust[1]). The gods too are the opposites of men: they bear the latter's form; have the latter's passions; live among themselves like men. Only in relation to, men are their powers superhuman.

This is the law of contrast. The point however must be emphasized; to the Babylonians themselves, it may not have been a law; they may not have been at all conscious of it. And yet it was ever-present in their literature, theology and life.

---

[1]) N. E. XII Col. IV—VI (K. B. VI, 1, 262—265).

Therefore it need not be at all surprising, that, in contrast to the evil spirits, good spirits also existed, whose duty was to protect man from the former's attacks. What the origin of this belief was, is hard to say. That they existed solely to ward off evil, points to a time when the evil spirits had come to be regarded, no longer as messengers of the gods, but as the inveterate foes of man. It is possible that the good spirits represent the remains of the belief in spirits as messengers of the gods' will, only now this was usually to protect man from the evil demons. It is also possible that the Babylonians came to see that not everybody, who became sick, died; in fact that not everybody became sick; that, in short, the power of the evil spirits must have been limited. Hence the idea, that there must be good spirits guarding man against evil. It is also possible, if any value may be attached to the law of contrast as a law, that the good spirits were conceived of as counterparts of the evil; if there are evil spirits, there must also be good. It is impossible to say which of these three theories is correct; in fact, it is highly probable that some kernel of truth lies at the bottom of each. At any rate, whatever the real origin be, this much is certain: the belief in good spirits followed, and was the direct outgrowth of, the belief in evil spirits.

Chief among the good spirits were man's own deities. Every man had from birth, his personal god and goddess[1]), who watched over him and protected him from evil. These were not new deities but some pair from among the great gods. Thus Ašur and Ašurītu were always the god and goddess of the king of Assyria, but of no one else[2]). It is possible that

---

[1]) This goddess, like most Babylonian goddesses, was merely the companion and pale reflection of the male deity, and was seldom referred to alone.

[2]) No matter what his god and goddess may have been, on ascending the throne, the king took Ašur and Ašurītu, the patron gods of the land, as his gods. Of course it is possible, that these were the god and goddess, not only of the king, but also of the whole royal family. But this is not probable, for then, in time, all the king's brothers would have had the same gods as he. The oldest son did not always succeed to the throne, and so the theory that this prince may also have had Ašur and Ašurītu for gods, is untenable. Besides, in case the crown-prince died, his

a man inherited his deities from his father, or else took that god and goddess as his own, in whose month he was born. Or again, it may be, that the god and goddess of the guild to which he belonged, were also his personal deities. Or finally, a man could perhaps choose his god and goddess at will.

Although belonging to the great gods, a man's personal deities were looked upon as something entirely different from these. They were merely the *ilu amēli* and *il ištar amēli.* the man's protecting deities, his guardians against evil, existing only in relation to that man alone. This is proved by the many passages in which the *ilu amēli* is mentioned as an especial deity in connection with the great gods[1]). When a man became sick, it showed that his personal deity, for some reason or other, had not been able to keep off the evil spirits. In such a case, the *ilu amēli* would entreat one of the great gods, whose power over the evil spirits was supreme, to drive the latter from the sick man's body[2]). After doing this, the great god would restore the man in perfect health to the protecting hands of his god and goddess[3]). This shows that these were deities of inferior rank, but little removed from the actual good spirits.

Related to the *ilu amēli*, but not so clearly defined, were the *ilu bīti*[4]), "the god of the house", and the *ilu ali*[5]), "the god of the city". Just as the *ilu amēli*, each of these had his

---

successor would have had to change his gods. Therefore we must conclude, that at least in exceptional cases, it was possible for a man to change his gods.

[1]) Cf. Beitr. I—XX 55—90, 127 ff. XXVI Col. IV 18, V 80.

[2]) IV R. 17 obv. 39.

[3]) B. M. S. XI 26.

[4]) IV R. 21 No. I (A) Col. I obv. 43; Beitr. XLI—XLII Col. I 15; U. L. tablet. G 6—7. In the last two pages, the *šēdu bīti* and *lạmassu bīti* are associated with the *ilu bīti* and the *il ištar bīti.*

[5]) Really there were two conceptions of the *ilu ali*; the first, the remains of the old local-cult idea, by which Marduk was the god of Babylon, Šamaš of Sippar, etc: the second, an *ilu ali*, who, like the *ilu amēli*, was merely a good spirit, protecting the city against evil demons. IV R. 21, No. 1 (A) Col. I obv. 43; Rm. 2, 159, obv. (Cr. II 9) 16—17. B. M. S IV 37, 46; VI 88; VII 19, 26.

female associate. They represented expansions of the idea of the *ilu amēli,* and so had absolutely nothing in common with the gods, except their names. They were merely good spirits, guarding the house and the city, and even as such, bore a very shadowy existence.

The real guardians of the house were the two good spirtis, the *šēdu* and *lamassu.* These were represented by the colossi, the so-called "winged bulls," that stood at each side of the entrances of temples and other buildings[1]). Every house had its *šēdu* and *lamassu*[2]), guarding all its entrances, so that no evil spirits might pass through. These images were, of course, mere representations of the good spirits. It is hardly probable that the Babylonians regarded them as the *šēdu* and *lamassu* themselves. These were actual, active spirits, and, while their chief station was the door, they were present throughout the house. It is possible that the image standing to the right of the door was the *šēdu,* and that to the left, the *lamassu,* but this is not certain[3]).

The etymology of the words is uncertain. *Lamassu* may perhaps be related to its Sumerian equivalent *la-am-ma*[4]). The ideogram for *lamassu* is *il* KAL; that for *šēdu il* ALAD[5]). The

---

[1]) Other images could also be used; cf. Tig. VI 62; Ašurb. VI 60; Beitr. XLI—XLII ff.

[2]) By this is not meant that every house had its colossi. These, of course, stood only before the temples and palaces, and perhaps the house of the wealthy. Poor people had to be content with small images, fastened to the doorposts. This was of course the same idea as that underlying the use of the מזוזות of the Bible.

[3]) U. L. III, 91—94; cf KAT^3, 456,1.

[4]) S b. 176.

[5]) S b. 175—176 seems to give the ideogram *il* KAL for both words, but as this ideogram is nowhere else used for *šēdu,* and there are indications in l. 175 that a wedge has fallen out, it is probably, with Delitzsch, to be read, *il* ALAD. Probably on the basis of these two lines King renders *il* KAL by *šēdu* (B. M. S. VI, 32; XIX, 29; XXII, 8, 64.). This is, of course, if we accept Delitzsch's emendation, to be corrected. Thompson ("Devils and Evil spirits") makes just the opposite mistake. Throughout his work he has transcribed 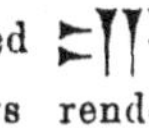 as ALAD, although, wherever the text is interlinear, it is always rendered *la-mas-su.* This is without doubt a mistake.

ideogram for *utukku* (UTUG) is also used for *šēdu*[1]), and is in fact the usual ideogram for this word in the series *Utukkē limnūti*. *Sēdu* may be an evil spirit as well as good[2]), and really this seems to have been its original meaning[3]). Then, by law of contrast again, the *šēdu* as a good spirit was conceived of. The two are respectively designated *šēdu limnu* and *šēdu damqu*[4]). As such the ideogram ALAD may be used for both. UTUG on the contrary denotes only the *šēdu* as a good spirit[5]), the counterpart of the *utukku limnu*[6]). In four passages[7]) the ideogram for *ekimmu* (GIDIM) is also used for *šēdu*. The *lamassu* was always a good spirit, called either *lamassu damqu* or *ilu mušallimu*. Delitzsch distinguishes between *šēdu* and *lamassu* as "Trutzgott" and "Schutzgott" respectively. It is not clear on what grounds he bases this distinction. As good spirits, their only function was to protect man and his property from evil demons. In this repect there was no difference between them. ALAD differs from KAL only in that it contains the additional element BE (⊢<). Whether one of the

---

[1]) Cf. above p. 13, note 1. The determinative for god always stands before KAL and ALAD, but never before UTUG, with the exceptions V. R. 51 a 29 and Cun. Texts XVII pl. 2, 8.

[2]) Cf. above, p. 13f.

[3]) In Hebrew and Syriac the word is used for evil spirits alone.

[4]) *Šēdu dumqu, damiqti*, or *nāṣiru* also occur.

[5]) One exception to this is found in U. L. tablet K 298/299, where UTUG=*šēdu*, as a bringer of poison. Note however that in this passage, Sin, Šamaš and Ištar, and other gods, as well as the *šēdu* and *labartu*, bring poison to man. This is also the only passage in this series, where *šēdu* occurs without the usual attributes, *limnu* or *damqu*.

[6]) In U. L. tablet. I, 10—11 ("Devils and Evil Spirits" I, 181) Thompson supplies [*u-tuk-ku dum-qi še-e-du dum*]-*qi*, without giving the passage upon which he bases this reading. Until he does, it can not, of course, be accepted. Also Delitzsch's reading *utukku damqu šēdu damqu* (H. W. B. 157 b) is to be corected to *šēdu damqu lamassu damqu*. In Cun. Texts XVII pl 2, 8—11 we find *il utukku* (UTUG) *damqu il lamassu* (KAL) *damqu il šēdu* (ALAD) *damqu* and KA-SA *damqu*. This shows that an *utukku damqu* existed, but still does not justify Thompson's emendation. KA-SA was probably also a good spirit, although, unlike the other ideograms, it lacks the determinative for god. Its reading is unknown.

[7]) IV R. 18 No. 3, Col. I. 24/26; U. L. tablet. G. 14—17; Cun. Texts XVII pl. 5, 35/36; cf. above, 13 note 1.

usual meanings of BE[1]) may be found in the BE of ALAD, is uncertain. The god Papsukal was identified with the *lamassu*, and Išum with *šēdu*[2]). It is noteworthy that, like the *šēdu*, Išum was a god of both good and evil.

Although the *lamassu* and *šēdu* were originally protectors of the house, they soon developed into protective spirits in general, so that little distinction existed between them and the *ilu amēli*. This evolution was just the opposite to that of the *ilu bīti*. This was a specialization of the functions of the *ilu amēli*, while the conception of the *šēdu* and *lamassu* as guardian deities of man himself was the result of the generalization of their functions as guardians of the house[3]). That they were closely related to the gods is shown by the determinative that always precedes their ideograms. The goddess Ištar is described as having a *šēdu* before her and a *lamassu* behind her, one to her right, and one to her left[4]). Finally, as a direct working of the law of contrast, just as the body of a sick man was regarded as the seat of an evil spirit, so the sick man prayed that a good spirit might enter his body and dwell there[5]).

Another fact, illustrative of this law of contrast, was that the evil spirits themselves could be used for good[6]). One method of counteracting the effects of witchcraft was for the exorciser to perform the same ceremonies against the witch that she had employed against the sick man. Since the evil spirits were usually subject to the witches, it is not at all sur-

---

[1]) Cf. Brün. 1494, 1499, 1512, 1518, 1519, 1527, 1528, 1533.

[2]) Cf. H. W. B. 381 b.

[3]) On the other hand, a specialization of the functions of the *šēdu* may perhaps be traced in the fact that, in addition to the *šēdu* of the house, other buildings also had *šēdu's*; Cf. IV R. 18 No. 6, 6—8, where the *šēdu* of the stable is referred to.

[4]) B. M. S. VIII 12—13. This probably means a *šēdu* to the right and a *lamassu* to the left; cf. above, p. 25.

[5]) A. S. K. T. XI Col. III, 11—12; Col. IV, 44—45; cf. *Šurpu* V/VI, 11/12, IV R. 18 No. 3, 24/27 a, and Cun. Texts XVII, 29, 25/28 where the man's personal deities are described as, under normal conditions, dwelling in his body.

[6]) Cf. above, p. 11.

prising to find the priest now sending them against the witches themselves. Thus[1]):

ina kibsiki rabiṣa ušēziz;
ekimma paqdāti ḫarrāniki ušassī.
In thy footsteps I will station the *rabiṣu*;
The *ekimmu* will I cause to remove thy guideposts.

These were the good spirits, that guarded man against all evil. Under their protection he was reasonably safe from the demons' attacks. Only in exceptional cases could the latter work their evil in spite of the good spirits[2]). But if the man sinned against his god or goddess, or against any of the great gods, they became angry and withdrew their protection. The man was now defenceless before the onslaught of the evil spirits. They entered his body, bringing with them all manner of ills, and established themselves firmly there. How expel them? The answer to this question is represented by the sum of all the magic and incantation texts of the Babylonian literature. The expulsion of evil spirits was the ever-present problem of the Babylonian religion.

Chap. IV.
Removal of Evil Spirits.

The need for some means to expel the evil spirits from the body was very urgent. Their presence meant continual sickness and suffering, and eventual death. Life therefore depended upon, and was, in a certain sense, the result of, their removal. The chief means, by which this was accomplished, were water and fire.

How this force came to be attached to these two elements is of course unknown. To all Semitic peoples they were the great purifiers, that cleaned everything from evil[3]). Fire too, associated with light, was directly opposed to the darkness of

[1]) *Maqlû* III, 146—147.
[2]) Cf. IV R. 18 No. 6, 6—8.
[3]) Cf. IV R. 14 rev. 14 ff. and in the Bible, Mal. 3, 2; Jer. 6, 29.

the night, when the evil spirits were most active. Fire and water were also the great benefactors of man, on which the very preservation of his life depended. Finally, even in the most ancient times, a certain medicinal force must have been attached to these elements, more so perhaps than to-day. Probably all these influences, and others as well, worked together, until finally, water and fire came to be regarded as the chief means employed in removing evil spirits. This is clear from the fact that the gods, most active in this work, were those of water and light.

These two elements were closely related in the Babylonian mind. They saw the sun rise every morning in the east, from out the *apsū* [1]), that surrounded the earth, and sink again every evening in the *apsū* to the west. The *apsū* extended underneath the underworld, and was in a vague way related to it. Consequently when the gods of light, Ištar, Tammuz, Nērgal, Išum, and others, spend part of the time in the underworld, they come into a certain connection with the *apsū*. Before being restored to the gods of heaven, Ištar is sprinkled with the water of life [2]). Gibil is *mār apsē*, "the son of the deep" [3]), and also *ša* ^il^ NIN-GUG-SIG *tappušu*, "the companion of Ea" [4]); while Nuzku, who is identical with Gibil, is called *tarbīt aspē binūt* ^il^ *Ea*, "the offspring of the deep, the child of Ea" [5]). And Marduk, originally a sun-god, came to be looked upon as the son and chief messenger of Ea against the evil spirits.

Of the two elements, water was by far the more important; was in fact the basis of all ceremonies for the removal of evil spirits. Besides fire and water, many other means were employed for this purpose, but all subordinate to the use of water. To thoroughly understand this subject, it is necessary to treat each separately. We precede therefore to the discussion of Water.

---

[1]) Since no English word exactly expresses the meaning of *apsū*, I have used this word itself throughout this work.

[2]) K. B. VI, I, 88, 34, 38.

[3]) IV R. 14 rev. 8/9.

[4]) Ibid. rev. 20/21.

[5]) *Maqlū* I, 124; cf. II, 111.

The home of the Ea-cult was the ancient city Eridu, at the mouth of the Euphrates and Tigris. This spot was especially sacred in the Babylonian religion. Thus we read[1]):

In Eridu groweth the dark *kiškanu*;
In an undefiled place it springeth forth.
Its appearance is shining lapis
Which reaches unto the Ocean.
The way of Ea into Eridu[2])
Is bountiful in luxuriance.
Where earth is, there is its place,
And the couch of the goddess Id, its home.
Into the undefiled dwelling, whose shadow, like a forest grove
Spreadeth out, no one enters[3]).
In its depths are Šamaš and Tammuz[4]).
At the opening of the mouth of the two streams
The gods Ka-Ḫegal, Ši-Dugal, (and) — — of Eridu
Have gathered this *kiškanu*, and over the man
Have performed the incantation of the deep.

Again Marduk is directed by Ea to take water from the mouth of the two streams and with it sprinkle the sick man[5]).

This was but natural. The waters of the Euphrates and Tigris were sacred; therefore efficacious in driving out evil spirits[6]). Consequently the place where they together flowed

---

[1]) U. L. tablet. K. 183—202. I have taken some liberties with Thompson's translation, thinking that a more literal rendering was better suited to the purpose of this work.

[2]) *Ša il Ēa tallaktašu ina Eridu* can mean only "the way of Ea into Eridu", and not as Thompson translates, "from Ea its way in Eridu."

[3]) The meaning of these two lines is not clear.

[4]) Although the tree of Eridu, and therefore of Ea, two sungods dwell in its depths. This again shows the close relationship between fire and water in this ritual.

[5]) IV R. 22 No. 1 (= Cun. Texts XVII pl. 26), rev. 10 ff. Cf. Cun. Texts, 38, 33/34.

[6]) Cf. *Šurpu* VIII, 66; *Maqlû* V, 132; U. L. IV Col. V, 63—66; V Col. II, 59—60.

into the *apsū* was especially sacred. The waters of the Euphrates were apparently the more potent; at any rate they were more often referred to[1]. However, the water of other rivers could also be used[2].

Water of springs too was sacred and often used in ceremonies[3]. Every temple needed pure water for this purpose. Those situated on a river probably used river-water[4]. Wherever this was not obtainable, spring-water had of course to be used. Possibly every temple had one or more sacred springs. We can understand the significance of the report, that a fox had fallen into a spring in the park of a temple of Ašur[5]. The water of this spring was thus defiled. Again we read of holy water from the spring of the temple of Marduk[6]; and in another passage[7],

> I have washed my hands, have cleaned my body,
> With pure spring-water that is in Eridu.

Thus even in Eridu, not only water from the mouth of the two streams was used, but also that from springs. This shows how sacred spring-water was. Both Ea and Marduk were called respectively lord and god of the springs[8].

However the real source of water used in the incantations was the *apsū*, the deep. All rivers and springs were parts of this. Man's great benefactor was Ea, the god of the *apsū*. From out its midst rose the sun-gods, bringing release from evils. Its waters were *mē ṭābūti*, "good waters," those of the

---

1) Cf. IV R. 14 No. 2; *Šurpu* IX, 111.

2) Cf. Rm. 2, 149 (Boiss. Doc. I p. 33, 9). This passage is extremely interesting. To cure scorpion-bite a man is directed to bathe (literally, "to dip") in the river seven times. Cf. II Ki. 5, 10.

3) Cf. IV R. 26 No. 7, 34; 56 Col. I, 15, 24; Cr. II pl. 8 rev. 6; U. L. IV Col. V, 65/66; V Col. II, 60; A. S. K. T. XXI, 35/38. Also Relig. Sem. 176 ff. and 135.

4) Cf. Bruce: "Three Inscriptions of Nabopolassar" (A. J. S. L. XVI, 178 ff.) I1 Col. II, 7—9.

5) K. 551 (= AL 4 p. 76; Harper's Letters. 142).

6) IV R. 60 obv. 21.

7) *Maqlū* VII, 115—116.

8) II R. 38 No. 2. rev. 54a. Col. III, 48.

tiāmat[1]), *mē limnūti*, "evil waters"[2]). These terms had a twofold significance. The ideogram ḪUL denoted both *limnu*, "evil"; and *marru*, "bitter". By "bitter" water, the Semites understood all water unfit to drink[3]). From the *tiāmat* the evil spirits went forth, bringing calamity to man. The water of the *apsū*, on the contrary, was sweet, good to drink, and brought release from these calamities.

The method of applying the water must have originally been very simple. The priest sprinkled the sick man, and that was all. From the great importance attached to this act, and the fact that it appears in almost all ceremonies, even the simplest, we must conclude that it was the original method of expelling evil spirits. But the tendency of religion, and especially primitive religions, is to heap up forms and ceremonies. Such was the case here. In time, in addition to the simple sprinkling of water, a prayer was spoken, at first, no doubt, merely supplementary to the use of water. But gradually, as the original purpose of the prayer was forgotten, it came to be considered of importance and efficacy, equal to that of water.

This ceremony was called *ašāpu* (ושף), from which *šiptu*, "that which expels evil spirits", was derived. *Ašāpu* however was used but seldom[4]). The act itself was always *šiptu nadū* (literally, "to cast the *šiptu*"). This is further proof that the sprinkling of water was the original method of expelling evil spirits. *Šiptu nadū* was a technical term, and came in time to be used for the recital of a spoken *šiptu*, the prayer accompanying the use of water as well. The expression *šiptu manū* "to recite a *šiptu*", was seldom used except in the technical meaning, "at such and such a place in the ceremonies, recite

---

[1]) The distinction between *apsū* and *tiāmat*, which at best could never have been very clear to the Babylonians, was in time almost forgotten, and *tāmtu* came to be used for both; cf. *Šurpu* VIII, 67, where *tāmtu* is used for the customary *apsū*. Cf. also K. B. VI, I, 559 f. and Z. A. XVII, 398.

[2]) U. L. IV Col. V 63/64; V Col. II 59.

[3]) Cf. Exodus, 15, 23; Numbers, 5, 18; 19, 24.

[4]) Cf. H. W. B. 247, and note that the verb was used only in the form II, 1, i. e., to perform the ceremony of the *šiptu*.

the *šiptu*"[1]). The complete service was called *āšipūtu* or *išippūtu*[2]).

The original ideogram for *ašāpu* and words derived from it, was ŠIB[3]). It was however seldom used for *šiptu*. The customary ideograms for this were NAM-ŠIB (-BA)[4]) and NAM-ŠUB (-BA)[5]). Of course in both NAM indicates a nominal formation. NAM-ŠIB was therefore the noun coming from ŠIB = *ašāpu*, and NAM-ŠUB that from ŠUB = *nadū*[6]), in the expression *šiptu nadū*.

In time *šiptu* came to denote also the prayer spoken in connection with the use of water. This change is apparent in its different ideograms. As we expect, NAM-ŠIB, being derived from ŠIB (= *ašāpu*), denoted *šiptu* in its most general meaning, "that which expelled evil spirits". NAM-ŠUB on the contrary, referred to the casting of the water, was therefore used almost without exception for that ceremony[7]). Another

---

[1]) In this meaning it is common in the directions for ceremonies. Jensen (cf. KAT[3], 604) sees in it a reference to the metrical form of the *šiptu*. The expression *šiptu ṣaraḫu*, "to call out the *šiptu*", was extremely rare. Cf. *Maqlū* VIII, 80, 85 (below).

[2]) Cf. H. W. B. 247 and 147 a. Delitzsch regards these words as coming from different stems. But that *išippūtu* meant just the same as *āšipūtu* is clear from V R. 4, 86 (*ina šipir i-šip-pu-ti parakkēšunu ubbib*); IV R. 25, 54/55 a (*pi-ka ina i-šip-pu-ti* NAM-ŠIB-BA *ip-ti*), and V R. 51, 71/72 b (*il Ea bēl išippūti*). The ideograms *išippu* (ŠIB) and *išippūtu* (NAM-ŠIB-BA) are the same as those for *āšipu* and *šiptu*. Therefore there can be no reason to doubt that they all come from the same stem. Whether *eššepū* and *eššepūtu* (H. W. B. 146 b) were also related to *āšipu* is hard to decide. *Eššepū* denoted "wizard", and *eššepūtu* "witchcraft" (*Maqlū* III, 42; VII, 88, 93; VI, 21). No feminine of *eššepū* is known, but singularly enough the feminine of *āšipu*, *āšiptu* (*sinniš* ŠIB) was used for witch (*Maqlū* III, 43; *Šurpu* VIII, 52). This is easily explained. Among all Semites, the priestly functions were confined to the male sex. But witches too worked with spells and water just as the *āšipu*. Consequently every woman that worked with spells and water (i. e. *āšiptu*) must have been a witch.

[3]) Brün. 10359, 10368, 10379, 10381; also 10364, 10375, 10376.

[4]) Ibid. 10379.

[5]) Ibid. 2130.

[6]) Ibid. 1434.

[7]) An exception to this is U. L. III, 96—8.

ideogram for *šiptu* was TÚ[1]), compounded of KA (= "word")[2]), and LI (= "pure")[3]). It denoted therefore "the pure (or "purifying") word", and naturally referred chiefly to the spoken *šiptu*. Another ideogram, identical in meaning and use with TÚ, was KA-AZAG (-GA[4]). TÚ could also be rendered in Assyrian, *tû*[5]), a reading related of course to the pronunciation of the ideogram[6]). Naturally it denoted only the spoken *šiptu*. TÚ-DUGGA[7]) was also used in the same sense. SAR[8]) was also equivalent to *šiptu*, but in what particular meaning is not clear.

As this ritual developed, the spoken *šiptu* increased in significance, until it finally became the most important part of the service. Water on the contrary was used less and less, until it came to be regarded, along with other ceremonies, as subordinate to, and accompanying, the spoken *šiptu*. The great incantation series, such as *Maqlû*, *Šurpu*, and *Utukkē limnūti*, are mere collections of spoken *šiptu*'s with, generally, short directions for accompanying ceremonies. Most of these ceremonies bore a direct relation to the *šiptu* they accompanied. Thus during the *šiptu*, beginning, "I have washed my hands," the man for whom it was recited, actually washed his hands.[9])

At the beginning of every spoken *šiptu*, the ideogram, EN[10]), was placed. This was merely the superscription of the spoken *šiptu*, and was itself not read. It was seldom used otherwise than in this technical sense[11]). At the end of each *šiptu*, TÚ-EN is usually found. The actual meaning of this ideogram is unknown, but it no doubt indicated the completion

---

1) Brün. 781; cf. 785.
2) Ibid. 518.
3) Ibid. 1103.
4) IV R. 22 No. 2, 14/15.
5) Brün. 782.
6) Delitzsch derives *tû* from *tamû*; "to exorcise": "Hiob" p. 168.
7) U. L. tablet C. 191; IV R. 7, 44a (= *Šurpu* V/VI, 50).
8) Brün. 4338.
9) *Maqlû* VII, 115—142.
10) Brün. 10857.
11) Exceptions are IV R. 55 No. 2, 19a; Cr. I pl. 59. 7.

of the *šiptu*[1]). At the beginning of the directions for the ceremonies accompanying a spoken *šiptu*, KA-KA-MA[2]) occurs. As the ideogram shows, this referred only to the spoken *šiptu*. Like ÉN, its use was technical, and it is rarely met with elsewhere, than in the above mentioned place[3]).

Thus in time the Babylonians came to look upon the spoken *šiptu* as the most efficacious means of removing evil spirits. The real force of the *šiptu* lay in the utterance of the names of the gods. Like other Semitic peoples, the Babylonians attached wonderful powers to the divine names[4]). When Aṣu-šunamir is sent to bring Ištar back from the underworld, Ea charges him, *tummēšima šum ilāni rabūti*, "exorcise her (Ereškigal) by the name uf the great gods"[5]). Again an *iṣ ḫulduppū*, into which the name of Ea has been spoken, is used to drive out evil spirits[6]). Many *šiptu's* close with the solemn recital of the names and titles of the gods invoked[7]).

Others close with the words *nīš il* — — — *lū tamātu* or *nīš il* — — — *utammēka*. This is to be translated, "in the name of — — — I exorcise thee"[8]). In this formula the name

[1]) Tallqvist's reading, *idī šiptu* (*Maqlū*, notes, p. 119 f.) has not been generally accepted.

[2]) Brün. 589. Since these directions are generally Sumerian, it is perhaps better to read, INIM-INIM-MA.

[3]) Exceptions are IV R. 4 Col. III (= Cun. Texts. XVII pl. 23) 32/33; U. L. tablet C. Col. III, 42/43; col. IV, 28/29; 143/144.

[4]) Note how Asarḫaddon has the people swear allegiance to Ašurbanipal in the name of the gods. Ašurb. I, 21.

[5]) Cf. K. B. VI, I, 86/87, 17. Jensen translates this, "lass sie aussprechen den Namen der grossen Götter." This is entirely too literal to convey the meaning of the text. Cf. also the effect which the mention of the name of Ninib has upon the *labbu*, K. 4829 (Hrozný in M. V. A. G. 1903, 5 pp. 16—17) obv. 11—14.

[6]) U. L. tablet. K. 141/142; cf. Beitr. XXXI—XXXVII St. II 17, and Cr. II pl. 4. 34.

[7]) Cf. *Maqlū* IV, 57—61; III, 180—183; V, 10. It is noteworthy that PAD, the usual ideogram for *tamū* (Brün. 9417. 9418), the customary verb in Babylonian for "to exorcise", is also equivalent to *zakāru*, (Brün. 9420) "to speak (the names of the gods)". Cf. IV R. 29 No. I rev. 15/17; K. 4829 obv. 11—14, and below, p. 36, note 2.

[8]) Cf. Jensen in K. B. II Ašurb. I, 21—22, VIII, 45, 50. For a somewhat different and less correct translation, although eventually with the same meaning, cf. Delitzsch, H. W. B. 482 f., AL' 178 a.

of any of the gods could be inserted. How *nīš* came to have this meaning is easily explained. The expression *šumu našū*, corresponding to the Hebrew נשא שם, must have existed in Assyrian. *Nīš ili* was a technical term for oath [1]. Speaking the names of the gods was usually the privilege of the priests alone; was too sacred for profane lips except when taking a solemn oath. Any transgression of this law was sin, and brought with it the usual calamities [2]. This is of course the same idea as in the third commandment [3].

Many *šiptu's* close in a manner similar to the following:

In the name of Heaven be thou exorcised! In the name of earth be thou exorcised!
In the name of Bēl, lord of the world, be thou exorcised!
In the name of Bēltis, mistress of the world, be thou exorcised!
In the name of Ninib, mighty warrior of Bēl, be thou exorcised!
In the name of Nuzku, the exalted messenger of Bēl, be thou exorcised!
In the name of Ištar, mistress of mankind, be thou exorcised!
In the name of Adad, the lord whose thunder is good, be thou exorcised!
In the name of Šamaš, lord of judgment, be thou exorcised!
In the name of the Anunnaki, the great gods, be thou exorcised! [4]

Often a longer list of gods is given [5]. The usual formula however is:

nīš šamē lū tamāta, nīš irṣitim lū tamāta [6]

---

[1]) In *Šurpu* VIII, 27 and K. 155 rev. 13, *nīš* is synonymous with *māmītu*, *arnu* and other words, denoting the evil, unclean and sinful state resulting from the attacks of the evil spirits. It can therefore mean only "curse", or perhaps better still "a charm spoken in the name of the evil spirits". Cf. Cun. Texts XVII pl. 34, 35—40.

[2]) *Šurpu* VIII, 43, *nīš ili zakāru*; cf. II, 14 (note) where MU = *nīš*. Cf. also ⨀ 116 (A. S. K. T. No. 4) Col. II, 42—43; II R. 40 No. 4, obv. 1/3; III R. 38, No. 1, obv. 12, and *Maqlū* VII, 130. Cf. also V R. VIII, 45, 50 with I, 21—22 and Asarh. (Prism A) I, 43.

[3]) Exodus 20 7. Cf. also Leviticus 24, 10 ff.

[4]) U. L. V Col. III 57-Col. IV 6.

[5]) Ibid. Col. II 9—54.

[6]) Ibid. Col. IV 38; Col. V 58; III 20, 168, 202, 228, etc.

In the name of heaven be thou exorcised! In the name of earth be thou exorcised!,

or still simpler:

nīš ilāni rabūti lū tamāta[1])

In the name of the great gods, be thou exorcised!

This was probably a stereotyped expression for the names of all the gods.

Sometimes the priest changes the formula to:

utammēki il Anum abū ilāni rabūti[2])

I exorcise thee by Anu, father of the great gods,

or,

nīš ilāni rabūti utammēka[3]).

In the name of the great gods I exorcise thee.

Often the words, *lū tatallak*, "that thou mayest depart", are added[4]). This formula may also occur just before the end of a *šiptu*, which then concludes with an exhortation to the evil spirits to leave the sick man[5]), or with the threat that, if they do not depart, they shall receive no food nor drink[6]).

In time the use of the *šiptu* was expanded. The possibility always existed that evil spirits might lurk in the objects to be used in the services. These were therefore first purified. Thus Ea directs Marduk, before using milk and butter, to first speak his *šiptu* over them[7]). This practice was carried so far that a *šiptu* was spoken over the water used against the evil spirits[8]). This was now *mū ellu*, "holy water"[9]). This shows how much the original conception of water had changed.

Another development was the recital of various *šiptu's* over the different parts of the body. Thus *šiptu's* were spoken,

---

1) IV R. 58 Col. I 59; U. L. III 123/4.
2) IV R. 56 Col. II 8—18.
3) U. L. tablet C. 63/64; G. 32; IV Col. I 20/21.
4) Ibid. C. 114/115. G. 32; IV Col. I 20/21.
5) Ibid. V Col. IV 23/26.
6) Ibid. Col. III 37/38; Col. II 55/63.
7) IV R. 4 Col. III (= Cun. Texts XVII pl. 23) 32/33.
8) IV R. 22 No. 1 (= Cun. Texts XVII pl. 25) rev. 12/13.
9) Cf. Num. 5 17. Note also the use of holy water in the Catholic church. For a different conception of the purpose of this *šiptu* and the efficacy thereby imparted to this water cf. M. A. 72 f.

respectively, over the head, neck, right and left hands and feet, breast, heart and hips (?) of a sick child; also over the objects placed at each side of the door, and suspended over the child's head[1]). Usually a *šiptu* was recited but once; very often however it was repeated three times[2]). From this it is clear that the purification ceremonies were often very complex and long drawn out.

The priest who performed these ceremonies was called *āšipu* or *mašmašu*. *Āšipu* is of course the participle of *ašāpu*. *Mašmašu* was probably derived from the Sumerian MAŠ-MAŠ. A verb *mašū* existed in Assyrian, with the ideogram NI[3]), synonymous with *namāru* and *uḫḫuru*. A verb, *mašū*, with the ideogram MAŠ, also existed. MAŠ was equivalent, not only to *namāru*[4]) and *uḫḫuru*[5]), but also to *ellu*[6]). Throughout the *āšipu*-ritual, *ellu* and *namru* were synonyms. We must therefore conclude that the two verbs, *mašū*, were identical. Furthermore, MAŠ-MAŠ was also the ideogram for *mullilu*[7]) which was in turn a synonym of *āšipu*. But *mullilu* meant, "the one who makes clean", "the purifier". Since *mašmašu* had the same meaning, it must have been closely related to *mašū*. From all this evidence it follows that, not only was *mašmašu* derived from the Sumerian MAŠ-MAŠ, but also *mašū* from MAŠ[8]).

Like *šiptu*, the original ideogram for *āšipu* was ŠIB[9]). It was however uncommon. Again, like *šiptu*, a great variety

---

[1]) IV R. 55 No. 1, 58-rev. 19.

[2]) Ibid. obv. 55; Beitr. XXXI-XXXVII St. I 15, 16, 21; XXVI Col. III 36 ff. Cf. below.

[3]) Cf. H. W. B. 429 b.

[4]) Brün. 1775.

[5]) Ibid. 1734.

[6]) Ibid. 1750.

[7]) Ibid. 1845.

[8]) מִשְׁעִי (Ez. 16, 4) may be related to *mašū*.

[9]) The close relation of the chief terms of the *āšipu*-ritual to the ideogram ŠIB (cf. Brün. 10359, 10368, 10375, 10376, 10379, and 10381) is significant. In Sumerian this is read *i-ši-ib* (Sb. 139). This tends to show that *ašāpu* was derived from the Sumerian. This is born out by the fact that it does not occur in any other Semitic language. Was perhaps, the whole *āšipu*-ritual of Sumerian origin? There is much in favor of this theory.

of ideograms were used for *āšipu*, most of them, singularly enough, designating him as the priest of the spoken *šiptu*. Among these were *amēl* TÚ-TÚ [1]), *amēl* KA-AZAG-GA [2]) or *amēl* KA-AZAG-GÁL [3]), *amēl* KA-NER [4]), *amēl* KA-UG [5]), *amēl* KA-KA [6]) and *amēl* KA-KA-MA [7]). Other ideograms, whose meanings were not certain, were *amēl* LUB-DUB [8]) and *amēl* ŠIM-SAR [9]).

It is significant, that among these ideograms, none indicate the *āšipu* specifically as the user of water. Certainly there must have been some such designation, and, because of the importance of water in this ritual, it could not have been uncommon; must therefore have come down to us. What could it have been?

A close examination of the terms, *āšipu* and *mašmašu*, shows that there was a distinction between them. In Beitr. XXVI the *mašmašu* acts merely as the assistant of another priest, belonging to the same class as himself, but apparently of higher rank [10]). Furthermore, Marduk-šakin-šum writes to the king, that the day fixed for certain purification-ceremonies being unpropitious for the *mašmašu*, he could not officiate; the writer would therefore officiate for him [11]). This shows that

---

1) = "the man of the spoken *šiptu*". U. L. III 129/130, 237/238, 262/263; IV R. 17 rev. 6; 20 No. 2 rev. 9; 18 No. 3 additions.

2) = "man of the pure mouth." Sm. 1674 rev.

3) = "man of the pure mouth." Brün. 750. Note also IV R. 30* obv. 23/24. MULU-TÚ-GÁL, A. S. K. T. XII obv. 11—12 and U. L. tablet B. 52/53, KA-TÚ-GÁL.

4) = "man of the pure mouth (?)". Brün. 743 and U. L. III 176/177.

5) Brün. 636.

6) Beitr. XXVI Col. VI 33. KA-KA=*tamū* (Brün. 578), "to exorcise". *amēl* KA-KA=*āšipu* = *tammā'u* cf. below p. 42.

7) Brün. 590.

8) Ibid. 7281 =*pāšiḫ kūru*, "the allayer of pain" (?).

9) Brün. 5174.

10) Notice the 2nd person, *tu-ḫap*, in Col. I 23, and that in the next line the *mašmašu* is referred to in the 3rd person; cf. also Col. II 19—21, III 17—19. IV 32—37.

11) K. 602 (Harper's Letters. 23) obv. 20—27. *šarra be-li ú-da* (21) *amēl mašmašu ūmu limnu ibbašē* (-*e*) *lā ṭābu* (22) *niš qāti lā i-na-aš-ši* (23) *ú-ma-a ri-eš dup-pa-a-ni* (24) *ma-'-a-du-ti lū XX lū XXX* (25) *damqāti*

Marduk-šakin-šum was not a *mašmašu*; yet he could perform this priest's duties. This and other letters show that Marduk-šakin-šum was either a physician or an *āšipu*. All evidence points to the latter. Thus, in another letter he instructs a *mašmašu* how to perform certain ceremonies[1]), and again he advises the use of images to remove the effect of witchcraft[2]), precisely as in *Maqlū*. In several letters[3]) he is associated with Adad-šum-uṣur, who must also have been an *āšipu*. This man says of himself[4]): *ú-ma-a* (13) *ú-da-a ki-i ni-me-qi* (*14*) *ša il E-a u il Silig-Mulu-Sár* (15) *u ši-tu qātā ša ardi-šu* (16) *i-šal-li-mu* "Now (the king) knows that the wisdom of Ea and Marduk, and his servant's raising (?)[5]) of the hands makes well"[6]). That he speaks in this way of "the wisdom of Ea and Marduk," which was almost a technical term for the *āšipu*-ritual in general, and uses here the ideogram for Marduk peculiar to this ritual, and also refers to the raising (?) of his hands in prayer as restoring health, proves beyond doubt that he was an *āšipu*. He too, like Marduk-šakin-šum gives instructions to the *mašmašu*[7]). Furthermore, he speaks of himself in

---

a-šár-ú-ti (26) *ú-ba-'* *a-na-aš-ši-a* (27) *a-šaṭ-ṭar*. "The king, my lord, knows, that the day is evil, not good, (for) the *mašmašu*; he will not raise his hands in prayer. Now the chief (?) tablets, whether twenty or thirty, many, propitious, favorable, I will bring, I will lift up, I will write." This passage is very significant.

[1]) K. 626 (Harper's Letters, 24).

[2]) K. 643 (Ibid. 11); K. 490 (Ibid. 18) K. 639 (Ibid. 25); cf. K. 583 (Ibid. 5) and K. 595 (Ibid. 6).

[3]) K. 643 (Ibid. 11); K. 1087 (Ibid. 14); K. 1197 (Ibid 15).

[4]) K. 618 (Ibid. 9), rev. 12—16.

[5]) This word I can explain only as a popular form of *nīš* from *našū* corresponding to the Hebrew שאת. Or can it perhaps be read *ši-pir*? Either reading however shows that this ceremony was a part of the *āšipu*-ritual.

[6]) For this meaning of *šalāmu* cf. below p. 45. The use of this word, a technical term in the *āšipu*-ritual, is further proof that this is an *āšipu*-letter.

[7]) K. 167 (Harper's Letters, 1), rev. 5—9; *ina ši-'-a-ri al-lak* (6) *a-mar-šu-nu šul-mu-šu-nu* (7) *a-na šarri a-qab-bi* (8) *amēl mašmašē* pl *ú-pa-qá-da* (9) *tul-lu-šu-nu e-pu-šu*. "In the morning I will go (and) observe their condition. I will report to the king. I will charge *mašmašu's*; they shall perform their ceremony".

connection with Arad-Ea, Ištar-šum-ēriš and Nabū-kullanu[1]), showing that they too were *āšipu's*. One of these, Arad-Ea, writes to the king[2]): *ana-ku ū-me mu-šu* (7) *ina muḫ-ḫi napšāte pl ša bēli-ia* (9) *u-ṣal-la* "I pray for the life of my lord, day and night"; additional proof that he was a priest, and not a physician.

This evidence shows that the *mašmašu* was a priest of the same class as, but subordinate to, the *āšipu*; that he received his instructions from him, and at times acted as the latter's assistant. It is surprising how seldom the name, *āšipu*, occurs in the directions for ceremonies. The usual officiating priest is the *mašmašu*. The ideogram for *mašmašu* designates him as "the purifyer", without the slightest reference to the use of the spoken *šiptu*. Both Ea and Marduk, who in the *āšipu*-ritual are essentially gods of the holy, purifying water, are repeatedly called *mašmaš ilāni*. They are also called *āšipu*, but this is comparatively rare; and besides, this was a general name for that class of priests to which the *mašmašu* belonged. As, in time, the use of water became secondary to the spoken *šiptu*, so also was the *mašmašu* subordinate to the *āšipu*. All this, though in itself hardly sufficient proof, would tend to show that the *mašmašu* was originally that priest who exorcised evil spirits by means of water.

Synonyms of *āšipu* were *muššipu* and *mullilu*. The former is, of course, merely the participle II_1 of *ašāpu*; the latter the same form of *alālu*. The two words were generally used together, the latter as complement of the former[3]). One ideogram for *muššipu*, *amēl* GIŠ-GAM-ŠU-UL[4]), designated him as "bearer of the *gamlu*". Since the epithet, *mullilu*, was originally applied to this utensil, it is clear how closely related the two terms, *muššipu* and *mullilu* were. An ideogram for *mullilu* was GIL-MÁ-DUB (= *sanga*)[5]).

---

[1]) K. 1428 (Harper 16).

[2]) K. 1040 (Ibid. 28), rev. 6—9.

[3]) K. 2866 obv. 28 (H. W. B. 247 a) *mullilu muššipu* [*ša?*] *šamē u irṣitim*; cf. *Šurpu* VIII, 24.

[4]) Brün. 1221.

[5]) Sb. Col. II, 11. The meaning of this ideogram is unknown; however it indicates the *mullilu* as the bearer of something.

Another priest-name, probably synonymous with *āšipu*, was *tammā'u*. It is found so far only once, and that in a syllabary. The ideogram is *amēl* NAM-ERIM-KUD-DA[1]), i. e. "the man who speaks a bann"[2]). *Tammā'u* is a form فعّال from *tamū* and indicates precisely what the ideogram literally meant.

Other synonyms of *āšipu* were *ramqu* and *pašīšu*. As Jensen has shown, these words denoted repectively, "the one who washes himself", and "the one who annoints himself"[3]). They were seldom used alone, but generally in connection with *āšipu* or *mašmašu*[4]). In fact the officiating priest was never designated otherwise than as *āšipu* or *mašmašu*, usually the latter.

The state of uncleanliness and sin, from which the sick man was to be freed, was called *māmītu*. There were really two words, *māmītu*, in Assyrian[5]). The first denoted "bann", "exorcism", that by which the evil spirits were removed; was therefore a synonym of *šiptu*. Its usual ideogram was ŠAG-BA[6]), equivalent in meaning to *pašāru*, a technical term for the removal of evil spirits[7]). The ideogram for the second *māmītu* was NAM-ERIM[8]), denoting "the state of evil"[9]), or "uncleanliness". Although the usual destinction between the two words and their respective ideograms was generally main-

---

[1]) Brün. 2183; cf. above, p. 39, note 6.

[2]) For the meaning of NAM-ERIM cf. below. Cf. also V R. 20, 9—10, e and f.

[3]) Cf. K. B. VI, I, 367 f., 462 f. I must differ somewhat from Jensen's explanation of these two words. It was the duty of the *āšipu* or *mašmašu*, before beginning his actual services, to purify himself. This he did, either by washing in holy water, or by annointing himself, or both. The two names then refer to these acts. This is born out by V R. 24, 5 c. d., where *ramqu* is given as a synonym for *ellu*. As we shall see, *ellu* is the state into which one comes after being washed in holy water.

[4]) Cf. U. L. III, 128—130.

[5]) H. W. B. 415 f.

[6]) Brün. 3533.

[7]) A. S. K. T. XI Col. III 18; cf. Brün. 3534 and 2181.

[8]) Brün. 2178.

[9]) Ibid. 4607.

tained throughout the religious literature, instances of their apparent confusion are not uncommon[1]).

A synonym of *māmītu* (II) was *'iltu*, derived from the stem אאל "to bind"[2]). It was probably based upon the idea that one method, by which the witches worked, was to bind knots, thus entangling man in the snares of their witchcraft[3]). The usual ideogram for *'iltu* was NAM-LAL[4]), denoting, "the state of being bound". A word apparently synonymous with both *māmītu* (I) and (II) was *uṣurtu*[5]). Its exact meaning however is unknown.

The usual verbs for sprinkling a sick man with water were *zarāqu* and *salāḫu*[6]), the latter the more common. The technical term for purifying the place where a ceremony was to be held, was *šabātu*. Sometimes, instead of merely sprinkling with water, the whole body or certain members were washed. The verbs for this were *ramāqu*, *mašū* or *šaḫātu*[7]).

---

[1]) For NAM-ERIM used for *māmītu* (I) cf. Brün. 2184; cf. p. 42 above, to *tammā'u*. For ŠAG-BA used for *māmītu* (II) cf. IV R. 7 (= *Šurpu* V/VI) obv. 7/8; also V R. 50, 33/34 a, where ŠAG-BA=*arāru*.

[2]) H. W. B. 2 a.

[3]) Cf. *Maqlū* II, 148—153; VII, 106, 113.

[4]) Brün. 1086. Another ideogram is KI-GA-A (IV R. 19, 12/13 b).

[5]) Cf. IV R. 16 No. 1, 1/2 and V R. 51 b 35/36, and A. S. K. T. VII rev. 5, and XII, 44.

[6]) Zimmern proposes the question whether the Hebrew סלח, "to forgive sin", be not identical with this word. When we remember that the Assyrian *salāḫu* also meant "to remove uncleanliness", therefore "to remove sin", there can be but little doubt of this.

[7]) Cf. H. W. B. 651 a. III שחת and IV R. 60 rev. 25. As oil came to be used for water (cf. below) the verbs *pašāšu*, *sakū* and *mašā'u* (cf. KAT[3] 602) became in part equivalent to *ramāqu* and *mašū*. *Pasāšu* was in fact even applied to the use of water. The phrase, *pašiš-apsē*, hardly meant, as Jensen explains (K. B. VI, I, 463), "ein Weltmeer-gesalbter", but refers merely to the ceremony of washing with holy water before the divine services. Jensen's explanation of the great *apsū* and little *apsū*, that Ur-Nina set up in the temple (K. B. III, I, 13), seems forced. Probably these were merely basins in which holy water of the *apsū* stood ready for use in the temple (cf. KAT[3] 525 f). Certainly a supply of holy water must have been present at all times. This may also be the explanation of the great sea that Solomon set up in his temple (1 Ki. 7, 23—26.) It rested on the backs of twelve oxen, and, as Jensen says, the ox was sacred to Marduk, therefore closely related to the apsū.

The act of expelling evil spirits was called *kuppuru*[1]). As Zimmern has shown, the original meaning of this word was "to wash away"[2]). In the sense of cleaning from evil spirits, it came to be applied to inanimate objects as well as human beings[3]). The noun, *takpirtu,* denoted both the ceremony itself[4]) and the uncleanliness removed. That this was something substantial: real, impure water, and not merely symbolic, may be inferred from the sentence *takpirtašu ana sūq irbitti* [— — —], "[cast?] his *takpirtu* to the four directions"[5]).

Another word, practically synonymous, was *quddušu*[6]). It meant simply, "to make pure", and was used transitively[7]), as well as reflexively. In the latter meaning it was the usual verb for the purification of the priest, preparatory to performing his holy duties[8]). A secondary meaning to the word, rare in Assyrian, but common in Hebrew, was "to dedicate something for holy purposes"[9]).

As the result of *kuppuru,* a sick man became *ellu,* "clean, pure, free from evil spirits"[10]). Naturally everything used in the ceremonies had to be pure. This was especially true of water. *Mū ellu*[11]) meant more than merely "clean water". It was "holy" water, fit for use in religious ceremonies, free from all impurities, ritual and otherwise, and therefore able to expel evil spirits. The water of the *apsū* was, in general, *ellu,* but

---

1) Cf. H. W. B. 348 a (II כפר). Beitr. p. 92, KAT³ 601 f. and K. B. VI, I, 393.

2) Ibid.; cf. also *ina šēri zumrišu kuppir* (Cun. Texts XVII. 30, 35/36).

3) Beitr. XLI—XLII St. I, 28—29.

4) Cf. 81—2—4, 49 (Harper's Letters, 370).

5) IV R. 13 rev. 51; cf. Beitr. XXVI Col. I, 18—20.

6) Cf. H. W. B. 581 b; KAT³ 602 f.

7) Beitr. XLVI—XLVII St. I, 1—3; LII, 2; LVIII, 2 (note); IV R. 56 Col. II 23.

8) Beitr. I—XX 30.

9) Cf. *Šurpu* II, 77. Note also the name, *qadištu,* for a priestess (?) of Ištar. Even if the word originally indicated Ištar herself as "the ritually pure" (KAT³ 423), it came finally to be used only for the priestesses. And without doubt, the Babylonians must have regarded this name as denoting "those devoted to Ištar"; cf. K. B. VI, I, 439.

10) That *ellu* was equivalent to טהור is clear from II Ki. 5, 10.

11) IV R. 25, 31 b; 55 No. 2, 14 a; 60 obv. 15, cf. Num. 5, 17.

even it, as we have seen[1]), could be rendered still more holy by speaking a *šiptu* over it.

The most common synonyms of *ellu* were *ebbu* and *namru*. Others were *zakū* and *quddušu*[2]). A partial synonym of *ellu* was *damqu*[3]). Therefore the hands of the gods were *qātā damqāti*[4]) as well as *ellāti*[5]). And just because a thing was *ellu*, dit it have power over the evil spirits. Therefore *ullulu*[6]) and *dummuqu*[7]) denoted "to purify", "to restore to health". Synonyms of these words were *šullumu*[8]), *pašāḫu*[9]), *nūḫ*[10]) *bulluṭu*[11]), *bunnū*[12]) and *ṭubbu*[13]).

The following passage[14]) serves to show how closely related these terms were, as well as other meanings in which they could be used:

266. *tāka ellu ana tēa šukun*;
pīka elli ana pīia šukun;
amātum ellītim dummiq;
qibīt pīia šullim;

---

[1]) Above p. 37.

[2]) קדש could also mean "pure", "clean", without reference to being dedicated to holy purposes; cf. I Sam. 21, 6.

[3]) Cf. IV R. 26, No. 5 (= Cun. Texts XVII, pl. 41) 11/12, *sinništu ša qātāša lā damqā* (= *lā misā*), and IV R. 14 No. 2, rev. 18/19, *ša ṣarpi ḫurāṣi mudammiqšunūti atta*. Here *dummuqu* = *nummuru* = *ullulu*. Note too that good spirits were never called *ṭābu* (cf. *utukku limnu*), but always *damqu* or *dumqu*.

[4]) IV R. 4 Col. III,3/4, (= Cun. Texts XVII, 22); Ibid. 46—48; 29 No. 4 (C.) II, 24.

[5]) IV R. 25 Col. IV, 44/49; K. B. VI, 1, 92, 13.

[6]) H. W. B. 71 f.

[7]) IV R. 3 Col. II, 25/26 (= Cun. Texts XVII, 21); 22 No. 1 rev. 29/30; cf. above, note 3.

[8]) IV R. 21 No. 1 (C.) III, 5.

[9]) U. L. III, 231/232 ff; IV R. 22 No. 1 obv. 54/55; No. 2, 14/15.

[10]) Cf. K. B. VI, I, 100, 17; U. L. III, 231/232.

[11]) U. L. III, 90/91; B. M. S. XII (= IV R. 57) 90; VIII, 17; IV, 32; VI, 75; VII, 13.

[12]) K. B. VI, I, 22, 24—26.

[13]) Cf. H. W. B. 300 b.

[14]) U. L. III, 266—291.

parṣiia ullulu qibī;
ema allaku lušlim;
amēlu alappatu lišlim;
ana pāniia egirtum damiqtim liqqabī,
ana arkiia ubānu damiqtim littariṣ.
lū šēdu dumqiia atta,
lū lamassi dumqiia attu.
ilāni mušallimu ^il^ *Marduk*
ema tallaktiia šalāmu liš[lim].

Add thy pure spell unto mine;
Add thy pure voice[1]) unto mine;
Make efficacious my pure charm[2]);
Endow with power to heal, the word of my mouth;
Ordain that my exorcism[3]) purify;
Wherever I go, let me be healthy,
Before me may propitious thoughts be spoken;
After me may a propitious finger be pointed:
Yea, thou art my guardian *šēdu*;
My guardian *lamassu* art thou.
O Marduk, (thou) who of the gods, bringest healing[4]),

---

[1]) Literally, "mouth".

[2]) This translation, differing from Thompson's, is based upon the following points: ll. 271—275 are clearly in parallelism; a variant of *amātum* is *amāti.* That in the final *i* of this last word, the suffix of the first person singular must lie, is clear from the Sumerian, KA-AZAG-GA-MU and the parallelism with the other two lines; *amāti (-tum)* = KA-AZAG-GA=*šiptu*; *dummiq* = "endow with power to heal" (cf. the intensive form of the verb in Hebrew and Arabic), = "make efficacious". *Šullim,* in the next line, has the same meaning.

[3]) Neither the usual translation of *parṣu,* "command", nor that offered by Thompson, "decision", suits the context here. But since *parṣu* is here in parallelism with *amātum* (KA-AZAG-GA) and *qibīt pīia,* both equivalent to *šiptu,* there can be no doubt that it has the same meaning. Notice also the expression *parṣu ša Eridu* (ŠIB NUN-KI-GA), U. L. tablet B. 46/47; cf. 62/63.

[4]) It is difficult to render this line exactly in English. The meaning is, "O Marduk, thou, who art that one of the gods, who bringest healing to men." This is then equivalent to *il Marduk mašmaš ilāni.* As we have seen (p. 45), *šullumu* is equivalent in every way to *ullulu.* *Mušallimu* then

Let me live in perfect health, wherever my path may be[1]).

A study of the Sumerian titles of some of the most important gods of the *āšipu*-ritual leads to interesting results. Marduk was called DINGIR-SILIG-NAM-ŠUB[2]), i. e. "controller of the *šiptu*". Again he was DINGIR-SILIG-NAM-TI[3]) or DINGIR-SILIG-NAM-TI-LA[4]), "the controller of life". Since one of the commonest epithets of Marduk was *muballiṭ mītū*, "the reviver of the dead", and this was brought about by means of the *šiptu*, the close relation between *šiptu* and *balāṭu* is at once apparent. It was the *šiptu* that restored life to the sick; hence the expression *šipat balāṭi*[5]).

Ea was also DINGIR-EN-TI[6]), "lord of life", and Damkina, DINGIR-NIN-TI[7]), "mistress of life". The latter was also DINGIR-NIN-ŠIB-ZU-AB[8]), "mistress of the exorcism of the deep".

A common expression for the waters of the *apsū* were *mē ṭābūti*, "good waters"[9]). The waters of the *tiāmat*, on the con-

---

is a synonym of *mullilu*. But *mullilu*, as we have also seen (p. 41), was a synonym of *mašmašu*. Note also the expression *ilu mušallimu* as epithet of the *lamassu* (above, p. 26).

[1]) This line literally translated is, "Wherever my path be, let the state of my health be complete". *Šalāmu* and *balāṭu* are synonyms in the sense, "to enjoy perfect health." It may be remarked here that *šalāmu* meant nothing more than "to be complete, perfect". However, a perfect body must be free from all bodily ills, i. e. free from evil spirits. Only such could participate in religious services. For this reason, in the Hebrew, as well as in the Babylonian ritual, priests with bodily defects were not allowed to officiate, since they were not *šalāmu*. They were perhaps regarded as being permanently possessed by an evil spirit; cf. Beitr. XXIV and Einl. p. 87.

[2]) II R. 54, 67 c.

[3]) Ibid. 66 c.

[4]) Ibid. 65 c.

[5]) IV R. 29, 35/36 a.

[6]) II R. 54, 45 c.

[7]) Ibid. 58 c. The ideogram TI-LA (= *balāṭu*) occurs also in the names of the gods, DINGIR-EN-UD-TI-LA, and DINGIR-NIN-UD-TI-LA (U. L. V Col. II, 21—22).

[8]) II R. 54, 56 c.

[9]) V R. 11, 27. Cf. Ezek. 47, 8-11, where the salt water of the sea is healed by that of the holy river flowing from the temple.

trary, were *mē limnūti*. From them the evil spirits went forth, bringing sickness and death unto man. They were therefore *mē mūti*, "waters of death". The health-bringing waters of the *apsū* were *mē balāṭi*, "waters of life"[1]). The Anunnaki had charge of these in the underworld, and through them Ištar was restored to life[2]). But the Anunnaki, together with the goddess Mammītum, decided the fate of those who entered the underworld. The expression "to decide the fate", was *šīmtu šāmu*[3]). This expression came to mean "to determine the time of death". The ideogram was NAM-TAR, the same as for the *namtāru*, the evil spirit, the messenger of Ereškigal, queen of the realm of the dead. Thus *šīmtu* came in time to denote death itself[4]). But there was a *šīmtu* of life as well[3]). Marduk, the bearer of the *dupšīmāte*, "the tablets of destiny", was the foe of the evil spirits, the giver of life to the sick[5]).

amēl qalū amēl ēdilu ultu ikribu [*ana amēli*]
il Anunnaki ilāni rabūti pa[*ḫru*]
il Mammītum bānat šīmti ittišunu šīmāte išīmma
ištaknu mūta u balāṭa
ša mūti ul uddū umēšu[6]).

After the watcher and the turnkey have greeted a man,
The Anunnaki, the great gods, assemble;
Mammītum, the one who fixes the fate, decides the fates with them.
They determine death and life,
But the days of death they do not fix[7]).

---

1) II R. 58 No. 6, 51, Cf. below.

2) K. B. VI, I, 88, 34, 38.

3) H. W. B. 653 b; cf. B. M. S. XIX, 21.

4) Note the expression *šīmti alāku* and *ūm šīmti*. H. W. B. 654 f.

5) Jensen has shown (K. B. VI, I, 405 f.) *uṣurtu* to be a synonym of *šīmtu*. In IV R. 16 No. 1 *uṣurtu* is synonymous with *māmītu*, referring to the *šiptu* of Ea, but at the same time retains the idea of *šīmtu* "fate". It is unchangeable; no god has power over it; when once fixed, neither god nor man can escape it. And yet it is, in this text, directed against the evil spirits alone; is therefore equivalent to *šīmat balāṭi* as well as *šiptu*.

6) N. E. X Col. VI 35 ff. (K. B. VI, I, 228. cf. notes).

7) Or, "they do not make known", or, "do not know", or, "are not made known"; cf. K. B. VI, I, 480.

This text describes the Anunnaki and Mammītum as passing judgment on man after he has entered the underworld, i. e. after his death. They decide not life and death, but death and life. Man's life has ceased; consequently the life here mentioned, can refer only to life *after* death, just as the order of the words *mūta u balāṭa* indicates[1]), Finally it speaks, not of the day, but of the *days*, of death. This can refer only to the days that the dead man must pass in the underworld. The thought conveyed by the text is therefore, that the gods mentioned decide death and life, i. e. whether a man is to be restored to life or not, after the days of his stay in the underworld are passed, but these they do not determine.

This text seems to show that the Babylonians believed, to a certain extent at least, in resurrection and future life[2]). True, the proof is slight. Had the conception of future life been well defined, we would expect to find many references to it in the literature. Such is however not the case. Yet this is easily explained. Even to-day, when the belief in future life is held by all orthodox Jews, Christians and Mohammedans, the conception of this life is, at the best, vague. What it is, when it shall come, and how, no one knows. Gabriel blows his horn, the dead arise from their graves, and judgment follows. Even the most orthodox does not conceive of much more than this. And we seldom refer to future life except in sermons or at funerals. The Babylonians, however, could not have gone even as far as this. At the most, they did not conceive of anything more than that the dead were restored to this life; otherwise, as Jensen has well asked[3]), why determine death and life? Consequently man had nothing to gain by that future life. It could be no better than the present, and

[1]) Jensen's explanation that the Anunnaki judge the dead, while Mammītum judges the unborn, of newborn, children (p. 479) seems forced. There is absolutely nothing in the text referring to such children. It states clearly that these gods sit in judgment on the dead, and decide *death and life*.

[2]) Of all Assyriologists, Jensen and Pinches alone hold this view. Others, like Zimmern (KAT[3] 638 f.), admit its possibility, but claim that the proof so far is not sufficient.

[3]) K. B. VI, I, 480.

before it could come, there was the long period in the underworld to be passed through, the length of which even the gods could not determine. And besides, there was the possibility that he would never be restored to life. No! For the Babylonian this life held all that was good; the underworld was for him a place of terrors; and did his thoughts pass beyond this to a future life, it was with but little anticipation of pleasure. This life was *ṭābu*, "good"; the underworld was *limnu*, "bad"; and the next life, he knew no more about it than that it might perhaps be. No wonder then that references to the future life were few, obscure, and apparently clouded with doubt[1]).

And yet the belief in resurrection was so well-suited to the Babylonians' view of life, that the wonder would be, not that they should have conceived of it, but rather that they should not. For to them, more than to any other people of antiquity, this belief lay ready to hand. They saw the sun rise and set from day to day, and to them it was a mystery requiring explanation. They pondered over it, and it found its place in their mythology and religion. They saw the passage of the sun from the summer to the winter solstice, and back again, year after year; the cycle of the moon's phases[2]); and Venus disappear as the evening-star only to reappear as the morning-star. And all these changes represented to them the life and death of the gods, and their restoration to life. Ištar, sprinkled with the water of life, leaves the realm of the dead, restoring thereby creative life to all the world. It would be strange indeed, had not the Babylonians, with such a lively conception of the return to life of the gods above them, and the animals and plants below, never asked themselves, "will not man too sometimes come forth from the underworld?"[3])

---

[1]) Cf. N. E. VII Col. 29 ff. (K. B. VI, I, 188—189.)

[2]) This must be the thought underlying U. L. XVI, where Sin, attacked by the evil spirits, is powerless before them. Nor can Šamaš, Adad nor Ištar help him, but only Ea and Marduk. Cf. KAT[3] 500.

[3]) This is in fact the question put by Gilgameš (NE X Col. III, 31 f.). "Will I also, just as he (Eabani), lay myself down; will I never rise again?" This question he put to Siduri-sabitu (X Col. II, 13—14), Ur-Nimin (Col. III, 31) and Ut-Napištim (Col. IV, 22). The latter answered this question apparently, but the entire column V and part of column VI are broken

Perhaps the answer to this question may be seen in the god Nin-Azu. He was lord of the underworld, husband of Ereškigal. However, when Nērgal entered the underworld, he became her husband[1]), and Nin-Azu sank into insignificance. Consequently we must picture him as the husband of Ereškigal at the time when Nērgal was no longer in the underworld; when, as a sun-god, he had gone forth and taken his place among the gods of heaven, i. e. in the spring and summer. Nin-Azu was, as his name indicates, "the lord who understands water", or "the physician," the god of healing. He seems to have been also a god of vegetation[2]). That he was not merely one of the gods of, but the lord of the underworld, and at the time when both gods and plants were restored to life, must have a deep significance; it can indicate nothing else than that this principle of restoration to life was active in the underworld, and that, to a certain extent at least, it must have affected the ghosts of mortals there.

But Nin-Azu was not the only principle of resurrection in the underworld. The water of life was there as well. And why were Nin-Azu and the water of life located in the underworld, if not that they bore a direct relation to its inhabitants, the dead? And granting this, what else can we conclude but that the restoration of the dead to life was an actual principle of the Babylonian theology?

But the real gods of the restoration to life were Ea and Marduk, especially the latter, acting in his usual capacity of messenger to his father. He, more than all other gods decided the fate of men; was *mušīm šīmāte*[3]), and as such, bore on his

away. The concluding lines of column VI are those cited above (p. 48). Must we not then regard them as the answer to this question: that every mortal must die, but that there *may* be a life *after* death? Gilgameš then asks Ut-Napištim (N. E. XI), "But how is it that you, who are seemingly a mortal, just as I, how is it that you did not meet this fate; that you too did not die?"

[1]) K. B. VI, I, 74 ff.

[2]) Ibid. 525.

[3]) Cr. II pl. 1, obv. 5. For these titles cf. Hehn: "Hymnen und Gebete an Marduk", p. 13 ff. Ea and Šamaš, who were most closely associated with Marduk in the removal of evil spirits, and also Bēl, were likewise called *bēl šīmāte* (B. M. S. X, 15—16; XIX, 6—9, VI, 112).

breast the tablets of destiny[1]). Again Marduk was *il* TU-TU, "the giver of birth to, and restorer of, the gods to life"[2]); *il Zi-ukkin*, "the life of all the gods"[3]), and *il Asar-ri*, "the god who brings forth vegetation"[4]). But above all, his most usual attribute, he was *muballiṭ mītu*, "the restorer of the dead to life"[5]). And along with this he was *bēl šipti ellītim*, "lord of the pure exorcism"[6]). He was also the *rīmēnu ša bulluṭu bašū ittišu*, "the merciful one, with whom rests the power to restore life"[7]), and *ša ina šiptišu ellītim issuḫu nagab limnūti*, "who with his pure exorcism, tears away all evil"[8]).

---

[1]) K. B. VI, I, 34 f. Notice also the seal of life held by Bēl-Marduk (K. B. VI, I, 47, 3).

[2]) *Mu'allid ilāni, muddiš ilāni*: K. 2107, 9 (cf. Hehn. p. 14); cf. also *mudiššu balāṭi mušallim napišti* (IV R. 21* No. 1 (C.) III 5).

[3]) K. B. VI, I, 34, 1.

[4]) *Šāriq mērišti mukīn iṣ(s)rati bānū šeam u qē mušēṣi urqīti*. (Hehn. p. 14); cf. IV R. 57 (= B. M. S. XII) obv. 30.

[5]) This title was born also by Ninib and Gula, the gods of medicine. With them however, and to a certain extent, with Marduk also, this meant merely, "the restorer to life of him who is sick unto death". That this was not the meaning everywhere, can not be disputed. It is interesting to note, not only this, but other attributes, common to Marduk, but applied to Jahwe in the Hebrew prayer: אתה גבור לעולם יהוה מחיה מתים אתה רב להושיע משיב הרוח ומוריד הגשם מכלכל חיים בחסד מחיה מתים ברחמים רבים סומך נופלים ורופא חולים ומתיר אסורים ומקים אמונתו לישני עפר, "Thou art powerful, O Jahwe, forever, reviver of the dead; Thou art mighty in salvation: (Thou) who causest the wind to blow, and bringest down the rain; who providest for the living in kindness; who revivest the dead in abundant kindness; who supportest the falling, curest the sick and freest the imprisoned, and fulfillest His promise unto those who sleep in the dust."

Since the so-called "Eighteen Benedictions", of which the above forms part, were introduced into the Jewish ritual by Gamliel II, probably before 100 A. D (Graetz: "History of the Jews" [English edition] II 363), it is hardly likely that they were influenced by Christian theology. It seems more probable that the doctrine of resurrection in both Christianity and Judaism goes back to a Babylonian origin. That the Jews held this doctrine before the time of Jesus, may be inferred from John 11, 24.

[6]) K. B. VI, I p. 34, 12, 19; IV R. 29 No. 1, 35/36 a.

[7]) Ibid. 34, 16; cf. above note 5, מחיה מתים ברחמים רבים.

[8]) K. B. VI, I, 36, 20.

To sum up: a man who has become sick, is in the power of the evil spirits. Accordingly, he prays through the *mašmašu* to be freed from the evil that has come upon his body. The priest then sprinkles him with holy water, and recites a *šiptu* to expel the evil spirits. If he succeds, the man is restored to health; if not, he dies, and enters the underworld, the home of the evil spirits. Here he remains, how long is not determined, until, sprinkled by the gods with the water of life, he returns to the upper world. The act is the same in both cases; through sprinkling with the water of life, the man is freed from the power of the evil spirits; is restored to life. However, not every one was thus blessed. Some were fated by the Anunnaki and Mammītum to remain forever in the underworld.

In contrast to the water of life was the water of death, the water of the *tiāmat*, that brought evil to man. It was A-ŠIŠ, "evil water" [1]), contrasted with the good water, the A-DUG-GA [2]). The ideogram, ERIM, denoted both *raggu*, "evil", and *tamtu*, "sea". When Ur-Nimin carries Gilgameš to Ut-Napištim, they pass over the "water of death", which Gilgameš is warned not to touch. Again the priest threatens the witch with "the water of death", i. e. with death itself.

Closely related to the water of life was the food of life. When the gods decided to confer eternal life upon Adapa, it was by means of the water and food of life [3]). It plays however no role in the actual religious literature. The *šam balāṭi*, "the plant of life", and the *šaman balāṭi*, "the oil of life", are also met with [4]).

In time the use of water so decreased in importance, that it became, together with other ceremonies, merely accessory to the spoken *šiptu*. The *šiptu* was all important, and the other ceremonies could apparently be omitted or prolonged to suit the occasion and the rank of the person for whom they were performed.

---

[1]) Cf. III R. 69, 73; U. L. IV Col. V, 63/64; V Col. II, 59.

[2]) Cf. V R. 11, 27, A-SI-IB-BA=A-DUG-GA=*mē* (*pl*) *ṭa-bu-tu*.

[3]) K. B. VI, I, 98, 24 ff.

[4]) For a thorough treatment of this whole matter, cf. KAT[3] 523—526.

At the same time water came to be used for specific purposes. All persons, priest and layman, who participated in any religious ceremony, as well as the utensils used, and the place where the ceremony was held, had to be ritually purified before the ceremony was begun. This was accomplished by sprinkling with, or bathing in, holy water[1]).

A direct development of the original use of water were the symbolic ceremonies of *mīs*[2]) *zumri*, *mīs qātā* and *mīs pī*, "washing of the body, the hands and the mouth." The last ceremony seems to have had a peculiar symbolic significance. It was always written ideographically KA-LUḪ-Ù-DA, and was almost invariably accompanied by the similar ideogram, KA-TUḪ-Ù-DA[3]), "opening the mouth"[4]). The real significance of these ceremonies, especially the latter, is not clear. They were applied to idols[5]), as well as men[6]).

Washing the hands or body symbolized the removal of all evil by means of holy water. Since the former was the more easily performed, it was naturally the commoner of the two. The symbolic nature of these lustrations will be clear from the following text[7]):

55. [*šipta*] *at-ti man-nu* *f* *kaššaptu ša* [— — —][8])
[*ṣalam*] *f* *kaššapti ša qīmu ina libbi erē nam-si-e* [*te-iṣ-ṣir*]
[*ṣalam ṭīti ša* *f* *kaššapti ina eli tašakkan*[9])(*-an*) *qātā-šu ana eli imissī*]
šipta ba-'-ir-tu ša ba-'-ra-a- [*ti*][10])
ṣalam *amēl* *kaššapi u* *f* *kaššapti*

---

1) Cf. below.

2) For the reading *mīs* cf. Cun. Texts XVII 39, 73/74.

3) Written once KA-TUḪ-ḪU-DA (Beitr. XI Col. IV, 20). It is probably a scribal error. But cf. Cun. Texts XVII 39, 73/74.

4) The usual expression is KA-LUḪ-Ù-DA (*mīs pī*) KA-TUḪ-Ù-DA (*pīt pī*) *tēpuš*. Cf. IV R. 25, 42 b—57 a.

5) Beitr. XXXI—XXXVII St. 1, 26 note.

6) Beitr. XI Col. IV, 20.

7) *Maqlû*. VIII, 55—91.

8) Probably the line is to be completed according to *Maqlû* IV, 62, V, 51, 82. or VIII, 9 or 11.

9) Read *tašakkan* instead of Tallqvist's *šitakkan*, because of the comparison with *teṣṣir* and *tanasuk*.

10) *Maqlû* VII, 80.

ša qīmu ina libbi erē nam-si-e te-iṣ-ṣ[ir]
ṣalam ṭīṭi ša amēl kaššapu u f kaššaptu ina eli ṣalam qīmu [tašakkan (-an)]
qātā-šu ina eli imissī (-si) ina ḫu-zab iṣ erīni ana III-šu i-kar-rid
[ina el]i ip-ši-ki ip-še-te-ki imissī[1] *[qātā?]*
[ina el]i riksē-ki riksāti mīs qātā iš-ḫi- [— — —]
[— — —] ana libbi erē nam-si-e ta-na-suk.
[šipta a]m-si qāti-ià ub-ba-ab zumri-ià[2]
[ina eli] ṣalam GAR-SAG-ÌL-*e*[3] *qātā-šu imissī(si)*
[šipta — — —] -bi še-e-ru[4] *mīš qātā*
šipta it-tú-ra še-e-ru[5] *mīs qātā*
šipta še-ru-um-ma še-e-ru[6] *mīs qātā*
šipta ina še-rim amsā (-a)[7] *qātā-a-a mīs qātā*
šipta am-si qātā-ià am-te-si qātā-ià[4] *mīs qātā*

šipta a-di tap-pu-ḫa[8] *iṣ bīnu šam DIL-BAT aban suluppi pū gaṣṣu unqu aban nisiqti riq GAM-GAM*[9]
burāšu qātā-šu imissī (-si)
šipta it-tap-ḫa il Šamaš a-kaš-šad[4] *mīs qātā*
šipta un-du f kaššaptu i-bir nāra[4] *mīs qātā*
šipta ul-tu il Ninib ina šadē ilsū (-ú) il A-la-la[10]
pū ana libbi karpati lā šuḫarrati idī (-di)-ma
ina pī-šu ana libbi nam-si-e ṣuruḫ (-uḫ)
šipta an-nu-u in-nin-na-ma
ṣalam f kaššapti ša ṭīṭu epuš (-uš) -ma aban šadē (-i) ina rēš libbi-ša tašakkan (-an)

---

[1]) That *imissī* is to be read in the third person is clear from *ikarrid* in l. 62 and *-šu* in l. 67. The second person refers to the priest; the third to the layman, for whom the ceremonies are performed.
[2]) *Maqlū* VII, 115.
[3]) Cf. below.
[4]) The beginning of a *šiptu* that has been lost.
[5]) Cf. *Maqlū* VII, 143.
[6]) Cf. B. A. IV, 162—167.
[7]) Ibid. reads *amsī*.
[8]) Cf. *Maqlū* VII, 152.
[9]) Perhaps to be read *kukru*; cf. A. B. M. 191, I, 24.
[10]) Cf. *Maqlū* VI, 46.

qātā-šu ana muḫ-ḫi imissī (*-si*)
ina ḫu-zab iṣ *erīni ana III-šu i-kar-rid*
šipta pu-u id-bu-ub lim-na-a-ti[1]) *mīs qātā*
šipta e-piš-tú muš-te-piš-tú ina še-ri dāmi[2]) *kiš-pi ru-ḫi-e*[1])
II akalē (pl) *I ta-a-an ṣalam* amēl *kaššapi u* f *kaššapti*
akal lē epuš-ma ina libbi akalē (pl) *ṣuruḫ-ma*
ina imni-šu u šumēli-šu išī-ma šipta munnū(*-nu*)*-ma*
ana kalbi u kalbati ta-nam-dim
šipta at-ta ṣillu mē karpat BUR-ZI-GAL-SAR *mullī-ma.*
At the exorcism[3]), "Who art thou, O witch, who [— — —]"

---

[1]) The beginning of a *šiptu* that has been lost.

[2]) Or *pagri*?

[3]) I have put *šiptu* in the accusative as a ظرف, and rendered it, "At the exorcism", i. e. "while the exorcism is being said", because the context shows that this is the meaning intended. This tablet is not only a list of exorcisms occurring in the first seven tablets of *Maqlū*, but also gives, as briefly as possible, directions for the ceremonies that accompany them (cf. VIII 11—12 and II 188—208). The use of the ظرف is not uncommon in Assyrian, thus, *ardatu ša muššiša šizba lā ibšū* (above p. 18), and, *asakku marṣu zumur amēli ittabšī* (K. 5182 [Cat. 696]). In fact the accusative can apparently take the place of a genitive and preposition in almost any shade of meaning; cf. IV R. 17 rev. 2; Beitr. XI etc. 2 and LXXV—LXXVIII 13.

A comparison of *Maqlū*, VIII, 11—12 with II, 188, 208 shows that they correspond exactly. The first passage must of course be translated:

At the exorcism, "Who art thou, O witch, that pursuest me?".

An image of tamarisk-, and one of cedar-wood (shall be present). This must also be the meaning of the last line of the second passage; INIM-INIM-MA UḪ-BUR-RU-DA NU-GIŠ-SINIG NU-GIŠ-ERID GAN. Tallqvist's rendering of UḪ-BUR-RU-DA as *muṣaprata*, has not been generally accepted. Zimmern has correctly rendered INIM-INIM-MA NAM-ERIM-BUR-RU-DA-GA (*Šurpu* V/VI, 170) "Beschwörung zur Lösung des Banns", equivalent in Assyrian to *šiptu ša ana pašāri māmītu*. The passage from *Maqlū* then would be in Assyrian *šiptu ana pašāri kišpu lū ṣalam iṣ bīnu iṣ erīnu* "at the conjuration for the removal of witchcraft, let there be an image of tamarisk-wood, and one of cedar-wood present." This last part has been correctly translated by Tallqvist. For GAN=*lū*, cf. Brün. 4041. That *lū* alone, denotes, "let there be", or "let there be present", is clear from the expression common in the letters, *lū šulmu ana šarri*. (For further references, cf. H. W. B. 373b, also 2 R. 13 No. 2, 59/60 and Cun. Texts XVII pl. 15, 25/26.) This also explains INIM-INIM-MA ŠU-ÍL-LA DINGIR . . . (cf. B. M. S. 13). This is to be rendered, "during the exorcism there shall be a raising of the hands to the god . . .". The expression, "raising the hands", is here to

An image of a witch out of meal shalt thou form in the copper wash-bowl;

A clay image of a witch[1] shalt thou put to it; he shall wash his hands above (them).

At the exorcism, "Catcher of Catchers,"

An image of a wizard and a witch

Shalt thou form out of meal in the copper wash-bowl;

A clay image of a wizard and a witch, shalt thou put to the image of meal;

He shall wash his hands above (them); with sap of cedar-wood he shall sprinkle (his hands) three times;

"Because of (or, above"?) thy[2] witchcraft, thy sorcery he washes (his) hands;

"Because of thy binding knots" washing of the hands shall he [— — —][3]

---

be taken literally, and not in the secondary meaning of "prayer", as King proposes. Also, the superscription of the *šiptu's* of *Utukkē limnūti*, INIM-INIM-MA UTUG-ḪUL A GAN, is to be interpreted, "at the *šiptu* of (against) the evil *utukku*, water shall be present". This shows that in this series, water was chiefly used.

Instead of translating INIM-INIM-MA, "at the *šiptu*", it is possible to regard it as a nominative, and render the above, "A *šiptu* against the evil *utukku*. Water shall be present". In fact, in such cases as *Šurpu* V/VI, 170 (c. above) where no directions are given, it must be so rendered. Such lines merely explain the purpose of the previous *šiptu*. In other colophon lines however, INIM-INIM-MA must be rendered *šipta*. This must of course be determined from the context.

[1]) These two lines are of grammatical interest, since they show that we can say *ṣalam kaššapti ša ṭīṭi* or *ṣalam ṭīṭi ša kaššapti*, with no difference in meaning (cf. also ll. 59—62, 67 and 87). Is there perhaps a shade of difference in emphasis between them?

[2]) Addressed to the images.

[3]) I have rejected Tallqvist's reading of IŠ-ḪI-[A?] for two reasons. In the first place, ll. 68—72 show that *mīs qātā* is a technical term. Wherever *qātā* follows LUḪ, it is to be so read. *Mīs qātā eprāti* would then mean, "washing the hands with dust (shall take place)" (cf. the use of *mīs qātā* in ll. 68—72). This would be a direction for a ceremony. But by comparison with the preceding line, this is impossible. Besides, not only does the ceremony of washing the hands with dust not occur elsewhere in ritual texts, but the very idea of dust is opposed to this. *Iš-ḫi-* then must be the beginning of a verb, the rest of which has been lost. *Mīs qātā iš-ḫi-*[. . .] was of course a parallel idea to *imissī* (*qātā*) in the previous line.

[— — —] shalt thou put in a copper wash-bowl.

At the exorcism, "I have washed my hands, have cleaned my body"

Above an image of a human form shall he wash his hands.

[At the exorcism, "— — —] dawn," washing of the hands (shall take place).

At the exorcism, "The dawn has passed," washing of the hands (shall take place).

At the exorcism, "At the dawn, the dawn," washing of the hands (shall take place).

At the exorcism, "At dawn have I washed my hands," washing of the hands (shall take place).

At the exorcism, "I have washed my hands, I have washed my hands clean," washing of the hands (shall take place).

At the exorcism, "Until thou shinest forth," tamarisk-wood, DIL-BAT-plant, a date-seed,

Straw[1]), gypsum, a ring, a precious stone, GAM-GAM-plant,

And cypress (shall be present)[2]); he shall wash his hands.

At the exorcism, "The sun shines forth, I conquer," washing of the hands (shall take place).

At the exorcism, "When[3]) the witch has crossed the river," washing of the hands (shall take place).

At the exorcism, "Because of (?) Ninib they call upon Alala in the mountain,"

Put straw into a "not narrow?" vessel;

Through its mouth call into the wash-bowl

The exorcism, and then.

Make a clay image of a witch; put a stone of the mountain at the top of its heart;

He shall wash his hands above (it);

---

[1]) Or "chaff"; cf. K. B. VI, I, 437 f. Cf. also *Maqlû* V, 57 and VI, 31 and Psalm 1, 4.

[2]) Tallqvist's translation, "he shall wash his hands with tamarisk-wood, etc.", is grammatically possible, but hardly practicable. It seems better to pause just after *burâšu*. We must remember that the language of these directions is as concise as possible; cf. ll. 68—72.

[3]) For this meaning of *undu* cf. Meissner: Suppl. 11 a.

With the sap of cedar-wood he shall sprinkle (them) three times.

At the exorcism, "The mouth has spoken evil things," washing of the hands (shall take place).

At the exorcism, "Witch, sorceress, in the flesh (and) blood (?) witchcraft, sorcery,"

Two food preparations, one apiece, for the image of the wizard and the witch;

A "medicinal food-preparation"[1]) shalt thou make; call into the food-preparations;

At his right side and his left side lift them up[2]), and recite the exorcism;

(then) give them to the dogs (literally, "to dog and bitch").

At the exorcism, "Thou art a shadow," fill a BUR-ZI-GAL-SAR-vessel with water[3]).

A study of this text reveals several interesting facts. We learn in the first place, how a *šiptu* was usually cited by its first words. We learn the manner of making and using images[4]), and the parts borne by the priest and layman in the services[5]). But above all, we learn the true meaning of the washing of the hands. We saw how the priest placed images of a witch in a wash-bowl, and how the sick man washed his hands over them. The idea, symbolized by this ceremony, was that the water, falling from the hands of the sick man on the images, would bring upon them, and therefore upon the images themselves, the uncleanliness and sin of the sick man[6]). We can now understand the real meaning of the lines[7]);

itti mē ša zumriia·u musāti ša qātāia liššaḫiṭma
ana muḫḫiki u lāniki lillikma anāku lubluṭ
ēnita l[i — — —]-an-ni-ma šērta limḫuranni.

---

[1]) Cf. H. W. B. 374.

[2]) With this ceremony compare the Biblical תרומה and תנופה.

[3]) For the translation of this line, cf. Beitr. p. 132, note 5.

[4]) Cf. below, p. 65.

[5]) Cf. below.

[6]) Cf. Deut. 21, 6. Here the washing of the hands indicates freedom from sin.

[7]) *Maqlû* VII, 77—79.

(May thy witchcraft) with the water of my body and the washwater of my hands be torn away

And come upon thee and thy body[1]); but may I live;

May it [free?] me from sin, take away iniquity from me[2]).

Sin was something material; with the washing of the body and the hands, actual uncleanliness passed into the water; this was now, ritually as well as physically, impure. The evil spirits had entered it[3]). And as the water dripped upon the images, the evil spirits passed into them, and so into the witch itself. She had now to suffer the same evil that she had caused the sick man.

The water loaded with evil spirits was unclean. Whoever touched it also became unclean; the evil spirits passed into him. Consequently it had to be put out of harm's way. Sometimes it was poured into the street[4]), symbolizing thereby that the evil spirits may also be poured out. But it was usually carried to a "clean place," an *ašru ellu*[5]), "clean" being here used euphemistically. Here there was no danger of coming in contact with evil spirits. As the result of the ceremony of washing the hands, came the idea that unwashed hands denoted ritual uncleanliness[6]).

Often ceremonies were held on the bank of a river[7])

---

[1]) Literally, "thy form".

[2]) Here "life" and "freedom from sin" are synonymous.

[3]) For further examples of the removal of sin in a material sense, cf.: *itti mē ša zumrika u musāti ša qātāka liššaḫitma irṣitim limḫur AN-gamlum aranka māmītka*, "with the water of thy body, and the wash-water of thy hands, may the vessel (?) of thy sin and thy evil (*māmītu*!) be torn away and taken up by the earth" (*Šurpu* VIII, 72—73). Cf. also *itti iṣṣuri šamē lū taparraš*, "with the bird of heaven, mayest thou (*labartu*) fly away" (IV R. 56, I, 8). With this passage cf. IV R. 4 Col. III (Cun. Texts XVII, 22), 1—2 and Leviticus 14, 4—7.

[4]) IV R. 16 No. 2 (Cun. Texts XVII, 31) rev. 50—58; 13 No. 3 (Ibid. 1), 50/51.

[5]) *Šurpu* V/VI 164/165; IV R. No. 2 rev. 1; Leviticus 4, 12. For the euphemistic use of *ašru ellu* and מקום טהור, cf. Haupt; Journal of Biblical Literature, 1900, pp. 55—81.

[6]) Cf. IV. R. 26 No. 5 (Cun. Texts XVII, 4) and *Šurpu* III, 44.

[7]) Beitr. XXXI—XXXVII St. I, 35—II, 9; IV R. 55 No. 2 obv. 17; 60 obv. 15; 25 Col. II, 31; K. 174 (Harper's Letters 53) obv. 11 ff. Cf. Le-

The chief reason for this must have been that the running waters might carry away the uncleanliness, that fell off the sick man. There was no danger of their becoming impure, since they were part of the *apšū*. And besides, the evil spirits, once in the water, were partly in their element. In the water of the *apšū* they could not stay; that was their great enemy. But it hurried them on to the *tiāmat*, and there they were at home; the sick man was released from their torments; was again clean, pure, and free from sin.

In time the functions of water were transferred to other liquids. This was no doubt due in part, to similarities in use, and in part to the association with water in the ceremonies themselves. Chief among these liquids was oil. The anointing of the body with oil is, for the Oriental, as necessary as washing with water. Consequently a semi-religious significance was attached to this act also; it too was considered able to expel evil spirits. Thus we read of the oil of life[1]), along with the water of life. This act of anointing was called *pašāšu*, while the term *pašīšu* became synonymous with *āšipu*[2]). Thus we read[3]):

šamnu ellu šamnu eb-bu šamnu nam-ru
šamnu mul-li-lu ša ilāni pl.
šamnu mu-pa-aš-ši-iḫ šir *bu-a-na ša a-me-lu-ti*
šaman šipti ša il *E-a šaman šipti ša* il *Marduk*
u-da-ḫi-id-ka šaman tap-šu-uḫ-ti
ša il *E-a id-di-nu a-na pa-aš-ḫa-a-ti*
ap-šu-uš-ka šaman balāṭi
ad-di-ka šipat il *E-a bêl Eridu* il *Nin-*[— — —]
aṭ-ru-ud a-sak-ku aḫ-ḫa-zu
[— — —] *šu-ru-ub-bu-u ša zumri-ka*
ú-šat-bi qu-lu ku-ru ni-is-sa-tú ša pag-ri-ka

---

viticus 14, 50. No doubt, the fact that the holy water which was used in the ceremonies, could be taken from the river, was another reason for the services being held on its bank. Probably too, because of its proximity to the holy water, the river bank was a sacred place. Cf. below.

¹) Cf. above p. 53.

²) Cf. above, pp. 42 and 43, note 7.

³) *Maqlū* VII, 31—48. The parts there missing are supplied by Weissbach: B. A. IV, 160—161.

u-pa-aš-ši-iḫ bu-a(?)-ni (?) *mi-na ti-ka lā ṭābāte* pl.
ina qi-bit[1]) *E-a ina šipat il Marduk*
ina ri-kis ra-ba-bu il [— — —]-*la*[2])
ina (?) *qātā II pa-aš-ḫa-a-ti ša il Nin*-[— — —]-*ga*[2])
il Nin-a-ḫa-kud-du bēl (-*it*?) [— — —][2])
pulānu mār pulānu šub-šu-ma il E-a šipat [— — —][2])
[— — —] *šu-ut Eridu*(-*dù*) *li-pa-aš-ši-ḫu SU-KI*[3]) (?)
[— — —].

Pure oil, clean oil, bright oil,
Oil that brings abundance[4]) to the gods,
Oil that eases the sinews of men,
Oil of the exorcism of Ea, oil of the exorcism of Marduk,
I have made thee trickle[5]) with the oil of easing,
Which Ea has given for easing;
I have anointed thee with the oil of life;
I have pronounced the exorcism of Ea, the lord of Eridu, NIN-[— — —]
I have expelled the *asakku*, the *aḫḫazu*,
The trembling of thy body;
I have driven out the cry of pain and anguish of thy body,
I have eased the sinews of thy afflicted limbs;
By command of Ea, king of the deep,
By the spell of Ea, the conjuration of Marduk,
By the binding of the — — — of [Gu (?)] -la,
By the two easing[6]) hands of Nin-[— — — — —]
Of Ninaḫakuddu, the mistr(ess) of the [holy-water-bowl]

---

[1]) The determinative, *il*, is here omitted, probably by mistake.

[2]) Weissbach offers the following suggestions for the conclusion of lines 45—48: (45) *il Gu-la* (?), (46) *il* NIN-DIN-BAD-GA (?), cf. Brün. 11084, (47) *a-gub-bi* (?), cf. IV R. 28 * No. 3 (48) *Eridu* (-*dù*).

[3]) *Zumru* (?).

[4]) II, I from ללא? Or shall we consider *mu-lil-li* written for *mul-lil-li* from אלל? But cf. דחד (a synonym of ללא) in l. 35.

[5]) Literally, "I have made thee abundant".

[6]) According to its form *pašḫāti* must be an adjective in the feminine plural; cf. l. 46. But how else translate it here? "Which Ea has given for the easing (hands)"?

N: N. the son of N. N. is restored to life[1]) (?), Ea, exorcism [— — — —]

[— — —] of Eridu may ease the body (?) [— — —].

Many kinds of oil were used in the ceremonies. In addition to that mentioned above, which seems to have been the usual olive or palm oil[2]), no doubt of a fine quality, we read of *šamnu-ṭâbu*, "good oil"[3]), *šaman rēšṭi*[4]) and *nigulu*[4]), "finest oil", *šaman iṣ erīni*[5]), "oil of the cedar-tree", *šaman iṣ šurmīnu*[6]), "oil of the *šurmīnu*-tree", *šaman šadē*[7]) (?) "mountain (?) oil", *šaman pūri*[8]), "pot oil", *šamnu ḫalṣu*[9]) and *šaman* NI-LID[10]). These were used principally for anointing, either the priest[11]) or layman[12]), or else the idol[13]), the house[14]), or whatever was to be purified. Sometimes more than one kind of oil was used, and sometimes they were used in connection with other objects[15]).

---

1) Permansive III, I of *bašū* (?). Literally, "is caused to exist".

2) Notice the ideogram for *šamnu*, 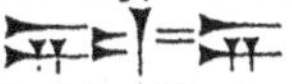 (*šamnu*) +  (*iṣu*).

3) IV R. 25, Col. III, 39; 28 No. 3, 3 b; 60 obv. 25; Beitr XL—XLI St. 1, 18; LII 6. Zimmern compares it to שמן טוב.

4) Asarḫad. VI, 40.

5) Beitr. XXXI—XXXVII St. I, 5; II R. 58 No. 6, 71, 73; K. 7845 (Cat. 878); Rm. 2, 160 (Cat 1653).

6) B. M. S. XII (IV R. 57) 15 a, 33 b; XXX, 26; cf. A. B. M. p. 88 f.

7) =NI-KUR-RA. Beitr. XLI—XLII St. I, 17.

8) Ibid. 18 (cf. note); IV R 58 Col. III, 27; N. E. XII Col. I, 16; K. 4075 (Cat. 592).

9) Purified (?) oil; cf. IV R. 60 obv. 25.

10) VI R. 28 No. 3, 3.

11) IV R. 57 (B. M. S.) rev. 33.

12) Beitr. XXVI Col. I 23—25.

13) Ibid. LII 6.

14) Ibid. XLI—XLII St. I, 17—18.

15) For the use of sap of the cedar-tree cf. above p. 55. Zimmern holds that the blood of slaughtered animals could also be used for purification. He bases this theory upon the single passage, Beitr. XXVI Col. III, 20. This passage is however fragmentary and a great deal must be supplied to support Zimmern's reading. Besides when we observe the great importance attached to the use of blood in the Hebrew and Arabic rituals, if we accept the theory that this custom was practiced by the Babylonians also, we must naturally regard it as common to all Semitic peoples. But then we would expect great significance to have been attached to it in Babylon as well as in Israel and Arabia. But instead, in only this one, very doubtful passage and in Cun. Texts

Having now completed the discussion of water, we turn to

Other Means of Removing Evil Spirits.

Next in importance to the use of water was that of fire. This was probably connected with the exalted position occupied by the gods of light in the incantations. Because of its nature the manner of its use differed from that of water. Its application to the body of a man, as water was applied, would

---

XVII, 5, 49/50 and 6, 12/13 is reference made to it! The sign, BE, which Zimmern reads *dāmu*, may also be read *pagru*, and the passage interpreted, "with the body of this lamb [touch?] the door-posts, etc." (For the ceremony of touching cf. p. 66 ff.). This translation too is very far-fetched, yet more in harmony with the Babylonian ritual than Zimmern's. In fact, Zimmern's translation is directly opposed to the entire ritual. (Cf. Relig. Sem. 33 f.).

It may be remarked here, that the great difference between the Babylonian and Hebrew sacrifices lay just in this use of blood in the latter, and its non-use in the former. In this respect the Hebrew ritual was, of course, closely related to the Arabic, before Islam. Startling resemblances however between the Babylonian and Hebrew systems of atonement must have already presented themselves to the reader. In fact the two systems were in their basic principles the same. The idea of direct atonement for ritual sin did not exist in Israel long before the exile. We must therefore conclude that the Israelites became aquainted with it during the exile, and that their whole system is based upon the Babylonian. The grafted it however upon their ancient system of sacrifice, which was in many respects, just as we have seen in regard to the use of blood, totally different from the Babylonian. Thus it is that in the Hebrew atonement ritual so much emphasis was laid upon the use of blood. It is the author's intention to develope this subject in a later work.

While differing from Zimmern in this matter, I may also remark that he has apparently attached far too great significance to the ceremony of "whispering" (*luḫḫušu*) (cf. Beitr. Einl. 92—3, LVI rev. 4, note, and KAT[3] 604). This ceremony is mentioned but four times in all the religious texts so far published, two of which (IV R. 21 No. 1 (B) add., and Beitr. XXXVIII, 12) are very fragmentary. Little is known of this ceremony or its significance. A *šiptu* seems to have been whispered into each ear of the image of a bull or lamb. More can not be said. Since the image of a bull is mentioned nowhere else in the ritual texts, it seems to have been used for this ceremony alone. However it is so seldom referred to, that but little importance can be attached to it in comparison with other ceremonies. Therefore when Zimmern apparently regards this as the usual method of reciting a *šiptu* (KAT[3] 604), he is clearly in error.

have been attended by just the contrary to the desired results. Therefore its destructive force had to be directed against the witches and evil spirits themselves. This was accomplished in two distinct ways.

The first of these, that used in *Maqlû*, was employed chiefly against the witches. Images of a wizard and witch were made and burnt; symbolizing thus the actual burning of the witch. But this was more than a mere symbolic act; it was actually believed that if certain acts, attended by magical ceremonies were performed upon the image of a man, they would likewise befall the man himself. This was one way in which the witches worked. They would make an image of the person they intended to destroy, and subject it to all manner of tortures; would burn it; would bury it in the high-road so that every passer-by might trample on it; would give it over to the dead and heap other similar indignities upon it[1]). In consequence thereof, the man was bewitched; the evil spirits had entered him. Therefore the priest made images of the witch and subjected them to the same spells that had been performed upon the image of the man. Now the evil spirits left the man and entered into the witch.

The images seem to have been made of materials easily destroyed by fire, usually, clay[2]), pitch[3]), wax[4]), tallow[5]), wood[6]), copper[7]), meal[8]), or sometimes a mixture of several of these substances[9]). The images were cast into the fire, and as they melted and disappeared, so too the witches[10]). That this method was used chiefly against the witches, was but natural.

1) *Maqlû* IV, 27—38.
2) Ibid. II, 122.
3) Ibid. 136.
4) Ibid. 113.
5) Ibid. 18.
6) Ibid. 208, IV, 39.
7) Ibid 91. This was usually called "copper from the river-bank" (cf. *Maqlû* VIII, 2), but could hardly have been copper as we understand it. It was probably some kind of a mineral or copperlike substance, found generally on river-banks and easily destroyed in fire.
8) *Maqlû* II, 168, 187.
9) Ibid. II, 147, IV, 40.
10) See next page.

It was easy to make images of them, because they were, after all, human beings. The evil spirits on the contrary changed their forms at will. Furthermore they were gods; of evil, it is true, but still indestructible; the priest could expel them but nothing more. The witches, on the other hand, being human, with the destruction of their images they too passed away.

The second method, that most common in *Šurpu*, was purely symbolic. During the recital of an incantation, the priest would cast different objects into the fire, burning in the censer on the altar, with the words, "As these things disappear never to return, so may the man's sins, uncleanliness and sickness disappear". Objects thus used were tamarisk-wood[1]), *maštakal*-plant[2]), cane[3]), wheat[4]), onion[5]), date[6]), palm-blossom[7]), sheep-skin[8]), goat-skin[9]), wool[10]) and seeds[11]). Or again, the priest would make a fire in the censer and then put it out with the words, "Like this fire which I have made and extinguished, so may the god Siris remove from the man the knots he has bound"[12]).

---

[10]) Cf. Ibid. II, 133—134:

kīma ṣalmāni annūti iḫūlu izūbu u ittattaku
amēl kaššapu u f kaššaptu liḫūlu lizūbu littattuku.

As these images tremble, melt, and pass away,
So may the wizard and the witch tremble, melt and pass away.
This method of witchcraft was in vogue until even modern times.

[1]) *Šurpu* IX, 1—8.

[2]) Ibid. 9—16.

[3]) Ibid. 17—23.

[4]) Ibid V/VI, 178—181.

[5]) Ibid 60—72.

[6]) Ibid 73—82.

[7]) Ibid 83—92.

[8]) Ibid 93—102.

[9]) Ibid 103—112.

[10]) Ibid 113—122.

[11]) Ibid 123—143.

[12]) Ibid 176—184. That in *Šurpu* the great majority of the ceremonies are purely symbolic, agrees well with the, for the incantation texts, advanced ethical conception of sin in these tablets (cf. above p. 2 note 6). It seems to indicate a time when some of the people, at least, had begun to feel that the ceremonies in themselves were not effective, but that through the direct intervention of the gods alone, could the evil spirits be expelled. The ceremonies in these tablets, are, with the exception of the

A third method may perhaps be seen in the use of the torch in various ceremonies. Many purification ceremonies were held at night, since that was the usual period of activity of the evil spirits. A torch was always used to light up the ceremonies, symbolizing at the same time the presence of the gods of light, and particularly the fire-god[1]), the deadly enemies of the evil spirits. Often a censer was used with the torch[2]), the underlying idea probably being that the holy smoke from these would remove all uncleanliness.

Another method of expelling evil spirits was by touching the *mašmašu*. The priest laid his hand upon the sick man, and straightway he became well. This seems to have been an old custom, and no doubt was at one time practiced independently. But in the magic texts it is completely subordinate to the spoken *šiptu*. The underlying idea must have been that contact with unclean bodies gave the evil spirits therein opportunity to pass over into that which had touched them, making this also unclean. Thus in both the Babylonian and Hebrew rituals, it was forbidden to touch a dead body[3]), for this, having been sick, was unclean, and having died therefrom, remained unclean; was completely in the power of the evil spirits. Furthermore it was forbidden in both rituals to touch any unclean person[4]) for the same reason. And for the same reason, food and water which no hand had touched, were used in the sacrifices and ceremonies[5]).

But if from contact with an unclean body, one became unclean, so also the mere touch of one endowed with power to expel evil spirits could restore cleanliness. There was no danger that the priest would thereby become unclean. He had washed himself in holy water, and Ea and Marduk had endowed

šiptu's themselves, mostly symbolic, and the assistance of the gods more directly invoked than in most incantation texts.

[1]) Cf. Beitr. XXVII, 5; U. L. tablet K. 145 ff.

[2]) Cf. below.

[3]) Cf. *Maqlû* IV, 27—31; Leviticus 11, 31—40; 21, 1, 11; Numbers 19, 11 ff.

[4]) *Šurpu* III, 115—125, 21, and Leviticus 15; 22, 1—16. For a detailed account of this cf. Relig. Sem. 146, 161, 446 ff.

[5]) IV R. 19 No. 2. 57 ff. cf. Leviticus 11, 32—38.

him with power over the evil spirits[1]). Consequently, at his touch the evil spirits had to leave the afflicted body; the sick man was restored to purity and health. Thus[2]):

ema allaku lušlim,
amēlu allapatu lišlim.
Let me be healthy wherever I go;
Let the man whom I now touch become healthy[3]).

And not only men, but also inanimate objects, principally houses, were purified by touching. It did not suffice that the sick man alone was freed from evil spirits; they had to be driven from his house as well, that they might not lurk there, awaiting an opportunity to reenter his body. The house was usually purified, not by the touch of the *mašmašu* himself, but rather by contact with holy objects in his hands[4]). Usually only those parts of the house, such as the outer and inner rooms, thresholds, doors, windows, roof, beams and court, where evil spirits were most likely to lurk, were purified in this way[5]). The final ceremony, usually a sacrifice, was then held, either in the court, or at the outer gate of the house, and some holy object was stationed there to prevent the evil spirits from ever again entering the house[6]).

---

[1]) U. L. III, 65—79; 108—125; K. 626 (Harper's Letters 24) obv. 10, 11. But cf. Cun. Texts XVII, 38, 9ff.

[2]) U. L. III, 276—279; cf. 151/152.

[3]) Notice how Jesus too drove out devils by his touch; Mark, 1, 31, 41; 5, 23, 41; 8, 22, 25; Luke 4, 40; 5, 13; 7, 14; 8, 54; 9, 13. Even the touch of his garment sufficed for this purpose. Mark. 3, 10; 5, 28. Luke 8, 54. Cf. also II Kings 4, 34—35.

[4]) Beitr. XXVI Col. II, 1—6; IV R. 59, 1, obv. 31 — rev. 10.

[5]) Beitr. XLI-XLII St. I, 17—20.

[6]) IV R. 58 Col. II 14; 55 No. 1 Col. I 8—9; Beitr. XXVI Col. II, 24, Col. III, 19; IV R. 13 No. 3; 59 No. 1 rev. 8; Cun. Texts. XVII 6 Col. III, 7—8. For the meaning of *bābu k(q)amū* cf. the Talmudic בבא קמא. In IV R. 55 No. 1 Col. I, 8—9 it is contrasted with the *bāb bīti*; must therefore be the gate of the court leading into the street. Furthermore in IV R. 13 No. 3, after the *takpirtu* is poured out to the four directions (cf. above, pp. 44, 60), probably into the street, grain is sprinkled at the *bābu k(q)amū*. In Beitr. XXVI Col. III, 19—22, the priest, after performing the ceremonies at the *bābu k(q)amū*, goes directly to the field, while in LXVI rev. 16 it seems to be the first door into which the messenger enters. This leaves but little doubt as to its meaning.

Evil spirits could also be expelled by means of a sacrifice or sin-offering. The primary purpose of this was to give pleasure to the gods in order to secure their help against the evil spirits. The sin-offering was usually offered to Ea, Šamaš and Marduk, the gods most directly connected with the *āšipu*-ritual. It could however be offered to other gods as well. Sometimes too a sacrifice of a peculiar nature was offered to the evil spirits themselves, to induce them to cease torturing the sick man[1]).

But the sin-offering had a secondary purpose as well. A man, possessed by evil spirits, sick unto death — his life was no more his own; was really forfeited to the gods whose anger he had caused. The sacrifice he brings is therefore in the nature of a gift of redemption. Thus we read[2]):

bulliṭ aradka litta'id qurdika
narbēka lidlula kāl dadmē
muḫur kadrašu leqē pidēšu
Cure thy servant that he may praise thy might,
That all lands may bow before thy greatness;
Accept his gift, receive his ransom.

Also[3]):

kasap ipṭeriia maḫrāta napišti qīšam
Accept my ransom, grant me life.

Thus, originally, the sin-offering had power to expel evil spirits. But in time it lost all this power, and, like the use of water, became subordinate to the spoken *šiptu*.

Another method of removing evil spirits was by substitution. Either an animal was slaughtered, or an image in the form of a man, with all its parts corresponding to the parts of the human body, was made, and various ceremonies performed with these. The purpose of this was that the animal or image should take the place of the sick man, and the evil spirits pass from him into them. This was a practice, common to all Semites. Whether, as Roberston-Smith maintains[4]), the

[1]) For a detailed treatment of the sin-offering, cf. below, Chap. VI
[2]) IV R. 54 No. 1 obv. 45—47 (= B P. 90, 38—40).
[3]) IV R. 59 No. 1, obv. 29, cf. 1, 24, [*kasap*] *ipṭerišu inašši*.
[4]) Relig. Sem. 364.

ultimate purpose of this ceremony was to deceive the evil spirits, and make them confuse the real man and his substitute, is not certain, for there is considerable evidence that the offering of the slaughtered animal or of the image was in the nature of a ransom, given with the knowledge and consent of the evil spirits[1]).

The ideogram for the image in human form is ALAM-GAR-SAG-ÌL-LA, variously rendered *ṣalam an dunānu, dinānu, pūḫu* and *zuqqurūtu*[2]). Literally the ideogram probably means, "the image with the erect head". This agrees with the apparent meaning of *zuqqurūtu,* "height", "loftiness"[3]). *Dinānu* and *dunānu* mean "bodily shape"[4]), and *pūḫu* has apparently the same meaning. Thus we read[5]):

IM-ABZU-TA *qiriṣma*
ṣalam *an* *dunānišu binīma.*
Pinch off a piece of clay from the deep and
Make an image in his shape.

And again[6]);

ṣalamšu idātsa ša tappinni eṣirma
Fashion an image of him, the sides of which are of dough[7]).

---

[1]) According to Cun. Texts XVII, 1, 40 and 2, 14, the substitution of an animal seems to have, in part at least, partaken of the nature of a sacrifice to the evil spirits. Cf. also Cun. Texts XVII, 6, 10—18. That this sacrifice was offered to the evil spirits, and not to the great gods, may be inferred from the fact that a swine was used. Cf. below. Notice also that, according to Cun. Texts. XVII pl. 1 6/7, the animal was thrown into an unclean place (note Thompson's translation, "Devils and Evil Spirits" II, and cf. above, p. 60) at the conclusion of the ceremonies, showing that the uncleanliness had passed from the sick man into it. That this was the common method of disposing of sacrifices to the evil spirits (cf. below) may be inferred from the comparison with *Maqlû* VIII, 88—90 (cf. above p. 56 f.), where, at the conclusion of the ceremonies, the "medicinal food-preparation" was given to the dogs.

[2]) Brün. 12034—12036. That there was still another rendering of the ideogram may be inferred from *Maqlû* VII, 133 and VIII, 67 and Cun. Texts XVII, 37, 15, where a phonetic complement follows. Another ideogram for *pūḫu* was KI-BI-IN-GAR-RA (cf. Brün. 9733—9737).

[3]) H. W. B. 262 a.

[4]) Ibid. 224 f.

[5]) Cun. Texts. XVII 29, 30 ff.

[6]) Ibid. 32, 1/2. Cf. V. R. 51 b. 57/58.

[7]) Cf. "Devils and Evil Spirits" II, 109 a.

These two incantations have the respective colophons:

INIM-INIM-MA ALAM-GAR-SAG-ÌL-LA IM-MA-GE

Incantation of the "image in human form" of clay,

and,

INIM-INIM-MA ALAM-GAR-SAG-ÌL-LA KU-ŠE KAN

During (this) incantation let an "image in human form" of dough be present[1]).

In time *pûḫu* and *dinânu* came to be used as technical terms, meaning "substitute." In this sense they could denote not only the "image in human form," but anything substituted for the sick man. Thus we read[2]), May Ea, *pûḫua ša ukinnu*, "my substitute which has been prepared," may Marduk, *dinânua ša ibbanû lišamgir*, "accept my substitute which has been made". And again[3]):

GI-SAG-DU-SA-A-*u binîma*
elišu šibirma lû dinânušu
Make a GI-SAG-DU-SA-A-*u* and
Break it above him and let it be his substitute[4]).

Examples of the substitution of an animal are common. The animals usually employed for this purpose were swine, lambs or kids. Thus we read[5]):

LU-UŠ LU-SAL LU-TI LU-BAD *šu limût*
anâku lubluṭ

A male sheep, a female sheep, a living sheep, a dead sheep, may it die,

May I live.

Also[6]),

šaḫâ(-a) a-na pu-ḫi-šu i-din-ma
še-ra kîma še-ri-šu da-me kîma da-me-šu i-din-ma lil-qu-ú

---

1) Cf. above, p. 56 note 3.

2) Cf. "Devils and Evil Spirits" II, 2 note b.

3) Cun. Texts. XVII, 15, 22—26; cf. Ibid 6, 22—25.

4) Note also the expressions, ana *dinân sukkalli bêlia lullik*, "may I go as the substitute for the messenger of my lord"; *ana dinân Šarrukên bêlia*, "instead of Sargon, my lord" (H. W. B. 224 b). Cf. also Meissner: Suppl. 32 a and 67 a and Bu. 88—5—12, 329, 20.

5) Cr. I pl. 18, 8—9.

6) Cun. Texts XVII 6, 10—18.

lib-ba ša ina rêš lib-bi-šu taš-ku-na
ki-ma lib-bi-šu i-din-ma lil-qu-ú
A swine[1]) shalt thou give as his substitute;
Flesh like his flesh, blood like his blood, shalt thou give and may he[2]) accept;
The heart which thou hast placed above his heart,
Shalt thou give like his heart, and may he[2]) accept (it).

And finally[3]),

ú-ri-[ṣa ina rêši-šu] ana mi-ḫir-ti-šu it-ta-din
ana abkalli is-si-ma
ú-ri-ṣu GAR-SAG-ÌL-LA-*ú ša a-me-lu-ti*
ú-ri-ṣa ana na-piš-ti-šu it-ta-din
qaq-qad ú-ri-ṣi ana qaq-qad amēli it-ta-din
ki-šad u-ri-ṣi ana ki-šad amēli it-ta-din
ir-ti ú-ri-ṣi ana ir-ti amēli it-ta-din
A lamb has he placed at his head, opposite him[4]);
Unto the *abkallu*[5]) he called;
The lamb, the substitute for mankind;

---

[1]) In Sumerian, "a young swine."

[2]) The evil spirit to whom the sacrifice is offered. Cf. above, p. 70 note 1.

[3]) Cun. Texts XVII, 37 Z.

[4]) Or perhaps better, "in exchange for him." Cf. Cun. Texts XVII, 1, 40, 2, 14, and Thompson's translation of these lines ("Devils and Evil Spirits" II 7, 9).

[5]) Here an epithet for Ea. In Cun. Texts. XVII, 6, 37/38 (cf. Thompson's "join" in "Devils and Evil Spirits" II pp. 20/21) the god is called *rubū rabū* (NUN-GAL) *bēl šipti*. Since NUN-GAL is also equivalent to *abkallu* (Brün. 2638), there can be little doubt that the passage is to be so explained (cf. A. S. K. T. XII obv. 11—12). The usual ideogram for *abkallu* is NUN-ŠIB (Brün. 2651), while NUN-ŠIB-TAG (Ibid. 2653) is uncommon. Possibly in ŠIB the idea of *ašāpu* (cf. above, p. 38f.) is contained. NUN-ŠIB-TAG denotes also *emqu, mūdū, ippišu, bēl têrti* and *mār ummāni*. Of these *bēl têrti* is another name for the *bārū*-priest (= *mūdē têrti* Beitr. Einl. p. 88). The first two words show that *abkallu* was equivalent to "very wise"; the last three, that he was a professional man (cf. IV R. 21 a Col. I, 40—41). The term is used as an epithet for different gods of the *āšipu*-ritual. Thus the Anunnaki and Adapa are called the *abkallē* of Eridu (V R. 51, 41, b; K. B. VI, I, 92, 5, 7), and the fire-god, the *abkallu ša ina māti šaqū*, "the *abkallu* who is exalted in the land" (IV R. 14 No. 2 rev. 6—7; cf. *Maqlū* IV, 61). One ideogram for the Igigi (cf. Brün. 2642—2643) designates them as the *abkallē* par excellance. But the term

He has offered the lamb for his life;
He has offered the head of the lamb for the head of the man;
He has offered the neck of the lamb for the neck of the man;
He has offered the breast of the lamb for the breast of the man.

The last two texts show clearly the nature and purpose of the ceremony of substitution.

Another method of expelling evil spirits, to which reference has already been made, was the application of the law of opposites. This method, for the same reason as in the use of fire, was employed chiefly against the witches. The underlying principle was, to cause the evil which the witches had brought upon the sick man, to revert upon themselves. To accomplish this it was necessary only that the priest repeat the ceremonies which the witches had performed. In fact the *āšipu* seems to have been nothing more than the good counterpart of the witch [1]. Both had power over the evil spirits, the one to cause them to attack men, and the other, to expel them; the witches worked with spells and charms of evil; the *āšipu*, with spells and charms of good. And just as by the law of opposites, good conquers evil, so too the *āšipu* prevailed over the witch, and caused her to fall a victim to her own evil.

Did the witch bind a cord to hold the victim enthralled in its magic knot, the priest did the same for her [2]. Did the witch speak a spell of evil [3], the *āšipu* spoke a spell of good; did the witch cast her spittle upon a man, the *āšipu* anointed

is most often applied to Marduk; is apparently synonymous with his more common epithet, *mašmaš ilāni*. In all probability then, the term was originally closely related to *āšipu*, probably designating him as "the one who understood the use of the *šiptu*" (cf. *mūdū* and *bēl tērti*). *Abkal šamni* was a technical term for the *bārū*-priest who worked with oil (Beitr. Einl. p. 85 note 6).

[1]) *Āšiptu* = witch; cf. above, p. 33 note 2.

[2]) *Maqlū* II, 148—168; cf. *Šurpu* V/VI, 146—165.

[3]) That there was a *šiptu* and *tū* of evil, used by the gods and spirits of evil, is clear from K. B. VI, I, 6 and 26, 91. Tiāmat speaks a *šiptu* and "casts" a *tū* in order to destroy Marduk. This shows that *šiptu* must have originally meant nothing else than the magic use of water, whether for good or evil, and *tū* merely a magic spell. This also shows how close was the relation originally between the *āšipu* and the witch.

the man with his spittle[1]); did the witch make images of the sick man, the *āšipu* made images of the witch and performed the same ceremonies upon them[2]). In this way the evil spirits were turned from the sick man against the witch herself[3]).

A common means of defence against the evil spirits was the use of different objects, supposed to contain some mysterious and holy power, that enabled them to drive away evil spirits. These objects may be divided into three classes, according to the influence they thus exerted. These classes however can not be distinguished from one another by hard and fast lines. Many objects in fact seem at one time to belong to one class, and again to another.

To the first class belonged such objects as exerted an active influence, and could of themselves expel evil spirits. Such objects were the MÀŠ-*gisillū*[4]), the *iṣ* *ḫulduppū*, the MÀŠ-*ḫulduppū*[5]),

---

[1]) Cf. IV, R. 29 No. 1, obv. 34/36; U. L. III, 76/77, 110, and note the expression *nid ru'ti*, II R. 35, 42 c. The use of spittle was a very common practice by the witch. The ideogram UḪ denotes *imtu*, "saliva" (Brün. 790), *ru'tu*, "saliva", (Brün. 792) and *kišpu*, "witchcraft" (Brün. 793). The wizard is the *amēl* UḪ-ZU, "the man who understands the use of saliva" (Brün. 794). The use of saliva by the *āšipu* does not seem to have been common, but singularly enough, in the N. T., it is one of the usual methods by which Jesus drives out evil spirits. Mark 7, 33; 8, 23; John 2, 6.

[2]) Cf. above, p. 65.

[3]) Cf. above, p. 27.

[4]) Probably a torch made of MAS (cf. the next note). Beitr. XXVI, Col. I, 21.

[5]) What the MÀS-*ḫulduppū* was, will become clear from the following remarks. The ideogram probably indicates it as the *pāšiḫ* (cf. Brün. 7030 and above, p. 45) *limutti*, "the aleviator of evil." There were really two *ḫulduppū*'s, one of wood, always written with the determinative *iṣ*, and the other with the determinative MÀŠ. Now MÀŠ is usually equivalent to *urīṣu*, "lamb" (Brün. 2030). Furthermore we read (Cun. Texts. XVII, 10, 73 ff.);

MÀŠ *piṣū ša il Du'uzi liqēma*
ina ṭiḫ marṣi šunīlma
libbašu usuḫma
ana qāti amēli šuāti šukunma
NAM-ŠUB NUN-KI-GA U-ME-NI-ŠUM.
urīṣa (= MÀŠ) *ša libbašu tassuḫu*
akala lī ša amēli šuātu kuppirma

Take a white lamb of Tammuz and
Lay it down near the sick man and
Take out its heart and
Put it on the hand of that man and
Speak the *šiptu* of Eridu.
The lamb, whose heart thou hast taken out,

Is *li*-food (cf. H. W. B. 374) with which thou shalt purify that man.

The *šiptu* of which this is a part has the colophon (cf. above, p. 56 note 3) INIM-INIM-MA MAŠ-ḪUL-DUB-BA-GE, which in Babylonian would probably be, *šiptu ša urīṣi pāšiḫ limutti.*

Another colophon (Cun. Texts XVII, 11, 67) reads, [INIM-INIM-MA] ....SU MAŠ-ḪUL-DUB-BA MULU-TUR-RA DUL-LA, i. e. "the *šiptu* at the covering of the body (?) of the sick man with the MAŠ-*ḫulduppū*". In ll. 54/55 of this *šiptu* we read that the sick man was actually covered with this, while lying on his bed.

A. S. K. T. XII, 37—39 reads as follows:

MÀŠ-ḪUL-DUB-BA ŠU-U-ME-TI
SAG-BI SAG-GA-NA U-ME-NI-GAR-GAR
LUGAL-E DU DINGIR-RA-NA U-ME-TE-GUR-GUR
Bring near a MÀŠ-*ḫulduppū.*
Put its head on the head (of the sick man).
Purify the king, the son of his god.

The colophon of this *šiptu* reads, INIM-INIM-MA MAŠ-ḪUL-DUB-BA KAM, "during the *šiptu* let a MÀŠ-*ḫulduppū* be present". In U. L. tablet D 30—34 we read of exactly the same ceremony.

Cun. Texts XVII 19, 42—48, is as follows:

šārat unīki lā pitīti liqēma
qaqqadi marṣi rukusma
kišād marṣi rukusma.
muruṣ qaqqadi ša ina zumur amēli bašū linassiḫ
Take the fleece of a virgin lamb and
Bind (it on) the head of the sick man and
Bind (it on) the neck of the sick man.

May the sickness of the head, which is in the body of the man, be torn away.

We read of almost the identical ceremony in Cun. Texts XVII, 20, 74 ff. The similarity of this ceremony with that above, where the head of the MÀŠ-*ḫulduppū* is bound on the head of the sick man, and moreover the similarity of the language of each, leaves but little doubt that they are identical. We must therefore conclude that by the MAŠ-*ḫulduppū* is meant, not so much the kid itself, as the skin with the head still attached. With this the sick man could be covered, while lying on his bed, and the head could be placed on his head, or it could be bound around the different parts of his body, according to the various directions.

The principle underlying the ceremony of binding the different parts of the MAŠ-*ḫulduppū* on the corresponding parts of the man's body, was probably that the evil spirits were thought to attack him in the same way. Thus we read (A. S. K. T. XI Col. II, 55—72) that the bed and the body of the sick man are bound with black and white woolen fillets so that the evil spirits

qaqqasunu	Their head
ana qaqqadišu	To his head,
qātišunu ana qātišu	Their hand to his hand,
šēpišunu ana šēpišu	Their foot to his foot,
ai iškunu	May not apply,
ai itḫū.	May not bring near.

It is also possible that this is the principle underlying the practice of substitution (cf. above, p. 69 ff.), where the head, neck, blood and other parts of the slaughtered animal are given for the corresponding parts of the sick man, and where the heart of the animal is placed above his heart, etc. It is noteworthy that the ceremony with the MÀŠ-*ḫulduppū*, quoted in our first text, is strikingly similar to that of the swine substituted for the man (cf. above, p. 72, and also II Ki. 4, 34.)

Furthermore it is both interesting and significant that Robertson-Smith (Relig. Sem. 474 ff.) describes exactly the same rite, as that with the MAŠ-*ḫulduppū*, in the worship of the Cyprian Aphrodite, as well as in the Greek and Roman rituals, in which either priests, or the person to be purified were clad in the skin of the sheep previously sacrificed; in which, in fact, at Hierapolis, "the sacrificer laid the skin on the ground and knelt on it, taking up the feet and head over his own head." Both here and in the Babylonian ritual, this was a ceremony of purification.

That by the MÀŠ-*ḫulduppū* is meant the skin of the animal, rather than its whole body, is proved by various passages. Thus we read (Beitr. LIL, 13), *ana mimma limni ṭarādi MÀŠ-ḫulduppū ina miḫrit bābi ulziz*, "to drive away all evil I have set up a MÀŠ-*ḫulduppū* before the door" (notice how the translation suggested above for MAŠ-ḪUL-DUB-BA agrees with the purpose given here);
and (Sp. I, 131, 22; cf. below, p. 78):

MAŠ-ḫulduppū ša ina rēš iṣ irši amēl marṣi innadi

The MÀŠ-*ḫulduppū* which has been placed at the head of the bed of the sick man;
and finally (Beitr. XXVI Col. 1. 20 ff.):

ina MÀŠ-*ḫulduppū ina* MÀŠ-*gisillū ina* LU-TI-LA etc. *ekalla tuḫap*, "with the MAŠ-*ḫulduppū*, the MÀŠ-torch, the living sheep etc. purify the palace."

Whether the *sugugallū*, "the skin of the great steer", and the LU-TI-LA, "the living sheep," so often, as in the last text, associated with the MÀŠ-*ḫulduppū*, were something similar to it, is not certain, although not improbable. What the MÀŠ-*gisillū* was, is not known.

the URUDU-ŠA-DAN-GA[1]), the LU-TI-LA[2]), the *qān uri-*

The nature of the *iṣ ḫulduppū* is not so certain. In one passage (U. L. tablet F, Col. III, 13) we read:

[........] GIŠ-MA-NU GIŠ-ḪUL-DUB-BA
Let him carve an *iṣ eru*, an *iṣ ḫulduppū*;

and also (Ibid. K. 140 ff.):

eri iṣ ḫulduppū ša rabiṣi
ša ina libbišu il Ea šumu zakru
ina šipti ṣirti šipat Eridu ša tēlilti
appa u išdi išāti luputma ana marṣi Sibitti-šunu ai iṭḫū
An *eru*, an *iṣ ḫulduppū* of the *rabiṣu*
Into which the name of Ea has been spoken
With the exalted *šiptu*, the *šiptu* of Eridu, of purification,
Touch with fire in front and behind that the "Seven" may not come near the sick man.

In Cun. Texts. XVII, 18, 8—15, we read of exactly the same ceremony with the *iṣ eru*, "the exalted weapon of Anu". As Delitzsch has seen (H. W. B. 125) *iṣ eru* can not here mean "tamarisk-wood," but must be a certain kind of vessel or implement. (But cf. "Devils and Evil Spirits", I p. 9 Note 2). A comparison of the above texts, shows that the *iṣ eru* and the *iṣ ḫulduppū* were probably identical. Although *iṣ eru* is synonymous with *šigaru* and *erinnu*, both of which mean "cage", (H. W. B. 135 f. and 640 f.), it is hardly probable that that was its meaning. It is impossible to tell what it was. The ideogram GIŠ-ḪUL-DUB-BA probably designated it as some kind of wooden implement that alleviated evil. In Beitr. LIV obv. 3/5 and rev. 11 (cf. also IV R. 59 No. 1 rev. 5—6) we hear of an *iṣ eru* made of the "heart of a palm-tree", held by the images of the "Seven".

In U. L. V Col. IV, 58, ḪUL-DUB occurs without either determinative (cf. IV R. 58 Col. I 58 and Brün. 9512, 9514).

The reading MAŠ for the sign , I owe to the kindness of Prof. Meissner, who called my attention to Scheil's article in Maspero's Rec. XIX 56 and M. V. A. G. 1903, 3, p. 13, note 16.

[1]) Beitr. XXVI Col. I, 22, II, 5; XXVII 8; XLI—XLII St. I, 23; XLIII, 6; IV R. 13, 18a; 6, 33c, (omitted in Cun. Texts XVI, 21); 21* No. 1 (C) II, 10; 59 No. 1, 5b; Sp. I, 131, 19—20; U. L. XVI, 247 (cf. note); A Col. I, 25 ff. 32; A. B. M. II, 56 b, [cf. also V R. 27, 17 a]. That this ideogram is to be read *ēru dannu* may be gathered from IV R. 13, 18 a. Often however it has the phonetic complement *u*, and in Sp. I, 131, 20 is written URUDU-ŠA-DAN-GU-U. This points to a reading other than *ēru dannu*. Thompson ("Devils and Evil Spirits") renders it "the potent meteorite of heaven." In A. B. M. II, 56 b the sick man is directed to carry it about until he becomes tired.

[2]) Beitr. XXVI Col. I, 21, II, 5, V, 4; XXVII, 13; XXVIII 3; XLI—XLII St. I, 22; XLIII, 6; cf. III R. 66 rev. Col. III, 33. LU-TI-LA

gallū[1]), the *sugugallū*[2]) and many others. Many of these objects were identified with different gods, and probably signified thereby that those gods were present during the ceremonies, and in consequence thereof, the evil spirits had to depart.

Thus[3]):

sugugallū (-*ú*) *u* URUDU-ŠA-DAN-GA *ša ina rēš amēl marṣi i-bi-en-ni*

20. *sugugallū*(-*ú*) *il A-nim* URUDU-ŠA-DAN-GU-U *il Bēl qān urigallē* pl

ša ina rēš amēl marṣi zu-uq-qu-pu il Sibitti-šunu ilāni pl *rabūti* pl *mārē* pl *il Iš-ḫa-ra šu-nu*

MÀŠ-*ḫulduppū*(-*u*) *ša ina rēš iṣ irši amēl marṣi innadī il* NIN-DAR-UTUL-AZAG-GA

amēl rēʾu(-*u*) *ana il Bēl niknakku gisillū ša ina bīt amēl marṣi šak-ni*

niknakku il Azag-šud gisillū il Nuzku

The "skin of the great steer" and "the strong copper" which have been placed at the head of the sick man,

20. The "skin of the great steer" is Anu, the „strong copper" is Bēl; the canopies

---

= "living sheep", but this was probably a technical term, and therefore gives no indication of its real meaning. Cf. above, p. 74, n. 5.

[1]) Beitr. XXVI Col. III, 24; IV, 49; XXXI—XXXVII St. II, 5—8; LIII, 14—15; A. S. K. T. XII obv. 13. Sp. I, 131, 20; 81—2—4, 49 (Harper's Letters, 370) obv. 11. Beitr. XXVI Col. III, 24 and Sp. I, 131, 20 show that it was something that could be erected (*qān urigallē pl ša ina rēš amēl marṣi zuqqupu*); it was something in which a man could remain for seven days, while preparing himself for certain ceremonies (81—2—4, 49 obv. 10—12 *ūmu* VII-*kan ina libbi qān urigallē ūšab*), and finally it was used in parallelism with *satukku* (Beitr. XXXI—XXXVII St. II, 5—8). Hence it could be nothing else than a small tent or canopy, that was erected over the head of the sick man. Whether this is the same as that mentioned in H. W. B. 720 a is not certain.

[2]) Beitr. XXVI Col. I, 22; XXVII, 9; XLI—XLII St. I, 24; XLIII, 6; IV R. 59 No. 1, 5 b; Sp. I, 131, 19—20. This denotes the "skin of the great steer," but was probably also used technically. Cf. above, p. 74, n. 5. With it may be compared the *gumaḫḫu* of Beitr. LVI, 11 (cf. IV R. 23 No. 1, obv. Col. I, 8—15). In U. L. V Col. IV, 14—16 GU-MAḪ-ḪU *ekimmu rabū*!

[3]) Sp. I, 131, 19—24.

Which have been erected at the head of the sick man are "The Seven", the great gods, the sons of Išḫarra;

The MÀŠ-*ḫulduppū* which has been placed at the head of the sick man is Nindarutulazagga,

The shepherd of Bēl; the censer and the torch which have been placed in the house of the sick man,

The censer is Azag-šud; the torch is Nuzku.

Another example, illustrating this idea even better occurs in the same text [1]):

gaṣṣu idda ša bāb bīt *amēl* *marṣi*

15. *lupputu* *pl* *gaṣṣu* *il* *Ninib iddu a-sak-ku* *il* *Nin-ib a-na a-sak-ku i-rad-da-ad*

With gypsum touch the pitch of the door of the house of the sick man;

The gypsum is Ninib; the pitch is the *asakku*; Ninib will pursue (drive away) the *asakku*.

The underlying thought of this passage is clear: just as the gypsum covers the pitch, hides it from view, and destroys its effect, so too Ninib will destroy the *asakku*.

It must not be supposed that the same god was always symbolized in one of these objects. This was apparently left to the will of the priest, or may perhaps have depended upon conditions of which we know nothing. Thus in the above text the URUDU-ŠA-DAN-GA represented Bēl, the MÀŠ-*ḫulduppū* Nindarutulazagga, the censer Azag-šud and the torch Nuzku. In Beitr. XXVII they represented respectively Ninsar and Nērgal, Kušu, Ninib and Gibil [2]). In this text too gypsum and pitch represent Utgallu and the river-god.

How these objects were used is not clear. Possibly, since they represented a god, their mere presence near the sick man sufficed to expel the evil spirits. They were used to purify the house [3]) as well as the man himself.

The next class consisted of those objects that exerted a semi-active influence on the evil spirits, i. e. alone they had

---

[1]) Ll. 14—15.

[2]) Gibil and Nuzku were however identical; cf. Chap. V.

[3]) Beitr. XXVI Col. I, 10—23, II, 4—6; XLI—XLII St. I, 17—27; cf. above p. 68.

no significance, but were used in various complex ceremonies. Such objects were a ring, a sword, a spindle, etc. Some of these objects were more important than others. In fact entire ceremonies seemed to center around these. Thus there were ceremonies with a reed[1]), upon which a complete *šiptu* was based, and the same with the fleece of a yellow goat or kid[2]). These ceremonies were various and so many different objects were used, that it is impossible to classify them. They were mostly symbolic, as the following example will show[3]):

The building shalt thou purify; clay from the building shalt tou take and make an image of the *labartu*

(And) place it at the head of the sick man. A censer shalt thou fill with fire; a sword shalt thou stick into it;

Thou shalt place it for three days at the head of the sick man; on the third day towards sunset

Shalt thou bring it[4]) out, cut it to pieces with the sword (and) bury it in the corner of the wall;

With meal shalt thou surround it; thou shalt not look behind thee.

Often the objects used in these ceremonies bore a close relation to the accompanying *šiptu*[5]). At times the ceremonies were long and complicated[6]), at others extremely simple[7]).

The third class consisted of those objects which were seldom used in the ceremonies themselves, but were rather to prevent the approach of evil spirits, or their return after having once been driven away. Chief among these objects were amulets and images. The latter differed from those used against witches[8]). Among them the most important were the images of the *šēdu* and *lamassu* that stood at the temple and palace doors[9]). Instead of these, people of the middle and lower

---

[1]) U. L. XVI 296–314.
[2]) Ibid. 315–329.
[3]) IV R. 56 Col. II, 23–27.
[4]) The image of the *labartu*.
[5]) Cf. *Maqlū* III, 118–127.
[6]) IV R. 55 No. 1 obv. 1–45.
[7]) Cf. the ceremony quoted above.
[8]) Cf. above p. 65.
[9]) Cf. above, p. 25.

classes seem to have had small images fixed to their door-posts. These were mostly images of gods[1]), but often hideous figures such as raving dogs, serpents, "Siamese-twins", mermen, etc. were used instead[2]). The purpose of these latter is not clear. Perhaps it was that the evil spirits, expelled from the sick man, might enter them. Certainly this must have been the purpose of images of the evil spirits themselves[3]). These images were usually made of clay or wood, and their preparation was generally accompanied by elaborate ceremonies[4]).

The amulets too were often very elaborate, composed even of precious stones, strung on vari-colored cords[5]). However, most amulets must have been simpler. Sometimes too they were inscribed. Thus[6]):

a-na il *Ištar be-el-tu*
šur-bu-tu šar-rat il *Igigi*
ù il *A-nun-na-ki*
ša ilāni pl *abē* pl *-ša*
be-lut-sa ú-šar-bu-u
To Ištar, the mighty lady,
Queen of the Igigi
And the Anunnaki;
Whose authority the gods,
Her fathers, made great.

Finally different plants were used in the ceremonies against evil spirits. This bordered on medicine; was medicine in fact. Probably some of these plants had merely a symbolic significance, but without doubt most were used because of their medicinal effects. Many of the same plants that were used in the incantations, are almost met with in the medicinal texts published by Küchler, and as more such texts are published, this number is bound to increase. And singularly enough, in these medicinal texts, showing how closely related medicine

---

[1]) Beitr. XLI—XLII—LVIII; IV R. 21 No. 1 (A) obv. 46; (C) III 32; K. 490 (Harper's Letters 18); K. 583 (Ibid. 5), rev. 4—5; K. 595 (Ibid. 6).

[2]) Beitr. L and LIV, and IV R. 58.

[3]) Cf. above, pp. 79 f.

[4]) Beitr. XLV—L.

[5]) IV R. 55 No. 1, obv. 4—22.

[6]) Rm. 2, 263 (Cat. 1662).

was to the *āšipu*-ritual, the physician would speak a *šiptu*, just as any *mašmašu*, to expel the evil spirits from the sick man[1]).

The use of plants against evil spirits must have been very old. When Marduk went against Tiamat, he held in his hand a "plant of exorcism"[2]). Furthermore, in the syllabaries, the names of plants such as the *qān tapšarti*[3]), "the reed of removal (of sin?)" and the *qān māmīti*[4]), "the reed of exorcism" occur. Whether these were the actual names of plants, or merely indicated their use in the *āšipu*-ritual, is not certain. Other plants bear the names of evil spirits such as *šam labartu*[5]) and *šam namtāru*[6]). Whether these were in any way related to these evil spirits, can also not be determined.

Thus there were many ways of removing evil spirits. No doubt most, if not all, were of independent origin and in themselves efficacious. But in time they were combined, and long and complex ceremonies came into existence. Only in this form are they found in the religious texts. Seldom or never do we meet there one method used alone.

This treatment of the methods of removal of evil spirits has furnished additional proof that sickness, evil spirits and sin were to the Babylonians one and the same thing, and that no distinction was made in the manner of their removal. Of the different methods, the most important was the spoken *šiptu*. All others were subordinate to it. But its efficacy lay chiefly in the pronunciation of the name of the god invoked. It is therefore necessary now to treat of the gods, directly connected with the *āšipu*-ritual.

---

[1]) A. B. M. I Sp. I, 5, II, 28, III, 29—72; II Sp. III, 3; Sp. II, 27—59. It is also noteworthy, as Fossey has shown (M. A. 91 f.), that few of these plants were taken internally by the sick man. They were usually compounded by the *āšipu* into a salve-like mixture and the patient was anointed therewith. Their efficacy therefore might have consisted in the fact that they had first been touched by the priest and were now applied to the sick man's body. Cf. above, pp. 67 f.

[2]) K. B. VI, I, 25, 62 *šammim tamē tamiḫ rituššu*.

[3]) II R. 24, 6—7.

[4]) V R. 32 No. 4, 35 and II R. 24 No. 1 obv. 3

[5]) II R. 37 No. 2, 34 and Sm. 341 (Cat. 1400).

[6]) K. 259 (Meissner: M. V. A. G. '04, 3, p. 46), 1—2; cf. Küchler: A. B. M. 191, I, 1 and 17.

Chap. V.

The Gods of the *Āšipu*-Ritual.

As we have seen, the *mašmašu* performed his ceremonies in the names of the gods. Through a certain semi-divine power, residing in him as their servant, did he have authority over the evil spirits. And in, and by, the names of the gods could he compel these to leave the sick man. A *nîš* could be spoken not only in the names of all gods, even the most insignificant, but also in the names of such things as the seven gates and bolts of the earth[1]), and *Upšukinakku*[2]), the holy dwelling. It seems that all things, which, by reason of their association with the gods, partook of a semi-divine nature, had power to expel the evil spirits. It may be laid down as a fundamental principle of the Babylonian religion: in the presence of the divine, evil can not remain.

However, while all gods possessed this power over the evil spirits, certain deities were directly concerned with their removal. Chief among these were Ea and his son, Marduk. Really the great god of the incantations was Ea alone. The association with Marduk was the work of a period when Babylon had become the supreme power in Western Asia, and the Marduk-worship was superseding, or rather, assimilating that of the gods[3]). This was of course the time of Ḫammurabi. Previous to this Ea must have stood alone as the supreme deity of the incantations. Indications of this are not lacking. He was the *bêl šipat balāṭi*[4]), "lord of the exorcism of life", the *bêl išippū(-ti)*[5]), "lord of the *āšipu*-service", the *mašmaš ilāni*[6]), "the exorciser of the gods", the *bêl šîmâte*[7]) "lord of destinies". Probably from being only the remover of sickness, he came to be considered the great benefactor of mankind. He

---

[1]) U. L. V Col. II, 45—47.
[2]) IV R. 56 Col. II, 17—18.
[3]) Jastrow: Relig. 116 ff.
[4]) K. 5004 (Cat. 682).
[5]) V R. 51 b. 71/72.
[6]) *Maqlû* VII, 104; IV. 6.
[7]) Ibid. VI, 57.

was the *bān kullāti bēl gimri*[1], "creator of everything, lord of all". He it was that saved Ut-Napistim from the deluge, attempted to save Adapa from the punishment of the other gods, that restored Ištar to life. He was the god of wisdom, the master of all handiwork. He was the lord of the *apsū*, and by means of its holy waters brought healing to man[2]- He endowed man with life[3]), was his creator and lord of his destinies. With him was associated his wife Damkina. In the incantations she appears but seldom, and then only in connection with Ea. Her different titles[4]) however show how closely identified she was with the *āšipu*-service. Still they only reflect the activities and powers of Ea, of whom she was but a mere, shadowy, feminine form.

However, so complete was the assimilation of the worship of the other gods by that of Marduk, and, in consequence thereof, so thorough the reworking of the incantations to accord with the new theology, that Ea was seldom mentioned alone in these texts. In fact, that Marduk took to himself the personalities and functions of Bēl and Ea especially may be inferred from the conclusion of the Creation-series. He seems to have completely absorbed the identity of Bēl, but his relation to Ea was diferent, as the lines indicate[5]):

See, he whose name his fathers have made glorious,
Like me, shall his name be, Ea.
All my commands shall he carry out,
All my orders shall he execute.

---

[1]) IV R. 56 Col. II, 9; cf. *Maqlū* V, 181.

[2]) The expression, *āšipu ša apsē* (V R. 51 b. 44/45) probably applies to Ea also. That Ea was the chief god of the incantations is proof that water was the original method of expelling evil spirits. Although water gradually lost its original significance, Ea still retained his exalted position. Cf. V R. 51 b. 48/49.

[3]) Cf. his titles, above, p. 48. In addition to these he was also *bēl naqbē*, "lord of the springs" (II R. 55, 48 c. d.).

[4]) Cf. above p. 48. Damkina was also the "mistress of the exorcism of the deep" (II R. 55, 56 c. d.), and the "mistress of the pure reed" (Ibid. 57).

[5]) K. B. VI, I, 36, 16—37, 19.

In just this relation to Ea does Marduk appear in the incantations, as his messenger, the mediator between him and the afflicted man. It is Ea who decides what is to be done for the afflicted man, but Marduk who carries this out. And to Marduk, and not to Ea, does the sick man address his prayer for help. This relation is illustrated by the usual dialogue between the two gods[1];

il Marduk ip-pa-lis-su-ma
50. *a-na a-bi-šu il Ēa a-na biti i-ru-um-ma i-šis-si*
a-bi ṭi-'u ul-tu Ē-kur it-ta-ṣa-a
a-di-ši-na iq-bi-šum-ma
55. *mi-na-a e-pu-uš amēlu šu-a-tu ul i-di ina mi-ni-i i-pa-aš-šaḫ*

Rev.

il Ē-a māra-šu il Marduk ip-pal
ma-a-ri mi-na-a lā ti-di mi-na-a lu-rad-di-ka
6. *il Marduk mi-na-a lā ti-di mi-na-a lu-rad-di-ka*
ša ana-ku i-du-u at-ta ti-i-di
a-lik ma-ri il Marduk

Marduk saw him and entered
50. The house unto his father Ea, and called out,
"My father, *ṭi'u*[2]) has come forth from the underworld"[3]).
A second time he addresses him,
56. "What that man has done, I do not know, (nor) how he will recover".

Rev.

Ea answers his son, Marduk,
"My son, what thou dost not know, what can I add to thy (knowledge),
6. Marduk, what thou dost not know, what can I add to thy (knowledge?)[4]).
What I know, thou knowest also.
Go my son, Marduk".

---

[1]) IV R. 22 No. 1. obv. 47—rev. 8.

[2]) A sickness (H. W. B. 207) demonified as an evil spirit. Cf. above, p. 16 note 2.

[3]) For Ē-KUR, = "the underworld," cf. Jastrow: Relig. 558, and above, p. 7.

[4]) Literally, "to thee."

Then Ea gives Marduk directions what ceremonies to perform, in order to heal the sick man. The *šiptu* then concludes[1]:
il Marduk māru rēštu ša apsē bunnū dummuqu kummu

O Marduk, eldest son of the deep, making clean and healing are thine.

This shows how the whole ceremony of purification was attributed not to Ea, but to Marduk, and how the thanks of the sick man were extended directly to the latter.

As mediator between Ea and man, Marduk came in turn to be regarded as the great god of purification. More and more he assumed the functions and titles of Ea. He was the *mašmaš ilāni*[2]) par excellance. He was also *bēl balāṭi*[3]), "the lord of life", *bēl āšipūti*[4]), "the lord of the *āšipu*-service", the *āšipu*[5]) himself. With his *šiptu* he restored life to mankind[6]). And above all other gods, he was the *muballiṭ mītu*[7]), "the restorer of the dead to life".

His usual ideogram in the incantations is *il* SILIG-MULU-SÀR[8]), the meaning of which is not certain, but which no doubt bears a close relation to his functions in the *āšipu*-service[9]). Other ideograms are also common. In fact the various ideograms seem at times to designate different gods. Thus he

---

[1]) Ibid. rev. 30.

[2]) Cf. above, p. 46 note 4.

[3]) *Šurpu* VIII 71; *Maqlū* VII, 107, 114.

[4]) Ibid. VI, 58; II, 158; I, 62. 72; VII, 20; IV R. 56 Col. II, 13, III, 49.

[5]) K. 2107; IV R. 58 Col. I, 8. This title was also borne by Damu (*Šurpu* VII, 79).

[6]) *Šurpu.* IV, 78—79.

[7]) Cf. above, pp. 46, 51 ff.

[8]) Brün. 925.

[9]) The ideogram probably designated Marduk as "the mighty one, who cures (lit. makes good. cf. above, p. 45 and Brün. 8239) man" (*šagapuru muṭīb amēlu*). This is borne out by the ideograms, *Dingir*—SILIG-MULU—SAR—NAM—TI (Brün. 928), i. e. "the mighty one who cures the life of man", and *Dingir*—SILIG—MULU—SÀR—NAM—ŠUB (Brün. 927), and *Dingir*—SILIG—MULU—SÀR—NAM—BAL—LA (Brün. 926). "the mighty one, who cures man by means of the *šiptu*." That NAM—BAL—LA is in all probability another ideogram for *šiptu*, is clear from Brün. 283. Cf. above, p. 42.

appears in one passage [1]) as three different deities, *il* AMAR-UD, *il* SILIG-MULU-SÀR and *il* TU-TU.

Other gods closely identified with the *āšipu*-ritual were the Anunnaki. We have seen that they were the guardians of the water of life in the underworld, and, together with the goddess Mammītum, decided the fate of the dead. In the incantations too, they were frequently invoked against the evil spirits [2]).

It has long been a question what the Anunnaki really were. The latest answer is that of Hrozný [3]), who holds the Anunnaki and Igigi to have been the deifications of the clouds. But although he has treated the matter with keen, scholarly insight, his answer can hardly be considered in every way satisfactory.

In a bilingual text [4]), the Sumerian A-NUN-NA is rendered in Assyrian *riḫût rubē*, "offspring of the *rubū*". Since A = "offspring", *riḫūtu* [5]), NUN(-NA) must = *rubū*. In A-NUN-NA-GE, as Anunnaki is usually written in Sumerian, the last syllable shows NUN-NA to be a noun. This Hrozný has seen. His great mistake however, on which his entire theory shatters, consists in regarding NUN-NA = *rubū*, almost without argument or proof, as denoting "heaven". It is true, as he says, that the Anunnaki were called "children of Anu", but this was merely a general name for all gods. Even the evil spirits were so called [6]). There is consequently not the slightest proof that NUN (-NA) meant "heaven". It remains therefore to see what it did mean.

The ideogram NUN (-NA) was not uncommon in names and titles of gods. Thus Ea was *Dingir*-NUN [7]), *Dingir*-DAR-NUN-NA [8]), and *Dingir*-ELIM-NUN-NA [9]). Marduk was *Dingir*-

---

1) *Šurpu* IV, 44—45; cf. 77—78.

2) IV R. 55 No. 1, rev. 33; U. L. V Col. II, 3—6; IV, 5—6; Beitr. XXVI Col. IV, 29; V. 26—43.

3) "Mythen von dem Gotte Ninrag": M. V. A. G. '03, 5, pp. 85—89.

4) K. 4829 rev. 5/6 (Hrozný pp. 18/19).

5) Brün. 11353.

6) U. L. V Col. I, 2—6, 22/23; V, 1/2; IV Col. I, 1/2.

7) Brün. 2625.

8) II R. 55, 29 c. d.

9) Ibid. 31 c. d.

SILIG-ELIM-NUN-NA[1]), while Damkina was always in Sumerian *Dingir*-DAM-GAL-NUN-NA[2]). Eridu was also NUN-KI (-GA)[3]). In addition to *Dingir*-DAR-NUN-NA, Ea was also *Dingir*-DAR-ZU-AB[4]). This together with the fact that the gods mentioned above, were all closely connected with the deep[5]), leaves but little doubt that NUN (-NA) = *rubū* was a synonym of *apsū*[6]). This explains the above names. Ea was *Dingir*-NUN, "god of the *apsū*," *Dingir*-DAR-NUN-NA and *Dingir*-ELIM-NUN-NA, "— — —[7]) of the *apsū*"; Damkina was *Dingir*-DAM-GAL-NUN-NA, "the great wife of the *apsū*". Eridu was NUN-KI-GA, "the city of the *apsū*"[8]).

---

[1]) Brün. 930. This ideogram occurs in the one sentence, often found at the end of a *šiptu* (cf. above, p. 86), *Dingir*-SILIG-ELIM-NUN-NA *Dumu-saggaku abzu*-GE SAG-GA TIL-TIL-LI-BI ZA-A KAN. *il Marduk māru rēštu ša apsē bunnū dummuqu kummu.* IV R. 3 Col. II, 25/26 (Cun. Texts 21); 22 No. 1. rev. 29/30; A. S. K. T. XI Col. IV, 57/58.

[2]) II R. 55, 53 c. d., cf. Brün. 11125.

[3]) Brün. 2645, 2649.

[4]) II R. 55, 27 c. d.

[5]) Cf. the Assyrian *rubū* = "the great" = the ocean, with the English "the deep."

[6]) Note also the common epithet of Ea, NUN-GAL = *rubū rabū*. Cun. Texts. XVII pl. 4 Col. II 17/18; pl. 6 Col. III, 37/38 (cf. above, p. 72 n. 5) and the expression Ē-NUN-NA-GE, A. S. K. T. XII obv. 24. In Hebrew a common epithet of the sea is רבה. Thus we read of the תהום רבה, Gen. 7, 11, Am. 7, 4, Ps. 36, 7. In fact this expression seems to be a technical term in the Bible and may perhaps be of Babylonian origin. Furthermore the expression מים רבים in Ez. 27, 26 clearly means "the sea" (cf. Cornill, Ez. 354—5. But cf. Gesenius 13 440 a), and in Jer. 41, 12, where it is modified by a subordinate clause, it means "the great pond near Gibeon." That the article is not used in either passage shows that in Hebrew מים רבים is a technical term.

[7]) Both DAR and ELIM must be titles similar to *bēlu*. For the reading ELIM, which is extremely questionable, cf. Brün. 8908 and 8882, and for the meaning, cf. nos. 8883 and 8887.

[8]) Other ideograms in which NUN (-NA) occur are (*nār*) UTU-KIB-NUN-KI, Sippar and the Euphrates, *Dingir*-KAM-NUN-NA (Brün. 4052), *Dingir*-BAB-SIG-NUN-ŠIB (Brün. 1202), *Dingir*-EN-BAB-SIG-NUN-ŠIB-UBARA (Brün. 2833—2835), *Dingir*-GAN-GIR-NUN-NA (Gud. Cyl. B. Col. XI, 9), *Dingir*-SA-DAR-NUN-AN-NA (*Šurpu* VIII, 17, cf. Nachtr.). These names can not be as yet satisfactorily explained, although NUN (-NA) is most probably equivalent to *apsū*. AB-NUN-NA-KI (Brün. 3834) designates

We turn now to the Anunnaki. Their Sumerian name was *Dingir*-A-NUN-NA (-GE [-E-NE]). But A-NUN-NA = *riḫût rubē*. It may possibly also be rendered *mū rubē*, "water of the *apsū*". However it seems best to accept the first reading. In the first place it is the only one of which we are certain. *Mū rubē* is only a very probable conjecture. In the second place, Adapa, the mortal son of Ea, was called "the very wise one of the Anunnaki"[1]). Consequently these must all have been children of Ea. And finally we read[2]):

mē pl *ellūti* [— — — — — —]
5. *mē* pl *Pu-rat-ti ša ina aš-ri* [— — —]
mu-ú ša ina ap-si-i ki-niš kun-nu-u
pu-ú el-lu ša il Ē-a ul-lil-šu-nu-ti.
11. *mārē* pl *ap-si-i si-bit-ti šu-nu*
mē pl *ul-li-lu mē* pl *ub-bi-bu mē* pl *ú-nam-me-ru*
15. *ina ma-ḫar a-bi-ku-nu il Ē-a*
ina ma-ḫar um-me-ku-nu il Dam-ki-na
li-lil li-bi-ib li-im-mir.

Pure water [— — — — — —]
5. Water of the Euphrates, which in a place [— — —]
Water, which is properly guarded in the deep,
The pure mouth of Ea has purified it.

Umliaš as the "house of the *apsū*". Another ideogram for Umliaš was *māt* A-A (Brün. 11693) = "land of the waters" (?) (cf. Jensen in K. B. III, I, 137, and VI, I, 370). There was also an *il* AB-NUN-NA-KI (II R. 47, 16d.). The ideogram for butter, NI-NUN-NA (Brün. 5349) designated it as "the oil of the *apsū* (?)." Ereškigal was Ù-A-NUN-NA (Brün. 9495) "mistress (cf. Brün. 9475, 8659 and 8660) of the Anunnaki." This agrees well with the account of the restoration of Ištar to life, where, at the command of Ereškigal, the Anunnaki are brought out and seated upon their throne. Furthermore *Dingir*-NIN-KAR-NUN-NA, which Hrozný renders "mistress of the damm of heaven" (pp. 114—116), is of course to be rendered "mistress of the damm of the *apsū*." This however only lends additional weight to his argument that this goddess is the deification of the rainbow. The damm of the heavenly *apsū* was that which hemmed its waters in, kept them from overflowing and falling on the earth. According to Gen. 9, 12—16, Jahwe placed the rainbow in the heaven to show that no flood would ever again come upon the earth.

[1]) K. B. VI, I. 92, 8; 94, 11.

[2]) IV R. 14 No. 2 obv. 2—19.

11. The children of the deep are seven;
They have purified the water, have cleaned it, have made it clear;
15. Before your father, Ea,
Before your mother, Damkina,
May it be pure, clean, clear.

Since, according to V R. 51 38/39, almost the same functions were attributed to the Anunnaki, there can be no question that they were identical with these seven children of the deep. Consequently A-NUN-NA (-GE[-E-NE]) is without doubt to be interpreted, "offspring of the *apsû*".

This text then indicates that the Anunnaki were seven in number. This leads to interesting results. Closely related to the Anunnaki were the Igigi. One ideogram, *Dingir*-NUN-GAL-E-NE[1]), or its equivalent *Dingir*-NUN-GAL-MEŠ[2]), designated them as the *abkallē*[3]). But *abkallu* was closely related to *āšipu*[4]). The usual epithet of Adapa, "the very wise one of the Anunnaki," was *abkallu*[4]). Marduk, the great god of the *āšipu*-ritual, the lord of the Anunnaki and Igigi[5]), was the *abkal ilāni*[4]), and Damkina, the goddess of the sea was the *abkallat* of the Anunnaki, the *mūdāt* of the Igigi[6]). This suffices to show that the Igigi, as the *abkallē*, were closely related to the waters of purification, the *apsû*.

The usual ideogram for the Igigi (𒀭 𒐛)[7]) designated them as "The Seven". However they were generally said to be eight and the Anunnaki nine[8]). And yet the Anunnaki were really seven. These apparently contradictory figures are easily reconciled. In the religious texts and syllabaries, a group of

---

[1]) Brün. 2642.

[2]) Ibid. 2643.

[3]) Ibid. 2638.

[4]) *Maqlû* I, 55; IV, 8, 60; cf. above, p. 72 note 5.

[5]) IV R. 57 (B. M. S. XII) 32 a; cf. Ibid. 88 a, *Šurpu* II, 152, Beitr. LXVI rev. 18; also Cr. II pl. 13, rev. 1–2, and B. M. S. XXVII, 2.

[6]) B. M. S. IV, 13.

[7]) Brün. 12195.

[8]) II R. 39 No. 2. additions; cf. also II R. 25, 69 g, 𒀭 𒐜 = the "Eight" (?) = 𒀭 𒐛.

gods, known as "The Seven," are often met with[1]). In several passages lists of these gods are given, and singularly enough the number is always eight. We have also seen, how, although there were seven evil spirits, no more than six were ever mentioned together. It seems that seven, being to all Semites a holy (or originally, unlucky?) number, they avoided direct reference to it as much as possible. Consequently eight gods instead of "The Seven", and eight Igigi instead of the seven indicated by the ideogram. And probably, to distinguish them from the Igigi, the Anunnaki were said to be nine.

The goddess Narudu was repeatedly called the sister of the "The Seven"[2]). In fact she was often included in this group[3]). In Sumerian she was Dingir-DAM-NUN-GAL-E-NE[4]), i. e. "wife of the Igigi." This together with the fact that "The Seven" were also regarded as children of Ea[5]), and that they and the Igigi were each seven (= eight) makes it highly probable that they were originally identical. Wife and sister were to the Semites closely related ideas[6]), and therefore this apparent discrepancy is no obstacle to this theory.

However, the Igigi and Anunnaki were not always reckoned as eight and nine. Thus[7]):

dim-me-ir an-na *ilāni* pl *ša šamē(-e)* (|) *dim-me-ir ki* (|) *ilāni* pl *ša irṣitim (-tim?)*

dim-me-[ir] gal-gal *ilāni* pl *rabūti* pl *ḫa-am-šat-su-nu* (|) *L-ne-ne*

dim-me-ir nam-tar-ra *ilani* pl *ši-ma-a-tim* (|) *VII-ne* (|) *si-bit-ti-šu-nu* (|)*-ne*

dimmer-A-NUN-NA *il A-nun-na-ku ša šamē (-e) V šu-ši* (|) *an-na-mu-uš V-bi.*

dimmer-A-NUN-NA *il A-nun-na-ku ša ir-ṣi-tum ni-e-ir-šu* (|) *ki-a-mu-uš X-bi*

---

1) Cf. below.
2) Beitr. XLI—XLII Col. II, 14; cf. note.
3) IV R. 21 No. (A.) obv. Col. I, 46.
4) Brün. 11116.
5) Beitr. LIV rev. 2.
6) Cf. Robertson-Smith, "Kinship and Marriage."
7) Reissner's Hymns, p. 92, 21—25; cf. Hrozný p. 87 f.

The gods of heaven, the gods of earth,
The great gods, fifty are they.
The gods of fate, seven are they.
The Anunnaki of heaven, three hundred[1]);
The Anunnaki of earth, six hundred.

Hrozný infers from this, and no doubt correctly, that the second and fourth lines refer to the Igigi, the third and fifth to the Anunnaki. This then gives the number of the Igigi, as great gods, as fifty; as gods of heaven, as three hundred; of the Anunnaki, as judges of fate, seven; as gods of the earth six hundred. Hrozný's explanation of these figures can hardly be considered satisfactory, and yet no better can at present be offered. However, some very interesting conclusions may be drawn from this text. From the ideogram 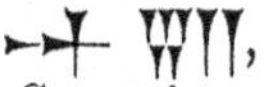, Hommel has inferred, and no doubt correctly, that the Sumerians regarded the Igigi as only five, and that the number seven was the result of Semitic influence[2]). At any rate there need be little doubt that five forms the basis of both numbers of the Igigi, fifty and three hundred (five sossoi). Furthermore, the number of the Anunnaki is here given as seven, the same as the sons of the deep. A not uncommon ideogram for the Anunnaki is *il* NER[3]), i. e. „The Six Hundred". This agrees with the number given in the last line of the above text.

The Igigi were the counterparts of the Anunnnaki; were generally regarded as gods of heaven, while the Anunnaki were gods of earth. The latter were clearly-defined deities in the Babylonian pantheon; they had their especial functions, as judges of fate in the underworld, and guardians and purifiers of the water of life. The Igigi on the contrary were but little more than the reflection of the Anunnaki. They seem to have had no particular functions, which is certainly significant in view of the highly important duties of the Anunnaki. Furthermore, in the above text they were called the Anunnaki of heaven, and

---

1) 5 × 60.
2) Hommel: "Semitische Völker", p. 491; Jastrow: Relig. p. 185.
3) IV R. 33, 46 b; Cr. I pl. 29 obv. 26, 30. B. M. S. IV, 13.

in another[1]), the ideogram *il* NER is used for them, i. e. they too, were designated as "The Six Hundred". They too, like the Anunnaki and "The Seven", were originally seven in number. And from another text[2]) it is clear that the Anunnaki, the Igigi and "The Seven" were all closely related. And, as we have seen, the Igigi and "The Seven" were probably originally identical. All this makes possible, although not certain, the theory that these three groups of gods were originally one. In time the Anunnaki came to be regarded as gods of the earth, i. e. of the earthly *apsū*. Therefore they were located, together with the water of life, in the underworld. The Igigi, on the other hand, became gods of heaven, of the heavenly *apsū*. And "The Seven", perhaps by the law of contrast, became the chief guardians of man against the seven evil spirits. As gods of the underworld, and therefore closely related to the dead, a *kipsu*, a sacrifice to the dead, was offered the Anunnaki[3]).

In conclusion, it may be added that the clouds, as bearers of rain, were part of the *apsū*, and therefore Hrozný's conception of the Igigi and Anunnaki as respectively the upper and lower strata of clouds, is in part correct.

Two other gods closely related to water were Azag-šud and Ninaḫakuddu. The phonetic readings of their names are not known[4]). They were usually associated in the incantations[5]); occasionally however they were mentioned separately, Ninaḫakuddu the oftener[6]). She was the *bēlit egubbē*[7]), "the mistress

---

[1]) IV R. 60, 33 a. Cf. also IV R. 29 No. 1 a 47/48 which speaks of "The Igigi of heaven and earth", where we would expect "Anunnaki" as usual.

[2]) K. B. VI, I, 582—584; cf. note to l. 18, p. 587.

[3]) Beitr. XXVI Col. IV, 43; cf. LXVI rev. 7 and note.

[4]) Tallqvist (Z. A. VII 275) proposes for *il Azag-šud, Zāriqu.* This is probable since AZAG-ŠUD is equivalent to *zāriqu ellu.* A god *Zāriqu* occurs in II R. 66 rev. 12 b.

[5]) Beitr. XXVI Col. III, 27—30; XXXI—XXXVII St. I, 14; XLI—XLII Col. I, 11—12.

[6]) U. L. III, 254; K. 170—173; IV R. 28 No. 3, 17 b; cf. Sp. I, 131, 24; IV R. 57 (B. M. S. XII) 17 b, and Sm. 997 (Cat. 1453).

[7]) IV R. 28 No. 3, 16/17 b; IV R. 29* rev. Col. I, 5.

of the holy-water-bowl", *bēlit šipti*[1]), "the mistress of the exorcism", and *bēlit tēlilti*[2]), "the mistress of purification". She too, like Marduk and Ea, drove out evil spirits by means of the exorcism of Eridu[3]). At her command the priest recited the exorcism[4]). In one passage[5]) she seems to have been the sister of Anu; in another[6]), the sister of Bēl; and again[7]), the daughter of Ea. Azag-šud on the other hand was the high priest (*šangamaḫḫu*) of Bēl[8]). Sometimes the god Ṣīrtu[9]) was associated with them; at others, different forms of Ea[10]).

Other water-gods played more or less important roles in the incantations. Of these the most important was the river-god[11]), invoked no doubt in connection with the water of rivers, so often used in the services. In *Utukkē limnūti* the goddess Id was often mentioned. She was the *bēlit egubbē elli*[12]), "mistress of the holy-water-bowl", and also the mother of Ea[13]). Adapa was also occasionally mentioned[14]).

Second in importance only to the gods of water, were

---

[1]) Cr. II pl. 15 rev. 11; K. 9274, 15—17 (cf. *Maqlū*, notes, p. 133); IV R. 56 Col. II, 14.

[2]) K. 145 (Meissner-Rost. B. S. 108).

[3]) *Ina tē ša il Ninaḫakuddu ina šipti ša Eridu šipat apsē u Eridu ṣīrti* (var. *ina šipti ṣīrtim ša apsē u al Eridi lā taršu liqqabī*). (cf. *Maqlū*, notes, p. 133).

[4]) IV R. 55 No. 1, 45 a.

[5]) U. L. III, 281.

[6]) III R. 68 No. 1 rev. 40.

[7]) 82—5—22, 1048 rev. (cf. Beitr. p. 142, note β).

[8]) II R. 58, 70—72 b; IV R. 18* No. 3 Col. IV, 13; 28* No. 3, 12 b. In one copy of IV R. 57 (B. M. S. XII), 17 b. we find *il Azag* (cf. Beitr. p. 142).

[9]) Zimmern's rendering of *il* MAḪ. Beitr. XXXI—XXXVII St. II, 15; XXXIX, 9 (cf. XXVI Col. III, 27); Cr. II pl. 16 obv. 16.

[10]) Beitr. XXXI—XXXVII St. II, 15—18, III, 6—10; XXXVIII, 20—21.

[11]) *Maqlū* III, 72, 77, 83, 88, VI, 70, 82, 91; Beitr. XXVII, 11; IV R. 29 No. 4 (C.) rev. 19. *Maqlū* IV, 70, 91 speaks of *il* ID (= A-ID) *mārat šamē rabūti*. Tallqvist infers from this that there must have been a river-goddess, as well as a river-god. This is however generally doubted. Probably the scribe here made a mistake for the goddes ID mentioned below.

[12]) U. L. III, 255/256.

[13]) Ibid. V Col. II, 36/37; cf. also III, 170/171.

[14]) Ibid. III. 107 e (cf. "Devils and Evil Spirits" I pp. 12—13); IV, R. 58 Col. I, 24.

those of light. This was but natural, since fire was second only to water as a means of expelling evil spirits. Moreover the gods of light, passing a part of the time in the *apsû*, were closely related to the water-gods. In fact Marduk was originally a sun-god[1]), and only after the completion of the theological system, by which he became the son of Ea, was he directly connected with water in the exorcisms. Probably before this time he occupied merely a minor position in the incantations.

Chief of the gods of light in the incantations was Šamaš. Sacrifices were usually offered him in connection with Ea and Marduk, although sacrifices to him alone were not uncommon. In the incantations he was seldom mentioned with the other two gods. He was usually referred to alone, or else associated with Gibil-Nuzku. This shows clearly that at one time, not long previous to the systemization of the Babylonian theology, Šamaš occupied a position entirely independent of, and of almost equal importance to, that of Ea. Marduk in time absorbed the functions and personality of Ea, but those of Šamaš remained practically undisturbed. His position in the ceremonies decreased somewhat in importance, as that of Marduk became supreme, but the exorcisms in his name could not well be changed nor modified so as to introduce Marduk. Consequently in them Šamaš usually appears alone[2]).

One significant fact in connection with his position in these texts, is the paucity of titles and epithets ascribed to him. We have seen how titles were given to both Ea and Marduk, illustrative of their exalted position and peculiar functions in the *âšipu*-ritual. They were however not directly connected with any other ritual. But Šamaš was the god of the *bârû*, even more than of the *âšipu*. He and Adad were here closely associated. As god of the *bârû*, he was the *daiiânu rabû*, "the great judge", who decided the decisions of man[3]).

---

[1]) Cf. K. B. VI, I, 562.

[2]) Cf. IV R. 17 and 28 No. 1.

[3]) This is expressed in the oft-recurring phrase of the *bârû*-ritual, *il Šamaš bêl dîni il Adad bêl birê*, "Šamaš, lord of judgment, Adad, lord of divination".

And precisely in this character, an under this title, does he appear in the incantations. This is the only specific attribute he receives. Otherwise he is merely "the destroyer of sin", "the remover of evil", titles illustrating merely the most general functions of the *āšipu*-ceremonies, and applicable to all other gods as well. Thus we read [1]):

ka-sa-a uš-šu-ru mar-ṣa [pašāḫu?] it-ti-ka i-ba-aš- [ši?]
ilu amēli aš-šu ma-ri-šu ka-a-ša áš-riš iz-za-az-ka
41. *be-lum ia-a-ti iš-pu-ra-an-ni*
EN-GAL DINGIR-EN-KI-GE-GA-E MU-UN-ŠI-IN-GI-EN
i-ziz-ma a-ma-as-su li-mad pu-ru-us-sa-šu pu-ru-us
46. *at-ta ina a-la-ki-ka ṣal-mat qaq-qa-di tuš-te-šir*
ša-ru-ur šul-mi šú-kun-šum-ma ma-ru-uš-ta-šu li-eš-te-šir
50. *a-me-lu mār ili-šu e-nu-un ar-nam e-mi-id*
meš-ri-tu-šu mar-ṣi-iš ip-šá mar-ṣi-iš ina mur-ṣi ni-il
il Šamaš ana ni-iš qa-ti-ia qu-lam-ma
56. *a-kal-šu a-kul ni-qa-šu mu-ḫur-ma i-la-am il-šu ana i-di-šu šu-ku-un*
ina qi-bi-ti-ka en-ne-is-su lip-pa-ṭi-ir
a-ra-an-šu li-in-na-si-iḫ.

Rev.

ka-su-us-su li-taš-ši-ir mar-ṣu-us-su li-ib-lu-uṭ
LUGAL-BI ḪE-EN-TI-LA
EN-E UD-DA AB-TI-LA NAM-MAḪ-ZU ḪE-IB-BI
5. LUGAL-BI KA-TAR-ZU ḪE-EN-SI-IL-E
U GA-E MULU-TÚ-TÚ URU-ZU GA-TAR-ZU ḪE-EN-SI-IL-E

To free [2]) the imprisoned, [to heal?] the sick, is thine [3]).
Because of his son, the god of the man comes humbly before thee.
41. "The lord has sent me,
The great lord, Ea, has sent me."
Go, learn his case, decide his decision,

---

[1]) IV R. 17 obv. 36- rev. 6.
[2]) Literally, "to make right"
[3]) Literally, "is with thee."

46. Thou guidest the black-headed race in thy course.
Prepare for him a sun-rise of good health, may his evil fate be changed to good[1];
50. Punishment for sin is laid upon the man, the son of his god,
His members are made sick; in sickness he lies sick.
O, Šamaš, have regard unto my prayer;
56. Eat his food, accept his sacrifice, and place at his hand the deity, his god.
At thy command may his punishment be removed,
May his sin be torn away.

Rev.

From his bondage may he come free; from his sickness may he be restored to life.
May that king be restored to life,
O Lord of day, who restorest life, that he proclaim thy greatness;
5. May that king be submissive unto thee,
And I too, the exorciser, thy servant.

Another sun-god who played a role in the incantations, second only to Šamaš, was Gibil-Nuzku, the fire-god[2]. He was invoked under both names, but there is no doubt, that they were identical. He was the deification of the fire itself, into which the images of the witches were cast, and their enchantments removed[3]. In consequence thereof, in *Maqlû* he played the most conspicuous role of all the gods. He shared the titles and functions of Šamaš, seems in fact, in this series, to have been but little removed from Šamaš himself. Of him it is said:[4]

tuš-te-eš-šir ilâni pl *u ma-al-ki*
ta-da-a-ni di-en ḫab-li u ḫa-bíl-ti
ina di-ni-ia i-ziz-za-am-ma ki-ma il *Šamaš qu-ra-du*
di-i-ni di-ni purussa-a-a purus(-us)
Thou guidest gods and princes,

---

[1]) Literally, "be made right."
[2]) For an exhaustive treatment of this god and his functions in the incantations, cf. *Maqlû*, Einl. pp. 25—30.
[3]) Cf. *Maqlû* IV, 47; II, 1—11.
[4]) Ibid. II, 115—118; cf. 23—25, 70, 94; I. 110—116.

Thou judgest the case of the evil man and woman;
Enter into my judgment, as Šamaš, the hero, and
Judge my case, decide my decision.

Once, as messenger of Bēl, Nuzku reported to Ea, in the deep, that the evil spirits had overpowered the moon-god, Sin[1]). Again he was called the *qarradu mār apsī*, "the hero, son of the deep"[2]), and *ša il Ea tappušu*, "the companion[3]) of Ea"[4]). Gilgameš seems to have been closely related to Gibil-Nuzku[5]).

Another sun-god, who occupied a peculiar position in the incantations was Nērgal. He represented the mid-day and mid-summer sun, with its fiery, destructive heat. Part of the time he spent in the underworld as husband of Ereškigal. Consequently he was a god of evil as well as good. As one of the gods of light, he protected man against the evil spirits, but as lord of the underworld, he sent these forth against man.

As a god of good he appears in the incantations not only in his own form, but in others as well. Chief of these were the twin gods, Lugal-Ùra and Šitlamtaēa[6]). Their importance may be inferred from the fact that sacrifices were offered to them, precisely as to Ea, Šamaš, and Marduk[7]). Their chief functions were to ward off the attacks of the evil spirits, rather than to expel them after they had once entered a man's body. They were usually represented in the form of images present at the bed-side of the sick man, or suspended on the door-posts of his house. Thus[8]):

ina imni bābi-ia u šumēli bābi-ia
ul-te-iz-ziz il Lugal-ù-ra u il Šit-lam-ta-ē-a

---

[1]) U. L. XVI, 112—127.

[2]) IV R. 14 No. 2 rev. 9/10.

[3]) Literally, "twin".

[4]) Ibid. 20/21.

[5]) Cf. *Maqlū* I, 38; K. 649 (Harper's Letters, 56) rev. 5 and K. B. VI, I, 266 ff.

[6]) Or *Almu* and *Alamu*, cf. II R. 54, 74—75 a.

[7]) Cf. below, p. 114.

[8]) *Maqlū* VI 123—124; cf. Beitr. XLI—XLII. II, 1 ff. and *Maqlū* IV, 15—17; VII Col. IV, 4—7 (Weissbach: B. A. IV); cf. also Beitr. XLI—XLII Col. I, 68 ff; XLVIII, 5; L Col. 3; LIII, 10—13; LIV, 21; IV R. 21* No. 1 (C) Col. III. 23.

To the right of my gate and to the left
Will I station Lugal-Ùra and Šitlamtaēa.

And again[1]):

napištu šur-ra-a-ša ^iṣ^ *iršu i-lam-mu-u* ^il^ *Lugal-ù-ra u* ^il^ *Šit-lam-ta-ē-a*

To save[2]) (?) the life, Lugal-Ùra and Šitlamtaēa surround the bed of the sick man.

Nērgal himself, as a god of good, was generally merely a protective deity, and was seldom directly invoked to drive out evil spirits[3]). And he too was usually represented in the form of an image. Other forms of Nērgal as the protector of mankind were Lugal-edinna[4]), Latarak[5]) and Išum[6]). He was also closely associated with "The Seven"[7]), and with Narudu[8]), their sister; seems in fact to have been their chief[9]). They too were merely protective deities, and as such their images were repeatedly used. As a god of evil, Nērgal appeared chiefly as Ùra, the plague-god, with Išum[10]), his counsellor of evil.

---

[1]) Sp, I, 131, 16.

[2]) II from שׁרא? cf. H. W. B. 687b. Is this the same stem as Meissner: Suppl. 97 b?

[3]) Exceptions are B. M. S. XI, 34, XXVII 21; Beitr. XXVII, 8, K. 2430 (Cat. 443); K. 3507 (Cat. 540); U. L. III, 145; IV Col. I, 20.

[4]) *Maqlū* VII Col. IV. 4—7 (Weissbach: B. A. IV).

[5]) Beitr. L Col. II, 6 ff; LIV obv. 27.

[6]) Ibid. LIII, 17; U. L. tablet K. 178—180; IV R. 21 No. 1 (A) Col. I obv. 44; B. M. S. VII, 39.

[7]) Cf. above, p. 92 f. It has already been said that "The Seven" were not always the same group of deities. Thus III R. 66 obv. Col. IV 12—19 reads, *il Sibitti-šunu il mārē-napišti il Na-ru-da il Ištar il* GAM *u il* [KIT] -GAM-TA *il* TI-ḪI *il Šamaš il Nērgal ša al Kar-Nērgal il La-ab-ra-nu ilāni ša bīt il Sibitti-šunu.* IV R. 21 No. 1 (A) obv. 43 ff. reads, *ilu bīti il ištar bīti ilu ali il ištar ali il Nērgal bēl šipti il I-šum sukkalu il Al-mu il A-la-mu šar-ri si-bit-ti.* In IV R. 21 No. 1 (B) (Beitr. LIV) rev. 9—11, images of two groups of seven gods are referred to. In Beitr. LIII 17, the image of Išum is associated with them; cf. also Beitr. XLVI—XLVII St. I, 15 ff.

[8]) Beitr. XLI—XLII St. II, 14; XLV Col. III, 1; XLVI—XLVII St. II, 13; LIV obv. 25.

[9]) IV R. 21 No. 1 (A) obv. Col. I, 44; Beitr. LIV obv. 12. Cf. LIII. 17.

[10]) Like Nērgal, Išum too, was a god of both good and evil.

Other sun-gods who played a less prominent role in the incantations, were Nin-girsu[1]), Nin-giš-zida[2]) and Siris[3]).

Two other deities, mentioned in the incantations, yet playing a role hardly commensurate with their greatness, were Ninib and Gula[4]). This is all the more surprising since Ninib was also a sun-god. They were the gods of medicine, and it seems merely as such, and because medicine was so closely related to the *āšipu*-ceremonies, did they find a place here. Gula was often called *muballiṭat mītu*, "the restorer of the dead to life"[5]), but this meant no more than "the one who cures the sick man with medicine". Damu, a form of Gula, was once called the *āšipu rabū*[6]).

Judging from their exalted rank, and the fact that they too were gods of light, we would expect to find Sin and Ištar playing important roles in the incantations. But just the reverse is the case; they are but seldom mentioned[7]). The explanation of this lies perhaps in the fact that they were gods of the light of the night, when the evil spirits were most active. Yet it is significant that other stars, especially Šibziana[8]), were occasionally invoked to remove evil. Furthermore a group of deities, known as "the gods of the night," seems to have played a fairly important role in the incantations[9]).

---

1) U. L. III, 10/11.

2) IV R. 21* No. 1 (C) rev. Col. II, 15; *Maqlû* VII, 11, cf. note.

3) Ibid.

4) *Maqlû* VI, 2, VIII, 78; Beitr. XXVII, 3, Sp. 1, 131, 14—15; Cr. II pl. 14, rev. Col. IV 8.

5) *Šurpu* VII, 77.

6) Ibid. 79.

7) Sin: B. M. S. I; K. 2430 (Cat. 443), *Maqlû* III, 100, 128; IV R. 56, 11 b; K. 602 (Harper's Letters, 23); K. 626 (Ibid. 24) rev. 14—15. Ištar: *Maqlû* III, 180, V, 59—60; IV R. 56 Col. I, 18, II, 16, III, 42; Beitr. XXVI Col. III, 54—55, V, 73; B. M. S. XXX—XXXII; K. 602 (Harper's Letters, 23). Although Ištar was but seldom referred to in the incantations themselves, in the sin-offering she occupied an important and peculiar position. Cf. below, pp. 109 ff.

8) B. M. S. L—LII; cf. XLVI—XLIX.

9) *Maqlû* I, 1; Cr. II pl. 8, obv. 13; Beitr. XXXI—XXXVII St. II, 17; 81—2—4, 49 (Harper's Letters, 370) rev. 2.

Finally, as we have seen[1]), a man's own personal god and goddess, and the protecting spirits of his house, also guarded him from evil spirits. They were however rather good spirits than real gods.

Chap. VI.
The Sin-Offering.

Sacrifice was, as we have seen, originally an independent means of expiating sin[2]). It was efficacious in itself, without being combined with other methods of expelling evil spirits. Originally it may have been nothing more than an offering to propitiate some angry deity, and thereby obtain remittance from the evil he had sent. In time however, expiatory force came to be attached to it. It was still a sacrifice to a deity, but it freed of itself. The question no longer existed, was the god propitiated or not. The number of gods to whom the sin-offering was sacrificed, was limited. Not every god was concerned with the removal of evil spirits. Consequently the sin-offering was first sacrificed to Ea and Šamaš almost exclusively. And, as the theological system reached its final form, Marduk was added to this group, and the great triad of the *āšipu*-ritual came into being. And, as was natural, the sacrifice, offered for a specific purpose, took on a fixed form. True, it could be altered somewhat to suit the occasion, but the underlying elements always remained the same, and differed essentially from all other sacrifices. And singularly enough, of the three gods composing this triad, it was not Ea, that played the leading part, nor yet Marduk, but Šamaš. True, but little difference can be noticed among them. All three usually appeared together; in only a few cases was a sacrifice offered to one of them separately. Yet what superiority there was, seems to have belonged to Šamaš. May we perhaps infer from this, that the sin-offering was originally peculiar to Šamaš, just as

---

[1]) Chap. III.

[2]) As such it was what is technically known as a "sin-offering".

the use of water was peculiar to Ea, and that, as the theological system was developed and systematized, first Ea, and then Marduk, the other great gods of purification, were associated with him?[1])

But in the texts that have come down to us, the original nature of the sin-offering has been greatly modified. In short, it has lost all, or almost all, its independent nature. It never appears unaccompanied by the recital of one or more *šiptu*'s, and often the use of water and other means of expiation, is added. And not only is the sin-offering accompanied by these, but it seems to be usually subordinate, a mere preparation for them, as it were. The efficacy of the service lies not in the sin-offering, but rather in the other expiatory ceremonies.

But few texts in which this sacrifice is mentioned, have as yet been published[2]), and many of these are too fragmentary for use. Examination of these texts shows that the usual formula for the sin-offering was as follows[3]):

maḫar il *Šamaš qaqqara tašabbit*[4]) *mū ellu tasallaḫ* GI-GAB *tukān*
šu' *niqē tanaqqē* šir *imittu* šir *ḫinṣa* (?)
šir *šumē tuṭaḫḫē*
suluppu KU-A-TER *tasarraq miris*
dišpi ḫemēti tašakkan adagura tukān
niknakka burāši tašakkan kurunna tanaqqē tuškēn

[1]) Not only the sin-offering, but sacrifices in general, seem to have been peculiar to Šamaš. In the *bārū*-ritual, he and Adad were supreme, and to them the real *bārū*-sacrifice was offered (Beitr. I—XX, 101—126). And also in the sacrifice of the *zammāru*, Šamaš seems to have played the chief role. It is significant too, that of the contracts, recording gifts or dues to temples, especially of such things as were used for sacrifices, fully ninety per cent were to the Šamaš-temple at Sippar.

[2]) In addition to Beitr. XXVI—LIX only IV R. 23, 25, 55 No. 2, 57 (B. M. S. XII) and 60, Cr. I 66—67 and B. M. S. XXI, XXX and LXII can be regarded with certainty as sacrificial *āšipu*-texts. In other texts, such as the *Labartu*-series, peculiar sacrifices to remove evil spirits occur, but they are not sin-offerings.

[3]) Beitr. XLVI—XLVII St. I, 4—9.

[4]) I have omitted Zimmern's question-mark, because this interpretation of the ideogram KI-SAR is so in accord with the underlying principle of the sin-offering, that there can be but little doubt of its correctness.

Before Šamaš shalt thou sweep the ground clean, sprinkle holy water, erect an altar.

5. A lamb shalt thou sacrifice, flesh of the right side, *ḫinṣa*(?)-flesh,

šumē-flesh shalt thou bring near.

Dates and A-TER-meal shalt thou pour out, a mixture[1]) of honey and butter shalt thou make; an *adagur*-vessel shalt thou place;

a censer of cypress-wood shalt thou light[2]); a libation of sesame-wine shalt thou pour on and prostrate thyself.

This simple and short ceremony is the complete sin-offering. We will now analyse it. The three ceremonies in the first line are more a preparation for, than a part of, the sacrifice. The place where the sacrifice is to be held is first swept clean and holy water sprinkled. The place is now both physically and ritually pure. The sacrifice may therefore be begun. First an altar is erected, for this is not a ceremony in a temple, but in the open air. A lamb is sacrificed and different kinds of meat are offered[3]). Then dates and A-TER-

[1]) For this reading and meaning of the ideogram, cf. IV R. 13 No. 3, 59/60.

[2]) This sentence Zimmern translates, "Censer, cypress, shalt thou place." This is altogether too literal to express the full meaning. In the first place *niknakku burāši* (Zimmern reads *burāša*) must mean a censer of cypress-wood, i. e. filled with this wood, and therefore ready for use (cf. *karpat kalli upuntu*, Beitr. LXXV—LXXVIII, 48; cf. also l. 46). And *šakānu* is used in the directions for ceremonies in any number of pregnant meanings. That this sentence means that the censer is to be lit, and incense offered, is clear from the fact that in all sacrifices no other verb is used with *niknakku*. And a censer is not merely placed for show, but is lighted and incense burnt on it. The expression, *mirsa sakānu* (ll. 7—8), also probably means more than merely "thou shalt make a mixture". In IV R. 13 No. 3, 59/60 this is *mirsa marāsu*. The above expression probably means "Thou shalt offer a mixture".

[3]) Just what these three kinds of meat were, is not clear. The first Zimmern translates, no doubt correctly, "flesh of the right side." Whether it denotes merely the right leg, or shoulder, as he renders it throughout Beitr. 1—XX, and is therefore to be compared with the right shoulder in Exodus 29, 22; Leviticus 7, 25, 26; 9, 21, etc. is doubtful (cf. Beitr. p. 95, note 3). The reading *ḫinṣa* for the ideogram ME-KAN rests upon Beitr. LVI, 8, where it is written phonetically *ḫi-in-ṣa* and stands between *šir*

meal[1]) are poured out; a mixture of honey and butter is offered; an *adagur*-vessel is placed on the altar (?); incense of cypress-wood is offered and a libation of sesame-wine poured out. The placing of the *adagur*-vessel has in itself no significance, but is merely for the libation. We have then in this sacrifice five elements: (1) the three meats of the lamb, (2) dates and A-TER-meal[2]), (3) the mixture of honey and butter[3]), (4) incense, and (5) a libation. At the close of these ceremonies the priest prostrates himself. Comparing this sacrifice with others[4]), we find them identical in every way. Not only are the elements the same, but also the order in which they are sacrificed, and the language employed. When we compare this again with Beitr. XLI—XLII St. I 6—12 and 40—46, we notice two differences. In the first place no incense is offered, and instead of sesame-wine the libation consisted of five different liquids used together, viz. fermented-wine, sweet-wine, honey, milk and oil. However this last fact is not significant. Either this group or parts of it, or sesame-wine alone, could be used for the libation. Whether there were rules for offering the one or the other, can not be determined; they seem however to have been employed at will. This much is however certain, that sesame-wine, as a libation, was unaccompanied by other liquids[5]). But the fact that the incense is here omitted is significant. It

---

imittu and *šīr šumē*. The phonetic writing also occurs in Neb. 247 obv. 9: *ḫi-in-ṣi* (cf. Beitr. note to LVI, 8). According to II R. 40, 27 b. it is a part of the body. Haupt compares *ḫinṣa* with the Hebrew חלצים, Aramaic حَصا "loins". Jensen compares *šīr šumē* with *šamū* (II R. 34, 71, a, b, ff.), شوى and the expression *šú-mi-e ši-i-ri* in NE. 17, 44, and infers that it means "roasted meat." This is probably correct, although, from the context, we would expect it to be another part of the body.

[1]) Neither the real meaning nor the reading of this ideogram is known.

[2]) These two always occur together in the sacrifices and consequently form one element.

[3]) No other substances are used in the mixture. *Ḫemētu* (cf. חמאה) was probably closer akin to "cream" than to "butter".

[4]) Beitr. XLVI—XLVII St. I, 1—9; L Col. III, 9—14.

[5]) The only exception to this rule is IV R. 60 obv. 20, where *kurunnu* and *karānu* are used together.

shows that after all, it was of only secondary importance in the sin-offering.

Turning now to other sacrifices, we find differences more or less striking. In Beitr. LVI the sacrifice is as follows: dates and A-TER-meal are poured out; the mixture of honey and butter is offered; the lamb slaughtered and the three kinds of meat brought near; incense is offered and *upuntu* [1]) poured on it; the "string (?) is drawn" [2]), and a pile of meal poured out. However, the real sin-offering seems to have ceased with the pouring of the *upuntu* on the censer. The rest of this text treats of a different ceremony. That *upuntu* is poured on the incense, is not of especial significance. It is not an uncommon act [3]), and merely heightened the effect of the incense. In this sin-offering however, several facts are noteworthy. In the first place, the order of sacrifice differs from that already discussed. The pouring out of dates and A-TER-meal and the offering of the mixture of honey and butter precede the sacrifice of the lamb [4]). And finally, the libation is omitted. From this we must conclude that, like the incense-offering, the libation was not an essential part of the sin-offering, and furthermore, that the order of the different parts of the sacrifice, as first treated of, was customary but not absolute, and could be changed according to the nature of the ceremony of which the sin-offering formed part.

The sin-offering in Beitr. XLIX Col. VI 4—6 presents other new features. In the first place, it is conducted on a rather grand scale, since seven complete sacrifices are offered

---

[1]) Halévy compares *upuntu* with אפן and translates it "peas". Zimmern, apparently more correctly, renders it "fine meal". Cf. Beitr. XCV, 4 and 12 and LXXXIX—XC 4 and 11, where it seems closely related to, if not used interchangeably with, *nisaba*.

[2]) *Šid-di tašuddad.* The meaning of this ceremony, which occurs also in the *bārū*-ritual, is entirely unknown.

[3]) Cf. Beitr. LXXV—LXXVIII 68—75 and Leviticus 2, 2, where incense and fine flour are offered together.

[4]) The language here differs somewhat from the usual *šu'* or *immēr niqē tanaqqē*. Here we read III *šu'ē ellūti tanaqqē*. Also, in l. 45, we read GI-GAB *tarakkas*, instead of the customary *tukān*. And in ll. 3—4 the directions are couched in unusual language. This indicates that the entire ceremony here is out of the ordinary.

at one time[1]). First, incense it burnt, then the lamb is sacrificed and the three meats brought near, and finally a libation of sesame-wine is poured out. Then follow other ceremonies. Not only is the order of sacrifice here unusual, but the pouring out of dates and A-TER-meal and the offering of the mixture of honey and butter are also omitted. These too then can not be absolutely essential to the sin-offering.

A sacrifice resembling this somewhat is that in B. M. S. LXII rev. 24—30. It forms part of a NAM-BUR-BI-service[2]), but the text is rather fragmentary. The ground is swept clean and holy water sprinkled. Here the text is broken away. Then dates and A-TER-meal are poured out, and the mixture of honey and butter brought near. Then comes another short break in the text. Then incense is burnt, the lamb sacrificed, and the three meats brought near.

A sin-offering very similar to this is found in B. M. S. XXI 28 ff. The ground is swept and holy water sprinkled; an altar erected; dates and A-TER-meal poured out; the mixture of honey and butter brought near; the lamb sacrificed and the three meats offered. Singularly enough this is a sacrifice to Adad.

The sacrifice in IV R. 60 obv. 15—20 is also similar. The ground is swept clean and holy water sprinkled. The usual preparations for the sacrifice are then made[3]). Incense is then burnt, the lamb slaughtered and the three meats brought near[4]); an *adagur*-vessel is made ready and a libation of sesame and sweet-wine is poured out[5]). Then follow other ceremonies, apparently closely related to, yet not an actual part of, the sacrifice.

The text in IV R. 23 No. 1 Col. III 24—29 is very fragmentary, yet, as far as can be learned, the sacrifice seems to

---

[1]) This is not uncommon. Cf. Beitr. XXVI Col. I, 26—32.

[2]) Cf. below.

[3]) *Riksu rakāsu* seems to be nothing more than a general term for all preparations for a sacrifice, such as cleaning the ground, setting up the altar, etc. Cf. Beitr. XXVI Col. IV, 17 ff.; XXXI—XXXVII St. II, 12—14.

[4]) The verb for this ceremony is always *ṭuḫḫû*, equivalent in meaning to the Hebrew הקריב.

[5]) Cf. above, p. 104, note 5

have been as follows: an altar is erected and preparations for the sacrifice made; the mixture of honey and butter is then offered; dates and A-TER-meal are poured out[1]); the lamb is sacrificed and the three meats brought near. The text here is broken away, but this suffices to show that the order of sacrifice here is different from any so far met with.

Likewise the text of Beitr. XXXVIII is too fragmentary to be of much service. The sin-offering there seems to have consisted of the lamb and the three meats, and a libation of honey and other substances, the names of which have been lost. This was probably not the complete sacrifice, the first part being entirely broken away.

In Beitr. LII we meet with a very peculiar ceremony, held for a man about to die. After the necessary images are made ready[2]), the place is swept clean, and holy water sprinkled as usual. White[3]) stools are placed for some god, whose name has been lost. Over these bright[4]) cloths are spread. An altar is erected and bread[5]) laid thereon before Ea, Šamaš and Marduk. Dates and A-TER-meal are then poured out, three[6]) *adagur*-vessels placed in position, the censers of incense[7]) lighted and different kinds of grain poured upon them[8]). Then follow ceremonies for the ghosts of the sick man's family. After these are finished, a lamb is sacrificed to Šamaš alone[9]), the

---

[1]) This is the first time that the mixture was offered before the dates and meal.

[2]) Cf. above, p. 74.

[3]) *Piṣâti*; perhaps to be read *ellêti*, "pure".

[4]) Or, "proper"; cf. Zimmern's note.

[5]) *Kurummatu*.

[6]) I. e. one for each god.

[7]) *Riqqê*. The word really means "evergreen-plants" (cf. A. B. M. pp. 79, 123). Incense consisted usually of cypress or cedar-wood, both evergreens. Therefore *riqqê* is hardly a new material for incense.

[8]) Cf. above, p. 105. This is precisely the same ceremony as pouring *upuntu* on the incense, and no especial significance need be attached to it. This is also additional proof that *upuntu* is a kind of grain, rather than peas. However, the latter could be included in the general term *še'u*, "grain".

[9]) This is however not certain. The expression *maḫar il Šamaš*, or *ina maḫar*, occurs almost invariably with the ceremony of sweeping the ground. Just what the expression, "thou shalt sweep the ground before

three meats brought near, and apparently a libation is also poured out, though the text here is too fragmentary to be sure of this [1]). This is a very peculiar sacrifice, rendered the more complicated by the introduction of the family ghosts and their ceremonies. That the sacrifice itself is a sin-offering, can not be doubted. The circumstances under which it is held, the materials composing it, and the gods to whom it is offered, all prove this. The striking facts then, are, first, that the mixture of honey and butter was omitted, and second, that other ceremonies could intervene between the different parts of the sin-offering.

IV R. 25 Col. II 30—38 corresponds fairly well to the usual sin-offering. Apparently an idol had just been completed and accordingly the sacrifice is offered not only to Ea, Šamaš and Marduk, but also to the god whom the idol represents. The ground is swept clean, and holy water sprinkled as usual. Preparations for the sacrifice are then made. Dates and A-TER-meal are poured out, and the mixture of honey and butter offered, and then, seemingly [2]), three lambs are sacrificed and the three meats brought near. A libation of sesame-wine is poured out, and then, strangely enough, the priest is commanded not to prostrate himself. This, and the fact that again no incense is offered, are the striking features of this sacrifice. When it is finished, other ceremonies are performed, directly concerned with the purification of the idol.

All these sin-offerings so far were to Ea, Šamaš or Marduk. Beitr. XLIX, L, LII and LVI were to these three gods together. As we have also seen, IV R. 25 was to them and the god whose idol had just been completed. IV R. 60 seems to have been to Ea and Šamaš together; IV R. 23 No. 1 to Ea alone; Beitr. XLI—XLII St. I 6—12 to Marduk alone, and XLV Col.

Šamaš", means, is not clear. We may perhaps see in the *ana maḫar il Šamaš* here the same expression. In that case the sacrifice of the lamb would be merely the resumption of the sin-offering, interrupted by the ceremony for the ghosts. Cf. לִפְנֵי יְהוָה Leviticus I, 3, 4 and passim.

[1]) Probably this consisted of sesame-wine, for the empty space admits of but little more than ŠAG-BI (= *kurunnu*).

[2]) III *niqē tanaqqē* can have no other meaning.

II 1—7 to Šamaš. XLI—XLII St. I 40—60 was to Azag-šud and Ninaḫakuddu. It is not stated to whom Beitr. XXXVIII and XLVI—XLVII were, but in all probability to the triad, or at least one of them.

Turning to Beitr. LVII we find a sacrifice, seemingly a sin-offering, although differing in some features, but offered to Ištar, Šamaš and Nērgal. Šamaš plays the principle part in this ceremony, and the other two deities seem merely to share in the sacrifice. This is as follows: as usual the place is first swept clean and holy water sprinkled. Altars are then erected to the three gods and wheat-bread laid on each. The mixture of honey and butter is then offered, dates and A-TER-meal poured out, three strong lambs (*šu'u dannūti*) sacrificed and the three meats brought near. *Upuntu* is then poured upon the censer of cypress-wood, which is no doubt burning. A libation is then poured out, consisting of honey, butter, wine, oil, and sweet-smelling (?) oil[1]). Then follow other ceremonies, no longer part of the sacrifice. The question is, is this a sin-offering? It is offered at a time when the enemy invades the land and makes war upon the king, Its obvious purpose is to avert all danger to the king's life. This seems to have little in common with the *āšipu*-services, and yet, when we remember that all in all, the purpose of these services was to avert danger to life, we may perhaps reconcile this apparent difficulty. The symbolic ceremonies that follow, smack too of the *āšipu*-ritual. An image of the king's enemy is made of tallow, and its face turned backward with a cord[2]). The king's eunuch (?), who bears the same name as the king, puts on (?) the latter's garments (?), steps before the image and recites a formula[3]). This

---

[1]) Cf. above, p. 104, where the libation was also composed of five liquids, but different from these here.

[2]) The purpose of this ceremony is not clear. Perhaps it symbolized he prayer, that the enemy may in that way be turned back, or destroyed, and his plans defeated.

[3]) *Minūtu*, from *manū*, "to measure". But *manū* also means, "to recite a prayer", and is in fact so used here. We may therefore probably translate *minūtu* by "prayer", almost synonymous with *šiptu*. Cf. B. M. S. II, 11; XI, 45; XL, 13.

has however been lost. The purpose of this ceremony was perhaps to deceive fate, as it were; that all evil that is fated, and can not be escaped, may come upon the eunuch, and the king thus be saved. The sacrifice too resembles the sin-offering very closely; true, the libation differs somewhat from the ordinary, the lambs are required to be strong, which is nowhere else the case, and we have the additional element of wheat-bread. None of these is however of much significance. It is not what is added to the usual sacrifice, that changes its nature, but rather what is omitted, and, as we have seen, even this cuts but little figure in the sin-offering. And finally, that the sacrifice is offered to Ištar, Šamaš and Nērgal, instead of the usual triad, likewise proves nothing. The next sin-offerings we shall treat of, are also offered to Ištar, while Nērgal, as we have seen, plays quite an important role in the *āšipu*-ceremonies. There seems therefore no reason to doubt that this is a sin-offering, but of a peculiar form, occasioned by the unusual purpose for which it is offered.

In IV R. 55 No. 2, 14—20 directions for a sin-offering to Ištar alone are given. It is offered at night-fall[1]) upon the roof of a house. As usual, this is first swept clean, holy water sprinkled and a altar erected. A censer of cypress-wood is then lit, a lamb slaughtered and the three meats brought near. A libation of fermented- and sweet-wine is poured out and different kinds of bread placed on the altar. Again a lamb is brought near. *Luluppu*-wood is heaped upon the altar, and a torch, lit from a fire on the river bank, is set to it. After the wood has been completely burned, different kinds of woods, reeds and plants are strewn upon it. Another libation of fermented- and sweet-wine is poured out, a *šiptu* is repeated three times before the goddess, and the afflicted man prostrates himself in prayer before her.

The noticeable features of this sacrifice, outside of the fact that it was offered to Ištar alone, are that it was held at night, and on the roof of a house; that bread again played a prominent part in it; the elaborate nature of the incense, and

---

[1]) For this meaning of the expression *kī šēpu parsat*, cf. Beitr. LXXIX—LXXXII St. I, 8 and note *a*.

the fact that apparently a second lamb, in addition to the one sacrificed, was used. This last however is not certain. And finally, it is also noteworthy that the mixture of honey and butter and the dates and A-TER-meal were omitted.

The sin-offerings so far treated of, seem to center about the lamb. All other parts of the sacrifice may at times be omitted, but this is always present, and the real expiatory force lies in it. This is proved by the sentence *urîṣu tanakkisma šarra tukappar*, "a lamb shalt thou slaughter and purify the king"[1]. That in this sentence *urîṣu* was used for the customary *šu' niqû*, and *nakāsu* for *naqû*, is not significant The fact remains beyond all doubt, that the expiatory force of the sin-offering centered in the lamb, and that all other parts of the sacrifice were secondary and without great significance[2]. We have now to consider a sin-offering in which the lamb is lacking[3].

This is a very simple sacrifice, also offered to Ištar, and again on the roof of a house. This is, as usual, first swept clean and holy water sprinkled. And altar is then erected before the goddess and twelve loaves of bread[4] put upon it. The mixture of honey and butter is then offered, dates and A-TER-meal poured out, and incense burnt[5]. Then a *šiptu* is spoken to the goddess.

A very similar sin-offering, also offered to Ištar, is as follows[6]: The roof is swept clean and holy water sprinkled;

---

[1]) Beitr. XXVI Col. II, 1.

[2]) Cf. the sin-offering in Leviticus 5 which consists of only an animal, usually a female lamb.

[3]) Cr. I pl. 66—67, obv. 12—14.

[4]) Or, "cakes".

[5]) It is interesting to compare with this text, Jeremiah 19, 13, which speaks of incense offered on the roofs of the houses to all the host of heaven, and of libations poured out there to other gods, and Ibid. 44, 15—19, where the women of Israel are said to burn incense, pour out libations and make cakes for the queen of heaven. This bears a very marked resemblance to these sacrifices to Ištar. The reference to the cakes is particularly noteworthy. The Hebrew word is כַּוָּן, which, as Jensen has shown (K. B. VI, I, 511), is equivalent to the Assyrian *kamānu*, which was especially sacred to Ištar.

[6]) B. M. S. XXX 20—29.

an altar is then erected to the goddess, and dates and A-TER-meal poured out; the mixture of honey and butter is then offered; an *adagur*-vessel put in place, and a libation of sesame-wine poured out. Then follow other ceremonies. This text forms the one hundred and thirty-fifth tablet of a series, probably the NAM-BUR-BI. The sacrifice preceding this, forms part of the one hundred and thirty-fourth tablet of this series.

In these two ceremonies no lamb is sacrificed. Yet that they are sin-offerings can not be doubted, for the one at least formed part of a NAM-BUR-BI-service. How this omission, which apparently contradicts our whole theory of the sin-offering, is to be explained, is difficult to say. Perhaps we have here a special form of the sin-offering, which permitted the omission of the lamb just as the other elements could be omitted on occasions. Singularly enough, all the sin-offerings in which the lamb was omitted, were sacrificed to Ištar. And in each the element, bread, entirely foreign to the sin-offering to the triad, was present and formed an important part of the sacrifice. We must therefore conclude that bread was especially sacred to Ištar, just as the lamb was sacred to the triad, and that, just as in the sin-offerings to the latter the real expiatory force lay in the lamb, so in those to Ištar it lay in the bread. This therefore explains why both bread and a lamb were used in the sin-offering to Ištar, Šamaš and Nērgal, in Beitr. LVII.

We have now to treat of a series of sacrifices closely related to the sin-offering, but differing from it in many, and very material, respects. These were not offered to gods, but were concerned more or less directly with images used in the *āšipu*-ceremonies.

The first of these[1]) is a very peculiar sacrifice, and very difficult to explain. It is apparently offered to the image of a bird made of bread-dough, and covered with gypsum[2]). The ground is swept as usual in the sin-offering, and holy water sprinkled. Then, seemingly, certain vessels are put in place,

---

[1]) Beitr. LVIII.

[2]) All this is however uncertain; cf. Zimmern's translation.

and a certain kind of bread laid on the altar. Dates and A-TER-meal are poured out, and the mixture of honey and butter offered. *Laḫanu*-vessels are filled with fermented wine, and apparently a libation is made. A lamb is then sacrificed, "corresponding to the figure of the bird"[1]). After these ceremonies, the man for whom they are performed seemingly takes his place at the left side of the altar, and says a prayer or *šiptu* to Šamaš. Whether this was a sin-offering of an unusual kind, or no sin-offering at all, is hard to say. Certainly it belonged to the *āšipu*-service, and was connected with Šamaš, although the directions seem rather to point to the image of the bird as the recipient of the sacrifice. But outside of the sacrifice of the lamb, the pouring out of the dates and A-TER-meal, and the offering of the mixture of honey and butter, we have no especial features of the sin-offering, and these could belong to other sacrifices as well[2]). The other features are entirely different from anything so far met with in the sin-offering. The text is however too fragmentary and incomprehensible to permit of any answer to this question. It must therefore remain open.

The next text[3]) is also very fragmentary. A sacrifice for a sick man has just preceded, but this part of the text has been lost. During this sacrifice, different images were present. After the remains of the sacrifice had been removed, the images were brought foreward[4]); incense was offered and apparently a libation poured out before them. That was the entire sacrifice. *Šiptu's* were then recited before the different images.

In another text[5]) we have a similar ceremony. Apparently a sin-offering to Ea, Šamaš and Marduk is to be held upon the roof of a house for a sick man. Images are to be used during the services. They are brought upon the roof; incense is burnt

---

[1]) *Tam-šil iṣṣuru šuātu.* The meaning of the words in uncertain.

[2]) The *bārū*-sacrifice for instance; cf. Beitr. I—XX.

[3]) Ibid. LIII.

[4]) I have supplied this verb, which has been lost in the original, to suit the context.

[5]) Beitr. LIII.

and a libation of sesame-wine poured out. Then the images are washed in holy water. This last act is probably only to make them ritually clean and fit for use in the services.

It seems that the sacrifice to images, if sacrifice it might be called, consisted merely of incense and libation. Just what its purpose was; whether it partook of the nature of a sin-offering, and if so, how far, can not be determined from these few texts. That it formed part of the *āšipu*-ritual is certain. More can not be said.

We have thus considered the sin-offering and found it peculiar in many respects. To sum up: It is offered usually to the triad of the *āšipu*-cult, Ea, Šamaš and Marduk, although it can be offered to any one of them alone. In fact, when offered to the three together, there are really complete sacrifices for each, on three separate altars. If any distinction can be made among them, it is in favor of Šamaš. However, at best, the difference in importance is slight. The sin-offering may however be offered to some other gods, as well as to the triad. It may be offered in precisely the same form as to the triad, to Azag-šud and Ninaḫakuddu. It may also be offered, but in a modified form, to Ištar. It may also apparently be offered to Nĕrgal and Adad [1]).

The sacrifice itself consisted of five elements; (1) the lamb, (2) the libation, (3) the incense, (4) dates and A-TER-meal, (5) the mixture of honey and butter. Other substances, such as *upuntu*, could be added to suit the occasion. Not all the lamb, but, just as in the other sacrifices, only the three kinds of meat are given to the god. What is done with the rest of the animal is not known [2]). The libation consists either

[1]) That Adad was not closely connected with the *āšipu*-ritual, is clear from the few references made to him. It is therefore surprising to find him sharing in the sin-offering. This can be explained only that, as the result of his close connection with Šamaš in the *bārū*-cult, he came to be associated with Šamaš in the *āšipu*-cult also. This theory would be born out by Beitr. LIX, 6. But is this an *āšipu*-text? There seems very little to prove it. Cf. also below.

[2]) Cf. *Maqlū* VIII, 90 (above, p. 56), where after completing the ceremonies, the priest gives the food to the dogs. Was this perhaps a general practice? Or did the priest eat the rest of the lamb? Cf. also above, p. 70 note 1.

of sesame-wine, or of fermented wine, sweet-wine, honey, milk and oil. The incense consists of cypress-wood, to which *upuntu* or other kinds of grain, wood, reeds or thorns, may be added. The dates and A-TER-meal, and the mixture of honey and butter, are always offered together, usually the former preceding. The real expiatory force of the sin-offering to the triad lies in the lamb, while in that to Ištar, it lies apparently in the bread. In both sin-offerings, any of the other elements may be omitted. However the lamb, or the bread, alone hardly suffice for a sin-offering.

Before concluding this chapter, we must discuss two other kinds of sacrifice, in no wise related to the sin-offering, yet, like it, an important part of the *āšipu*-ritual, viz. the sacrifices to the dead and to the evil spirits.

The technical term for the sacrifice to the dead was *kispu*; the verb *kasāpu*. As Jensen has shown [1]), the original meaning of the expression was, "to leave the remains of food for the dead." *Ūm kispi* was equivalent to *ūm nubatti* [2]). K. 602 [3]) shows that the *nubattu* was a part of the NAM-BUR-BI-services, and was conducted by the *mašmašu*. In *Maqlū* II 157—8 and VII 18—19, Marduk is called the *bēl nubatti* and *bēl āšipūti* [4]). From this there seems to be a close connection between

---

[1]) K. B. VI, I, 446.

[2]) I accept Jensen's reading for the usual *nu*-BAT-*ti*.

[3]) Harper's Letters, 23. *Nubattu*-services for Arad-Ea, who had probably died, are here referred to.

[4]) Two different ideograms are used for the god here. As AMAR-UD (i. e. "son of light", cf. K. B. VI, I, 562) he is *bēl nubatti*, and as SILIG-MULU-SÀR, he is *bēl āšipūti*. It is noteworthy that in Beitr. XLIX, 11, where a *kispu* is offered before (to?) Ea, Šamaš and Marduk, the ideogram for the latter is AMAR-UD. In the sin-offering, the ideogram invariably used for Marduk is SILIG-MULU-SAR, unless there be a reason for using AMAR-UD. No other ideogram is used for Marduk in the sin-offering itself. Outside of the above passage, AMAR-UD occurs in only three places; in Beitr. XXXI—XXXVII St. II, 10, where Marduk, in common with eight other deities, and with no especial reference to his functions as god of the *āšipu*-services, partakes of a daily-offering (cf. below, p. 124); ibid. XXVI Col. V, 78, where the name occurs, not in a sacrifice, but in a *šiptu*, and ibid. XLI—XLII St. I, 6, where a sin-offering is sacrificed to Marduk alone (cf. above, p. 108). These are all exceptional cases, and

the *āšipu*-service and the *nubattu* and *kispu*. This belief is strengthened by the fact that *kispu's* were offered before, and apparently to, Ea, Šamaš and Marduk, the triad of the *āšipu*-ritual, and also before the Anunnaki[1]), the guardians of the water of life in the underworld. That in this last passage the *kipsu* was offered directly to the gods, is proved by the language used[2]). And although the language used for the *kispu* before the driad is different[3]), there need be no doubt that it was offered to them too. Again we find a *kispu* offered to the family ghosts[4]), in connection with a sin-offering for a man about to die[5]). The question now is, what was the purpose of the *kispu?*

The purpose of the sacrifice to the ghosts is clear from the following passage[6]):

Until thou departest from the body of the man, the son of his god,

> Thou shalt have no food to eat;
> Thou shalt have no water to drink;
> Thou shalt not stretch forth thy hand
> Unto [the table] of father, Bēl, thy creator.
> Neither with sea-[water], nor with sweet water,
> Nor with bad water, nor with Tigris-water,
> Nor with Euphrates-[water], nor with spring-water,
> [Nor with river-water] shalt thou be covered (?).

From this we see that the ghosts required food and drink, and also to be covered (?) with water[7]). And if they did not

---

Beitr. XLIX, 11 must also be so regarded. Wherein then lies the exception to the usual rule, if not that, because of his connection with the *kispu*, which is in turn related to the *nubattu*, the ideogram for Marduk as lord of the latter, viz. AMAR-UD, is used?

[1]) Beitr. XXVI Col. IV, 43; cf. LXVI rev. 7.

[2]) *Kispa ana il Anunnaki takassip*; cf. LII, 14.

[3]) *Kispa takassipšunūti*; cf. Zimmern's note.

[4]) Beitr. LII, 14.

[5]) Cf. above, p. 107.

[6]) U. L. IV Col. V, 55—56; cf. V Col. II, 54—61, III, 37—38; Cun. Texts XVII pl. 37, 8/9.

[7]) Cf. U. L. IV Col. V, 9/10. To the evil spirits belongs,
ekimmu ša kasap (sip?) kispi lā īšū.
The ghost who has no one to offer a *kispu*.

refrain from attacking the sick man, the priest threatened to withold the sacrifice from them.

But what could have been the purpose of a *kispu* offered to just those gods, most closely connected with the *āšipu*-ritual? That it is a *kispu*, points to a connection with the dead; that it is offered to these gods, points to the use of *āšipu*-service by them, in behalf of the dead. This can indicate nothing less than the belief in resurrection. At some time, not necessarily in the immediate future, Ea, Šamaš, Marduk, and the Anunnaki, by virtue of their innate, divine power, are to restore the dead to life[1]). It is significant too that the twenty-eighth and twenty-ninth days of the month were *nubattu*-days for Sin and Nērgal[2]). These two gods spend part of their time among the dead[3]), and are then restored to their place in heaven. The third of Ab was also the *nubattu*-day of Marduk[4]). We must remember that Marduk was originally the deification of the spring-sun[5]). It is just about Ab[6]) that this gives way to the burning, mid-summer sun. Just like that of Sin then, the *ūm nubatti* of Marduk was the day of his disappearance. The twenty-eighth of Ellul was the day of the disappearance of Nērgal, his *ūm nubatti*. These days were the days of the deaths of different gods, all of whom were later restored to life.

We have then here two kinds of *kispu*'s, one to the gods and one to the family ghosts. Possibly no distinction can be

---

[1]) It is interesting to compare with this idea the *šiptu* recited to the triad after the *kispu* is offered them. It is significant in the first place that a *šiptu* was seldom recited to the triad together. This one begins:

Ea, Šamaš and Marduk, you gods . . .,
Judges of what is above and below;
To restore the dead to life, to free the imprisoned, is yours.

[2]) Cf. K. B. VI, I, 446 and H. W. B. 446 a.

[3]) We have no reference to Sin ever being in the underworld, but that during the three days that he is not visible, he was regarded as among the dead, is shown by U. L. XVI, where it is the evil spirits that cause him to disappear. And it is by Marduk, the lord of the *nubattu*- as well as of the *āšipu*-service, that these are overpowered.

[4]) V R. IX, 11; cf. *Šurpu* VIII, 25.

[5]) But cf. K. B. VI, I, 562.

[6]) About the middle of July.

made between them in form, but certainly there was a difference in purpose.

Turning now to the sacrifice to the evil spirits proper, we see that its purpose was similar to that to the ghosts. One passage reads[1]):

> Thy food is the food of ghosts,
> Thy drink is the drink of ghosts.

Sacrifices were offered to the evil spirits but seldom. They were usually exorcised in other ways. But at times certain peculiar sacrifices were given them, to propitiate them as it were, and thus bribe them to leave the sick man's body. Thus we read[2]) of a sacrifice to the *labartu* consisting of twelve loaves of bread, made of a certain, unknown kind of flour, a libation of spring-water, a black dog, a swine's heart and certain fruits, oil and other food. The text is here broken off. Again[3]) the same kind of fruit is given her[4]); water and fermented wine are poured out as a libation, a young swine is slaughtered, and its heart put in the mouth of her image. Whether these may be regarded as real sacrifices, is not certain, yet there seems no reason to doubt it. It is entirely different from any sacrifice offered to the gods, and is probably a typical sacrifice to the evil spirits. The noteworthy part about it is that the animals sacrificed were unclean[5]).

---

[1]) U. L. tablet, A, Col. IV, 17—20.

[2]) IV R. 56 Col. I, 22—27; cf. 55 No. 1 rev. 20—24.

[3]) IV R. 56 Col. IV, 5—8.

[4]) Myhrman reads *akalē*, "bread", but says in a note that the sign is partly erased, and that *mē* is possible. Because it forms part of a libation, it seems better to read *mē*.

[5]) It is not certain whether the Babylonians regarded the swine as unclean, or not. That it is here associated with a black dog, would seem to indicate the affirmative. But it was the sacred animal of Ninib and Gula. And in Cr. II pl. 5, 4—5, a swine is sacrificed to Šamaš. Whether the recipient of the swine sacrificed in Cun. Texts. XVII, 6, 10ff. (cf. above, p. 72) was a god or one of the evil spirits, is not certain. That the swine and dog were especially sacred to the evil spirits, is clear from the so-called "Hades Relief", where Ereškigal holds a sucking swine and dog on her breast. In Cun. Texts XVII, 1, 40 and 2, 14, a young swine is offered to the *asakku*. For a detailed investigation of this matter cf. Relig. Sem. 290—4 and 449. Cf. also above, p. 71 note 5, and "Devils and Evil Spirits", II p. XLVII.

We have thus treated of all the sacrifices peculiar to the *āšipu*-service. It is now necessary to analyse some of the more important ceremonies, in order to gain a deeper insight into the principles underlying these services, their application and internal relations.

Chap. VII.

Analyses.

In analysing the most important of the ceremonies already published, it is out of the question to present a complete picture of the *āšipu*-ritual, since every text reveals so many new features. It will therefore suffice to illustrate by these analyses the most general features of the ritual, the use of the sin-offering and the *šiptu*, of water, medicinal plants and other objects, of fire and other means of purification, and to give a general idea of the nature of symbolic ceremonies. For this purpose it will be best to begin with simple ceremonies and advance to the more complex.

Beitr. XLVI—XLVII describes a ceremony attendant upon the cutting of wood from which to make images used against evil spirits. No impurity of any kind might come upon the wood. Consequently the tools to be used had first to be purified. To suit the solemn occasion these were made of gold and silver. They were purified by means of the censer, the torch and the bowl of holy water[1]). This was a very common method of purification. Sometimes the censer and the torch were used alone. Just how this ceremony was conducted is not certain, but probably smoke from the censer and torch was allowed to come upon the object, which thereby became clean. Holy water from the holy-water-bowl[2]) was then sprinkled upon the object, thus rendering it doubly pure. The images were

[1]) Zimmern has a question-mark after the last.

[2]) The word for this vessel was *a(e)gubbū*. It was derived from the Sumerian A-GUB-BA, which meant "holy water" (*mū ellu*).

to be made of a branch of an *ēru*-tree[1]). Apparently the ground was swept clean in a circle twenty-eight cubits in diameter, around the tree[2]), and holy water sprinkled, just as was usually done before a sin-offering. This was to render the place ritually clean so that no impurity might come upon the sacrifice. The regular sin-offering[3]) was then brought. After this was completed, the priest approached the tree and recited a *šiptu* addressed to the *utukku*. This was to drive out the evil spirit, who may perhaps have resided in the tree. This accomplished, the last possibility of anything becoming unclean was removed, and so the real object of these ceremonies could be proceeded with. The priest touched the tree with the holy instruments and then cut it down. The ceremonies were now really completed. Therefore the holy water, which had been sprinkled, was brushed away, the sacrificial utensils removed, and the priest prostrated himself. The tree was then cut into pieces suitable for transportation and brought into the city. The priest then made from it images of various forms.

In this ceremony it will be noticed how apparently insignificant was the part the sin-offering played. The real purification consisted of the sprinkling of holy water, and the use of the censer and torch; i. e. purification by water and fire. The sin-offering seems merely to have accompanied these ceremonies, but was not in itself invested with especial purifying force.

We turn now to a text[4]), alas, quite fragmentary describing the purification of a house. The text begins with ceremonies following the making of images of Lugal-Ùra and Šitlamtaēa. These were brought to the house and set upon a pedestal facing the east. They were then purified with the bowl of holy water, the censer and the torch. As soon as the sun had set, the

---

[1]) Just what kind of a tree this was, is not known; it was however closely related to the cedar. Thompson ("Devils and Evil Spirits" I, 173, 13, 197, 40) translates it "tamarisk." However the commonly-accepted word for this was *bīnu*.

[2]) This is not certain; cf. Zimmern's notes.

[3]) Cf. above, pp. 103 ff.

[4]) Beitr. XLI—XLII.

house was cleaned[1]), and a sin-offering sacrificed to Marduk alone[2]). After this, the regular evening sacrifices[3]) consisting of merely a lamb, were offered to three separate groups of gods, respectively, Anu, Bēl, Ea, and another god whose name has been lost[4]), Azag-šud and Ninaḫakuddu, and the house-god, the house-goddess and the house-*šēdu*. Each of these received a lamb. Now came the real ceremony to which everything so far had been merely preparatory. Apparently the house had been in some way rendered unclean. Possibly a sick man had resided in it, and after he had been purified, it was necessary to clean the house[5]). This explains the use of images at the door. After the house was once cleaned and the evil spirits driven away, these were to prevent the latter's return[6]).

The ceremonies were as follows: the rooms of the house, the threshold, the court, the roof, the beams and the windows were touched with asphalt, gypsum, "mountain-oil", honey, butter, "good oil", a holy-water-bowl, seven censers and seven torches. After this the house was symbolically cleaned with seven *ḫulduppū's*, torches, LU-TI-LA's, young date-trees, URUDU-ŠA-DAN-GA's, *sugugallū's*, with a copper tambourine (?), a dark cloth,

---

[1]) This is Zimmern's suggestion, but, although probable, is not certain.

[2]) Cf. above, p. 108.

[3]) That this was the regular evening עלה, has become clear to me as the result of my investigation of the complete sacrificial system. Space and time however forbid me to discuss this subject here. I must therefore beg the reader's indulgence until opportunity offers to publish the results of these investigations.

[4]) Zimmern suggests the house-god, but since he is included in the third group, this is hardly probable. Nor is there anything in the text to warrant this assumption. We would rather expect here some god closely related to Anu, Bēl and Ea, cf. Beitr. XXXI—XXXVII St. II, 10 ff.

[5]) The house seems to have been already cleaned once (cf. above, note 1). However, if this reading be correct, it refers only to the cleaning preparatory to the sacrifice, and corresponds to the usual sweeping of the ground and sprinkling of holy water. We come now, however, to the thorough purification of the house, which is the purpose of these ceremonies.

[6]) Perhaps the images that were formerly there, had been removed, for, since the house had become unclean, these had lost their efficacy; the evil spirits had prevailed over them. Consequently new images had to be set up.

a whip, a QA-GAZ-vessel and different kinds of grains, and then the unclean things were carried out of the house [1]. Then a *šiptu* was recited, and the house again cleaned as at first, preparatory to a sacrifice [2]. The two images were again purified by means of the holy-water-bowl, the censer and the torch. A sin-offering was then sacrificed to Lugal-Ùra and Šitlamtaēa, the gods they represented, and then a series of *šiptu's* were recited before them and other images. The text then becomes very fragmentary.

In this text we see that the first sin-offering, that to Marduk alone, was merely preparatory to the regular evening sacrifice, while this in turn preceded the cleaning of the house. Really we have here a double ceremony of purification, the first part consisting of touching the unclean parts of the building with things, in which lay a power compelling the evil spirits to flee, and the second apparently consisting of touching the unclean parts of the building with things, into which evil spirits entered, and were thus carried away. Then followed another sin-offering, which seemingly, in connection with the *šiptu's*, was to purify for the last time the two images at the door and thus render them, not only free from, but efficacious against, the evil spirits.

We turn now to a ceremony, similar to the last part of the preceding, i. e. where an idol, after having been completed, was purified by various rites, in order that it might become

---

[1]) The verb used for this ceremony is *kuppuru* (cf. above p. 44). As the house had been already purified, this second purification must have been purely symbolic. The idea must have been that the various objects here mentioned were touched to the different parts of the house, so that any evil spirits that might still have been lurking there, in spite of the previous ceremonies, might pass into those objects. These thereby became unclean. That the word *takpirāti* can refer to nothing else but these objects, is clear from the context. It says, "the *takpirāti* shalt thou bring out of the door." And the only objects that could be brought out were these.

[2]) This and the first reference show that the cleaning of the place where the sacrifice was to be held, was an indispensable part of the sacrificial ceremony, for here, where the house had been already purified, the ceremony was still performed preparatory to the sin-offering.

thoroughly clean and holy, fit to represent the god. This seems to have formed part of a very large text[1]), a good part of which has been preserved and gives a fair insight into such a ceremony. The beginning, probably describing the making of the idol and accompanying ceremonies, is lost. What has been preserved begins apparently with a description of a necklace for the idol, made of all manner of precious stones, annointed (?)[2]) with different kinds of oil, strung on white, gray and blue wool, and put around the neck of the idol. Then follows a short ceremony, incomprehensible because of the condition of the text. During this a *šiptu* is repeated three times. The idol is then cleaned by the usual method of the censer, torch and holy-water-bowl. It is then washed all over with holy water. The ground is now swept and holy water sprinkled; incense of cedar- and cypress-wood burnt and a libation of sesame-wine made. A heap of meal is then poured upon the holy-water-bowl, and two *šiptu's* recited, each three times, before it. The usual preparations for a sin-offering are then proceeded with: a lamb sacrificed, incense of cypress-wood burnt, and a libation of sesame-wine poured out. The priest then raises his hands and recites a *šiptu* referring to the holy water of the Tigris three times before the holy-water-bowl. This completes the first part of the ceremony.

Here we see the great importance attached to the use of water in the *āšipu*-ritual. This entire ceremony centered about the water-bowl; and even the sin-offering was interrupted by a ceremony with this vessel. In addition to this interruption the sin-offering here is noteworthy for the fact that an additional offering of incense, consisting of both cypress- and cedar-wood, was made.

The meaning of the next lines is not quite clear. The priest apparently goes to a certain house, erects an altar and looks toward the river. Then in the house where the idol was made, the place[3]) is swept clean, and holy water sprinkled,

---

[1]) Beitr. XXXI—XXXVII.

[2]) The verb here is lost; Zimmern suggests *rakāsu*.

[3]) It seems better to read *ašra* here for KI, rather than the usual *qaqqara*, since this is inside the house.

preparatory to a sin-offering to Ea, Marduk and the god of the idol. Incense is burnt for each and a libation of sesame-wine poured out. Then follow the ceremonies of washing and opening the mouth [1]), applied to the idol. It is then purified again with the censer and the torch and washed in water from the holy-water-bowl. The priest then recites a prayer to that god three times, prostrates himself, takes hold of the idol's hands, shows (?)[2]) him a lamb, and then marches solemnly from the house where the idol was made, to the river-bank, by the light of torches, all the time repeating a certain *šiptu*. The text here for a few lines is again fragmentary. Apparently the idol is removed from the house to the river-bank, and the tools of the workmen, who made it, laid beside it. The idol is placed on a pedestal on the river-bank, and canopies are erected. A sin-offering is then sacrificed to Ea and Marduk. The text here is again fragmentary, and while there seems to have been some unusual features to this sacrifice, outside of the fact that it was offered only to Ea and Marduk, we can not learn what they were. The text then breaks off completely.

When it begins again, we read that the sacrifice that had been held before Ea shall be removed. Then the idol is placed on a pedestal among the canopies and tents [3]). The pedestal is covered with a linen cloth. The face of the idol is turned towards the east, while the utensils used in its service, as well as the tools of the workmen, are placed at its side. The priest then goes away[4]) and offers the evening sacrifice to two groups of nine gods each, respectively, Anu, Bēl, Ea, Sin, Šamaš, Adad, Marduk, Gula, and Nindaranna[5]), and Ṣîrtu[5]), Azag-šud, Ninaḫakuddu, Ninkurra[6]), Ninagal, Guškinbanda, Nini-

[1]) Cf. above. p. 54.

[2]) This translation is suggested by Zimmern as the most probable of several doubtful ones.

[3]) *Qân urigallû*; cf. above, p. 77f.

[4]) Cf. Zimmern's translation and note λ.

[5]) A form of Ištar.

[6]) This and the next four gods were forms of Ea, as god of the different handicrafts.

ginangargid, Ninzadim, and the god of the idol. The sacrifice consists of incense and a lamb, and is accompanied both times by the ceremonies of washing and opening the mouth. In the sacrifice to the first group a libation of sesame-wine is also poured out, while in the second the gods are called upon by name. The sacrifice to the first group of deities is offered in the direction of the evening-star, that to the second group in the direction of the gods of the night[1]).

Then, early in the morning, the priest places three thrones in the canopies of Ea, Šamas and Marduk. He spreads out something, the meaning of which is not clear[2]), and puts a linen cloth over it. Then follow the beginnings of what is apparently a sin-offering to the triad. Only a few lines are however preserved. In these we read that the libation consisted of fermented wine and milk and probably other liquids, the names of which have been lost, and also that *qānu ṭābu*, "good cane"[3]), was used. The text again breaks off here, and when it begins again, we read that the morning sacrifice, consisting of incense, a lamb and a libation of sesame-wine, is brought to the seven gods, Azag-šud, Ninaḫakuddu, Ninkurra, Ninagal, Guškinbanda, Niniginangargid and Ninzadim. The sacrifice is again accompanied by the ceremonies of washing and opening the mouth. The idol is then once more purified with the censer and torch, and again washed in water from the holy-water-bowl. The priest then goes away. Here the text breaks off again. Fragments of four lines are still preserved, but nothing is to be learned from them.

This text shows the necessity of purifying an idol before it could be ready for use. We see that the ceremonies were both long and complicated, and are in many respects still very obscure. The part played by the daily sacrifice, as well as the importance attached to the use of water, as a means of purification, are of especial interest.

---

[1]) The meaning of these two expressions is not clear.

[2]) Cf. Zimmern's note.

[3]) Damkina was called the "mistress of the pure cane": II R. 5, 57 c. d.

We treat now of a very peculiar ceremony, viz. that where a man lies on the point of death[1]). The dwelling[2]) is first purified and *upuntu* poured out, Then comes a short break in the text; then two incomplete lines, one of which is Sumerian of uncertain meaning. Images of a wizard and a witch are then made. Then comes another short break in the text. These images are then clad in a garment for every day[3]), and are anointed with "good oil". The place is then swept clean and holy water sprinkled. White stools are placed for a certain god, whose name has been lost. Cloths are spread over these, and an altar erected. Then follows a sin-offering to Šamaš, Ea and Marduk[4]). During this stools are placed at the left side of the sacrifice for the ghosts of the sick man's family. A *kispu* is offered and many presents given them[5]). Once more the text becomes fragmentary. Then a libation of water is[6]) poured out for them. The sin-offering is then concluded, and a *šiptu* recited. The remainder of the text is lost.

We now come to a very interesting, but complicated and difficult text[7]), the greater part of which has been preserved. It treats of the purification-ceremony for the king and his palace. Apparently the king has been sick. At any rate both he and the palace have become unclean, and must be purified.

The greater part of the first seventeen lines has been lost. From what remains we learn that the *mašmašu* recites a *šiptu* over the king. There are also some ceremonies around the king's bed, which lends weight to the theory that the king has been sick and these are ceremonies attendant upon his recovery[8]). When the lines become complete, the priest[9]) is

[1]) Beitr. LII., cf. above, p. 107.

[2]) Cf. Zimmern's note.

[3]) It is not clear what this is.

[4]) In the order named. The usual order is Ea, Šamaš and Marduk.

[5]) The nature of these presents is not clear. Probably they were similar to the things buried with the dead.

[6]) Zimmern has supplied this.

[7]) Beitr. XXVI.

[8]) Cf. the ceremonies at the purification of a leper and his house; Leviticus 14.

[9]) Notice in this text the difference between the priest, probably an *āšipu*, and the *mašmašu*, his assistant. The latter is always addressed in

directed to purify the king[1]) and bring the means of purification and the resulting uncleanliness[2]) out the door. Then purify the palace with the *ḫulduppū*, the torch, the LU-TI-LA, the URUDU-ŠA-DAN-GA, the *sugugallū* and certain seeds. The *mašmašu* shall anoint man and woman[3]) with a certain salve; shall mix honey and butter and anoint himself with it, and shall clad himself in dark-red[4]) garments. You shall erect seven altars in the court of the palace; put different kinds of bread, dates, A-TER-meal and different kinds of oil, flour, honey, butter, milk and a certain sweet drink upon it, and station seven censers and seven vessels of wine there. The remainder of this column is lost.

In col. II we read: a lamb shalt thou slaughter and with it purify the king[5]). Then follow precisely the same ceremonies as in col. I, agreeing word for word. From this we can complete the account of the above ceremony. After the seven vessels of wine have been put in place, do the same with seven vessels of fermented wine; strew cypress and a certain plant upon the censer for incense. This is the beginning of the real sacrifice. All before this has been preparatory. After the incense, pour out a libation of sesame-wine, sacrifice the lamb and bring near the three meats; make a libation of wine and fermented wine and pour out seven heaps of meal[6]). The

---

the third person, the priest always in the second. To emphasize this fact, I shall employ the same method. It is also important to notice the functions of the king in these ceremonies.

[1]) *Takpirāti ebbēti šarra tukappar.*

[2]) This is all included in *takpirāti*. It is difficult to give the exact meaning of this word in English. Cf. above, p. 44.

[3]) It is not known to what this refers

[4]) For this meaning of *sāmtu* cf. K. B. VI, I, 570.

[5]) Cf. above, p. 111.

[6]) Whether this is an actual part of the sin-offering or not, is not sure. Here it seems to be a part of it, since seven different heaps of meal are poured out, corresponding to the seven altars. But from Beitr. XLI—XLII St. I, 33, and XXXI—XXXVII St. I, 12, it is clear that independent purifying force was ascribed to the heap of meal. And while it has occured in several texts already discussed, just after the sin-offering, it has been invariably separated from this by other ceremonies. And although this is not absolute proof, it still seems to indicate that, in spite of the

mašmašu shall place himself behind the sacrifice but facing it, and recite a *šiptu*. He shall then sprinkle a mixture of honey and butter to the four winds, and then go out through the outer door[1]) and perform certain sacrificial ceremonies there. These ceremonies are too fragmentary to be understood or described. They conclude however in a *šiptu*, spoken by the *mašmašu*. The rest of this column is lost. This apparently concludes the first part of the ceremony.

We notice in the first place the magnitude of this ceremony. It differs in many respects from the usual simple sin-offering, being conducted on a far grander scale. This is no doubt to be attributed to the fact that it is a ceremony for the king[2]). The number seven plays an especially important role. There are seven altars, seven censers, seven vessels of each kind of wine and seven heaps of meal. And, as we have seen, there are two priests officiating. The sin-offering too is on a large scale. The libation consists of sweet and fermented wine, as well as the usual sesame-wine; is in fact two libations. To the usual incense of cypress-wood a certain plant is added. The meaning of the ceremony of scattering the mixture of honey and butter to the four winds is of course not clear. Although there is no mention of the usual dates and A-TER-meal, that they were nevertheless used, is clear from the reference to them at the beginning of the ceremonies. Or it may be that the sin-offering began with the erection of seven altars. As we have already seen, the preliminary purification-ceremonies were likewise very elaborate. Why this entire ceremony, including the sacrifice, was performed twice, is not clear.

In col. III, we learn of the part the king takes in the ceremonies. The first few lines are fragmentary, and therefore a complete description of these ceremonies can not be given. The king seems though to perform different sacrificial rites, such as pouring a libation of fermented wine, at the same time

above text, the pouring of the heap of meal while closely related to the sin-offering, was not actually a part of it. And even if it were a part of this, it would be that part that was most frequently omitted.

[1]) Cf. above, p. 68, note 6.

[2]) Cf. Leviticus 5, where various sin-offerings are prescribed for the different classes of people.

repeating different prayers, asking that his sins be removed, the results of his follies be taken away, and that he become pure. During one of the prayers he asks, "May the tablet of my sins be broken"[1]). This no doubt refers to an actual tablet, upon which the king's sins, real or imaginary, were inscribed, and which is now broken. After these ceremonies, which may perhaps have been closely connected with the previous sin-offering, the king washes himself, puts on a clean garment and then washes his hands. This is preparatory to the ceremonies now about to be held.

The *mašmašu* now goes out through the outer door of the palace, sacrifices a lamb[2]) there, and then performs certain purification-ceremonies, the nature of which is not clear[3]), but which are probably the last act in the ceremonies for cleaning the palace. He then goes into the field and builds a bath-house[4]), apparently in the names of Ea, Šamaš and Marduk. Thou shalt erect the king's tent[5]) in the bath-house and put *mandittu*-wood in it; erect a house for Azag-šud and Ninaḫa-kuddu; place fourteen[6]) bowls of holy water, and make preparations for three sacrifices. Then sacrifice three lambs. Here is a short break in the text. Then come directions for a sacrifice, consisting of incense and a libation of sesame-wine to the following deities: Anu and Anatu, Bēl and Bēlit, Ea and Damkina, Ninib and Gula, Sin and Ištar, Nabū and Tašmet, Nuzku, "The Seven", the Šibziana-star, and eight other deities whose names have been lost. Each of these sacrifices is accompanied by a *šiptu* in the name of the god to whom the sacrifice is

[1]) Col. III, 5; cf. *Šurpu* IV, 58.

[2]) *Uriṣu*! Note that in Col. II, 1, the king was purified with a lamb alone.

[3]) Cf. above, p. 63, note 15.

[4]) *Ramāqu* means "to wash oneself" (cf. above, p. 42, note 3), and of course, in these texts refers to the ritual washings. The ceremonies in the *bīt rimqi* were the final ceremonies for the purification of the king. As we have learned, after a purification-ceremony, the unclean things were removed to a "clean place" (cf. above, p. 60), usually a field. Possibly this is the reason for erecting the bath-house in the field.

[5]) *Qān urigállū*.

[6]) Cf. Zimmern's note.

offered. The simple nature of this sacrifice as well as the fact that in this long list of gods, the names of Šamaš and Marduk do not occur, show that this is in no wise a sin-offering. Its purpose is probably merely to propitiate the different gods and thereby render the various *šiptu's*, spoken in their names, effective.

Other services to Ea, Šamaš, Marduk and the king's protecting deity follow. They are, of course, purification-ceremonies, or rather preparations for such, but the text is here again too fragmentary to gain a clear insight into their nature. We can gather only a few facts here and there. We learn that NAM-BUR-BI-services[1]) are performed; that there are sacrifices to the Anunnaki and another god[2]); that in these sacrifices, honey, oil, butter, sesame-wine, water, bread and sweet-smelling cane are used in different ways. When these preparations are completed, the king waits until sunrise. Then he washes himself again, puts on a clean, sacrificial garment, and seats himself in the bath-house. The *mašmašu* shall light all the censers that have been made ready, and pour thorns upon them; then slaughter all the lambs and bring near the three meats of each. On the *ḫinṣa*-meat he shall sprinkle *upuntu* and cypress-wood, and then offer a libation of fermented wine, milk and sweet wine to Ea, Šamaš and Marduk; pour out a heap of meal, sprinkle holy water; offer a *kispu* to the Anunnaki, and sacrifice a lamb. Here again the text becomes too fragmentary to be discussed. We have here had a sin-offering of peculiar form.

Now follows a series of *šiptu's* apparently in connection with such objects as the *ḫulduppū* and the LU-TI-LA, and their attendant ceremonies. Then once more, just as at the beginning[3]), the priest is directed to purify the king, and then wash him in holy water. Then fill two BUR-ZI-GAL-SAR-vessels with water from the holy-water-bowl; put cedar- and cypress-wood in it and place two purifying-vessels[4]) in position. The king

[1]) Cf. below, pp. 137 ff.

[2]) Zimmern suggests Bēl.

[3]) Cf. above, p. 127.

[4]) *Mullilu*, equivalent to *gamlu*; cf. above, p. 41.

shall take one of these in each hand and wave them seven times in all four directions[1]). This is accompanied by other ceremonies, the nature of which can not be learned because of the fragmentary condition of the text. During the ceremony the king recites a prayer, apparently to Ea. Then comes another break in the text. When this becomes once more legible, we have a series of *šiptu*'s recited by the priest. The king then takes his place before the sacrifice that has been offered to Šamaš, while the priest recites an incantation to the triad[2]). This ceremony is repeated before the sacrifice to the king's personal god and goddess. The rest of this column is lost, while Col. VI is so fragmentary that nothing can be learned from it, other than that more *šiptu*'s were recited before the end of the ceremonies.

This text shows how long and complicated the purification-rites could be made to suit the occasion. The king was purified many times during the course of this ceremony; how many, the fragmentary condition of the text does not let us learn. In fact this forbids all but the most general conclusions. The significant fact about this ceremony is the prominent position occupied by the different sin-offerings. There were probably three of these, two identical, offered at the beginning of the services, and the other offered the next morning at sun-rise. These seem to be of equal importance with the use of water and the *šiptu*. In fact, all three methods of expiation play very important roles in this ceremony. But of the three, the sin-offering seems the most important. The *šiptu*'s are spoken, for the most part, in connection with its different ceremonies, while the use of water is also worked into the different ceremonies of the sin-offerings. Purification by fire (censer and torch) and by touching with different objects is also conspicuous.

---

[1]) Cf. תרומה and תנופה in the Bible.

[2]) Zimmern seems to think that the king recited the *šiptu*. But this was always recited by the priest, and just because of this was it efficacious. There is no reason to consider this passage an exception. This passage is also significant in showing the importance of Šamaš in the sin-offering. His altar occupied the place of honor between those of Ea and Marduk. And

We now turn to an entirely different kind of ceremony[1]), one that well illustrates the use of medicinal plants and other substances. It begins:

1. In order that the evil of sickness — — — — — — may not approach a man.

Do as follows: in the night sweep the roof clean; sprinkle holy water; place an altar before Marduk;

---

1. *Ana murṣi* DI-BAL-A ZI-TAR-RU-DA KA-DIB-BI-DA *dubbubu ana amēli ul ṭeḫē*

---

epuš annām ina mūši ūra tašabbit mū ellu tasallaḫ ana pān il Marduk GI-GAB *tukān* (*-an*)

pour out dates and A-TER-meal; offer a mixture of honey and butter;

place an *adagur*-vessel; pour out — — — grain; light a censer of cypress;

5. pour out sesame-wine, place blossoms of — — — wood, blossoms of — — — wood, blossoms of — — — wood

at the front of the preparations; draw over (it) a gorgeous robe; behind the preparations place GIŠ-SAR-plant;

sacrifice a lamb; offer up the flesh of the right side, *ḫinṣa* (?)-flesh, *šumē*-flesh;

take oil in a salve-box of *urkarinnu*-wood, and into that oil

put gypsum, gold, tamarisk-wood, *maštakal*-plant, EL-plant, cypress,

---

suluppu KU-A-TER *tasarraq* (*-aq*) *miris dišpi ḫemēti tašakkan* (-an)

karpat a-da-gur tukān (*-an*) *še-am na-aḫ-la tasarraq niknakka burāši tašakkan* (*-an*)

---

although the *šiptu* was recited to the triad, the king stood before the altar of Šamaš.

[1]) IV R. 57 (B. M. S. XII).

kurunna tanaqqē (*-qi*) *ana pān riksi arē* pl *iṣ* [sign] *árē* pl *iṣ* MA *arē* pl *iṣ* ŠID-MÀ-KAN-NA
tanaddē (*-di*) *ṣubātu ḫuššu ina eli tašaddad* (*-ad*) *arka riksi* šam GIŠ-SAR *tanaddē* (*-di*)
immēr niqē tanaqqē (*-qi*) *šīr imittu šīr ḫinṣa* (*?*) *šīr šumē tašakkan* (*-an*)[1]
šamnu ina iṣ napšašti iṣ urkarinnu taleqqē(*-qi*)*-ma ana libbi šamnu šu-a-tu*[2]
gaššu ḫurāṣu iṣ bīnu šam maštakal šam EL *burāšu*

NIM-wood, thorns, TAR-MUŠ-plant, ŠI-ŠI-plant, ŠI-MAN-plant, ARA-RAD;
place it at the side of the preparations; some AN-ḪUL-plants[3]), one piece of alabaster,
one piece of gold, one lapis-lazuli, one seal shalt thou bring (?)[4]); the alabaster, the gold,
the lapis-lazuli, the seal into[5]) the AN-ḪUL-plants in the — — — shalt thou — — —,
thou shalt put it at the side of the preparations in a BUR-ZI-GAL-vessel; the — — — of those AN-ḪUL-plants
shalt thou mix with oil of the *šurmīnu*-tree; in a salve-box of *urkarinnu*-wood shalt thou put it, beside the preparations;
take the hand of the sick man and recite the exorcism, "Marduk, [lord of the lands?]" three times.

---

[1]) Notice the use of *šakānu* here instead of the usual *ṭuḫḫū*; cf. above, p. 103, note 2.

[2]) Repeated in l. 11, probably because of the many words occurring between this phrase and the verb.

[3]) King considers AN-ḪUL-MEŠ an epithet for Marduk, as "the god of joys". That this is a mistake is clear from the following facts: in l. 13 different things are put into it; cf. also ll, 101, 103, 104 and 105. Ll. 101, 104 and 115 show that it must be the ideogram for a plant-name. In l. 67 it is written merely *šam* AN-ḪUL-LA pl. This is clearly the same as *šam* AN-ḪUL-LA in *Maqlū* VI, 84.

[4]) Cf. the expression *immēr niqē epēšu*. Is this similar?

[5]) For *birit* cf. K. B. VI, I. 508. *Ina birit* = *ina libbi* (?).

iṣ NIM iṣ *ušāgu* šam TAR-MUŠ šam ŠI-ŠI šam ŠI-MAN ARA-RAD
ana libbi šamni tanaddī (*-di*) *ina idi riksi tašakkan* (*-an*)
ša AN-ḪUL pl I *ša* aban *parūtu*
I *ša ḫurāṣu* I *ša* aban *uknū* I *ša* iṣ *kunukku tēpuš* (*-uš*)
aban *parūtu* aban *ḫurāṣu*
aban *uknū* aban *kunukku ina bi-rit* AN-ḪUL pl *ina GU-GAD tašakkak*(?)(*-ak*) *ina idi riksi ina* karpat BUR-ZI-GAL *tašakkan*(*-an*) *KU ša* AN-ḪUL pl *ša-šu-nu*
ina šaman iṣ *šurmīni tuballal ina* iṣ *napšašti* [iṣ *urkarinnu ina idi*] *riksi tašakkan* (*-an*)
qāt amēl *marṣi taṣabbit-ma šiptu* il *Marduk* [*bēl mātāte?*] *III-šu munnū-šu*

Now come the words of this exorcism. A part[1]) of this is as follows:

May the AN-ḪUL-plant, which has been placed on my neck, let no evil approach;
The evil curse, the impious mouth may it dash aside.
Like alabaster may my light shine forth; may I not suffer affliction;
Like lapis-lazuli may my life be precious before thee; may it establish mercy;
Like gold, O my god and my goddess, may I enjoy prosperity[2]);
In the mouth of men may I find favor[3]);
Like a seal may my evil deeds be removed;
May the curse, evil (and) not good, not approach nor oppress (me),
May my name and posterity be pleasing unto thee[4]);
May the plants and ointments, which have been placed before thee, tear away my evil;

---

[1]) Ll. 67—94.

[2]) Literally, "may prosperity be with me". *Šulmu* means here not only "good health", but also "exemption from evil".

[3]) Literally, "may I be for favor". Cf. לחן לחסד ולרחמים.

[4]) With *ina pāniki lišir*. cf. ישר בעינים.

May neither the rage nor the anger of a god bring near[1]) me
Wrong-doing, transgression (and) sin; from curse (and) evil
May the raising of my hands, the speaking of the name of the great gods free (me).

At thy mighty command may I approach; command thou life!
Like the heaven may I be clear from the enchantments that possess me,
Like the earth may I be free of witchcraft, not good;
Like the midst of heaven may I be pure; may the power of my evil deeds be removed;
May the tamarisk-wood purify me; the DIL-BAT-plant[2]) free me; the pith (?)[3]) of the palm-tree remove my sin;
May the censer and the torch of the fire-god and Azag [-šud] purify me;
By command of Ea, king of the deep, father of the gods, lord of wisdom[4]),
May the raising of my hand quiet thy heart, O Marduk, *mašmašu* of the great gods, *abkallu* of the Igigi[5]),
May the word of Ea be glorified, and the queen, Damkina, grant prosperity.

May I, thy servant, N. N. son of N. N., live, enjoy perfect health,
And may I revere thy divinity; may I bow in submission before thee.

---

[1]) With *qurrubu itti*, cf. "בוא ב and اتى ب (??).

[2]) A plant not mentioned in the directions, but from this reference we must infer that it too has been used in these services. It is purely medicinal, and occurs often in connection with ŠI-ŠI- and ŠI-MAN-plants.

[3]) *iṣ libbu giššimaru*.

[4]) Literally, "lord of the pure eye".

[5]) Notice the parallelism between *mašmaš ilāni rabûti* and *abkal il Igigi*; cf. above, p. 72, note 5.

O my god, let me revere thy power;
O my goddess, let me tell of thy greatness;
And may I, the *mašmašu*, bow in submission before thee.

During this *šiptu* the priest is commanded to raise his hands to Marduk[1]). Then follow other ceremonies, a part of which, owing to the condition of the text, can not be translated. Another *šiptu* is then spoken three times, and part of the sacrificial utensils removed[2]). The sick man now returns to his house without looking behind him. The priest then mixes AN-ḪUL-plants, in[3]) which are NI-GUL-LA-and UGU-GUL-LA-plants with oil of the *šurmīnu*-tree, puts this near the preparations that remain, and anoints his body. He does this three times and then takes up some of the AN-ḪUL-plants and places them, together with the stones mentioned in the first set of directions, upon the ḪAR[4]). He then speaks a *šiptu* over them, beginning, "Thou, O AN-ḪUL-plant, guardian of the salvation[5]) of Ea and Marduk". Then follow other directions: Concerning the AN-ḪUL-plants, thou shalt command that he put it on his neck[6]). Into the oil which has been put into the salve-box of *urkarinnu*-wood speak an awe-inspiring *šiptu* three times, meanwhile salving[7]) the sick man continually. Then bring the holy-water-bowl, the censer and the torch near to him. The text then concludes with the words:

ilu u-šal-la-ṭú mimma en-šu mimma limnu ul iṭeḫē-šu šum-šu ana damiqti (-ti) izzakar (-ár)

---

[1]) Cf. ll. 79—88.

[2]) Only those utensils used in the actual sin-offering are removed.

[3]) King reads *ištu*, but *ina* is better.

[4]) What this is, or how to be read, is not certain; perhaps *tērtu* (??).

[5]) The idea of *šulmu* here is probably "health-giving power"; therefore I have rendered it "salvation".

[6]) Cf. l. 67. These seem to be general directions for the treatment of the sick man, instead of directions for additional ceremonies after the sick man has gone away.

[7]) *Pušuš* must be read here instead of *dumum*, as King proposes.

The god will prevail[1]; nothing weak nor evil will approach him (the man);
His name will be spoken for good[2].

This text centered around the AN-ḪUL-plants. Not only did they play an important part in the ceremonies themselves, but the different *šiptu's* also were based directly upon the symbolic idea of these ceremonies. They are associated with a great number of objects, the use of which is purely symbolic. Even such plants as ŠI-ŠI, ŠI-MAN, TAR-MUŠ and DIL-BAT, which play a great role in medicine, have here seemingly only symbolic significance. The whole ceremony is directed to Marduk, and the sin-offering, which plays but a minor role, is to him alone.

Of great importance in the *āšipu*-ritual were the so-called NAM-BUR-BI-services. The reading of this ideogram is not certain, although *tapširtu*, proposed by Zimmern[3], is probable. That these ceremonies were of great importance is proved by the fact that a series, consisting of at least one hundred and

---

1) King reads *šamū-ú šal-la-tú* which offers no meaning; cf. B. M. S. LXII, 11 *mu-šal-li-tu qe-e lumni.* Meissner (Suppl. 95 b) renders this "who cuts the cord of evil", from a stem שלח. This can not however be the meaning here. It seems better to consider the verb here a form II, 1 from שלט.

2) King reads *tazakar.*

3) Beitr. p. 113 note v. BUR=*pašāru* (Brün. 344). NAM-BUR-BI could very well then = *tapširtu.* IV R. 17 rev. 14—17, seems to bear this out:

il Šamaš at-ta-ma mu-di-e rik-si-šu-nu
mu-ḫal-liq rag-gi mu-pa-aš-šir NAM-BUR-BI-e
idāte pl ittāte pl limnēti pl šunāti mašdāti pl lā ṭābāti pl
Thou, O, Šamaš, knowest their enchantments (litorally "their knots").
Overthrower of evil, remover by the NAM-BUR-BI-services of
Evil signs and visions, of dreams, oppressive, not good.

In this sentence if the reading *tapširtu* be correct, *puššuru tapširāti* would be a مفعول مطلق; cf. *kuppuru takpirāti* (Beitr. XXVI Col. II, 2). The only objection to this reading is that the phonetic complement, *e*, usually follows the ideogram, indicating a noun whose final vowel is long. Meissner (Suppl. p. 65 f.) reads the ideogram phonetically, *nambulbu*, which is certainly incorrect.

thirty-five tablets[1]), was devoted to them, and also from the numerous references to them throughout the Babylonian literature[2]).

That they were ceremonies for the removal of sin is clear from many passages. Thus we read[3]):

ma-a ar(?)-ni-šu a-na ili lip-ti ma-a
NAM-BUR-BI *li-pu-uš ma-a lū e-ti-iq*
Now let him confess his sin unto the god;
Let him perform NAM-BUR-BI-rites; may it (the sin) go away.

And again[4]):

ūmu VII-kan
ina libbi qân *urigallē*
ú-šab tak-pi-ra-a-ti
in-ni-pa-ša ni-eš-šu
tul-lu-šu ki-i ša amēl *marṣi*
in-ni-pa-aš

Rev.

ina VII ū-mi nīš qāti ili
ša ina pān ilāni pl *mu-ši-ti*
u NAM-BUR-BI *limutti kalama*
is-si-niš in-ni-pa-aš

---

[1]) Cr. I, 66—67 is the one hundred and thirty-fifth tablet of the series; K. 6313 (Cat. 778) is the ninth, and K. 6052 (Beitr. XLIII) the one hundred and twenty-second. K. 2587 (IV R. 60) also belongs to the series. Most of the tablets of this series have been lost, or at least can not be identified (cf. Cat V, 2054a). Zimmern suggests (Beitr. p. 152) that all texts beginning *šumma amēlu* and not dealing directly with omens, may have belonged to this series.

[2]) In addition to the above texts, and the passages cited in Meissner's Suppl. (p. 66), cf. 80—7—19, 36 (Harper's Letters, 470); K. 939a (Ibid. 46), rev. 15; 81—2—4, 49 (Ibid. 370); D. T. 98 (Ibid. 337); 83—1—18, 37 (Ibid. 355); 83—1—18, 38 (Ibid. 367); K. 6365 (Cat. 782); B. M. S. LXII, 12; Beitr. XI, rev. etc.

[3]) 83—1—18, 37 (Harper's Letters 355), left-hand edge. Cf. NAM-BUR-BI *limutti kalama* IV R. 60, 35 b, Beitr. XXVI Col. IV, 23; 81—2—4, 49 (Harper's Letters 370), rev. 3.

[4]) Ibid. obv. 10—rev.

VII ū-mi ša ina libbi *qān urigallē*
kam-mu-su-u-ni da-li-li-šu-nu
a-na ili-šu *il* *iš-tar-šu*
i-dal-lal a-ki-i
iṣ-ṣu-ri šarru iq-qab-bi
ma-a ú-ma-a ip-ša
ūmu VIII-kan ṭābu a-na e-pa-ši

Seven days[1])
in the tent[2])
shall he dwell; expiatory ceremonies
shall be performed; his prayer,
his ceremony, like that of a sick man
shall be made.

Rev.

During the seven days, prayer
which (is) before the gods of the night,
and the NAM-BUR-BI for all kinds of evil
shall be performed together.
During the seven days which (he passes) in the tent,
prostrate and submissive
to his god and goddess
shall he show himself[3]). Just as
the king now will command
shall it be performed.
The eighth day is favorable for performing (the ceremonies).

Again[4]) we read that weeds had grown up in the temple court and on its walls. NAM-BUR-BI-services were therefore held to remove them and purify the place.

And again[5]):

mi-i-nu ḫi-iṭ-ṭu NAM-BUR-BI-*šu e-pi-iš*
According to (?) the sin, is its NAM-BUR-BI performed.

---

[1]) Or, "the seventh day"? But cf. rev. 5.
[2]) Cf. above, 78, note 1.
[3]) Literally, "shall he be submissive".
[4]) 83—1—18, 38 (Harper's Letters. 367).
[5]) III R. 54, 36 c.

Furthermore NAM-BUR-BI were held to remove the evil effects of an eclipse of the moon[1]. They seem also to have often lasted a whole day. Thus[2]:

ina eli NAM-BUR-BI *limutti kalama*
šarru be-li iš-pur-an-ni
ma-a a-na ši-ia-a-ri
e-pu-uš ū-mu lā ṭābu
10. *ūmu XXV-kan nu-ša-aṣ-bat*
ūmu XXVI-kan ni-pa-aš
Concerning the NAM-BUR-BI for all kinds of evil, (with which) my lord, the king, commissioned me: "To-morrow
perform", the day is not good.
10. On the twenty-fifth day we will begin (?),
on the twenty-sixth we will perform (them).

They seem at times to have been of a rather terrifying nature, for the king is on one occasion charged not to be frightened[3]. On another occasion he was forbidden to speak while they were being performed[4]. IV R. 60 and Cr. I 66—67 show that the NAM-BUR-BI-services differed in no wise from other purification-services. In fact it seems highly probable that they were a particular, but commonly used, form of purification-services.

---

[1] 80—7—19, 36 (Harper's Letters 470) and B. M. S. LXII.
[2] K. 21 (Harper's Letters 51), obv. 6—11.
[3] Ibid. rev. 7: *šarru be-li lū lā i-pa-laḫ*.
[4] K. 939a (Ibid. 46):
ina ši-a-ri šārru a-na amēl ardi-šu lā i-qab-bi-i
ma-a amēl arda ša abi-ià lā ta-a-ta-a
lā ta-am-li-kan-ni lā tu-šaḫ-kim-an-ni
In the morning the king shall not speak to his servant;
The servant of my father shalt thou not see.
Thou shalt not advise me nor give me instructions.
Cf. also K. 21 (Harper's Letters 51), rev. 2.

Chap. VIII.

Recapitulation.

We have seen how various was the nature of the purification-ceremonies: sometimes consisting of but little more than a *šiptu* and sprinkling of holy water; at others lasting several days, and embracing almost all the different methods of removal of sin, many of these repeated several times. The nature of the ceremony seems to have depended partly upon the purpose for which it was employed. Thus ceremonies attendant upon the cleansing of an idol, in order to prepare it for use, differed greatly from those performed for a sick man. Again they seemed to vary somewhat according to the deity invoked. The sin-offering to Ištar differed from that to Ea, Šamaš and Marduk. And finally they seemed to vary according to the rank of the person for whom they were employed. We have noticed the magnitude of the ceremonies for the king.

The ceremonies could vary in different ways to suit the occasion. Either new methods of purification could be introduced and others dropped, or the old method could be repeated, or different parts of the ceremonies could be magnified, either by repetition or by the introduction of new features. Thus, a *šiptu* was very often recited three times[1]), while on great occasions seven complete sin-offerings might be sacrificed.

The actual purification-ceremonies were usually carried out at sunrise, although ceremonies at sunset were not uncommon[2]). In exceptional cases ceremonies could be performed at night. Thus the sin-offerings to Ištar were usually offered at that time, due, probably, to the conception of the goddess as the evening-star. When the ceremony was to be conducted on a large scale, it was customary to begin the preparations during the night[3]) or even on the day before[4]). Then a daily sacrifice

---

[1]) In IV R. 59 No. 1, 23 b. and Cr. II pl. V, 8, the *šiptu* is to be recited seven times daily.

[2]) IV R. 56, Col. II, 25, cf. *Maqlû* I, 3 and IV R. 55 No. 1 rev. 24.

[3]) Beitr. XXVI Col. IV, 33—35; L, 6—9.

[4]) Cf. above, p. 140.

at evening and morning could be offered to the great gods [1]). Whether this was customary however, the evidence is too meager to show. Sacrifices could also be offered to ghosts and evil spirits. Simple ceremonies, unattended by a sin-offering, were also often performed at night by the light of torches [2]), no doubt because this was the time when the evil spirits were most active. But most ceremonies, especially those where a sin-offering was employed, seem to have begun at sun-rise. This may have been due, partly to the fact that that was the time for the daily morning sacrifice, but even more so, to the supreme position occupied by Šamaš in the sin-offering.

This was always sacrificed towards the rising sun, and the priest faced the east at all times [3]). When images were used in the ceremonies at sun-rise, they too were placed with their faces towards the east, while in the ceremonies at sunset they faced the west [4]). This shows that the idea of *Qibleh* was well-defined in the Babylonian ritual, and was always, during the day, in the direction facing the sun. Was this perhaps due to the position of the sun-god in the sacrifices? We have also seen that sacrifices offered after sunset had a different *Qibleh*. Thus the evening sacrifice to Anu, Bēl, Ea and the other great gods was offered towards the evening star; that to Azag-šud, Ninaḫakuddu and their companion deities, toward "the gods of the night" [5]).

Purification-ceremonies could not be held at all times. Some days were unfavorable for them; some days more favorable than others. Then too, other facts might arise to prevent them. Thus we have seen that, because the day was unfavorable for his profession, no *mašmašu* could officiate in the NAM-BUR-BI-services, and these had to be carried out by an *āšipu*.

---

[1]) Beitr. XXXI—XXXVII Col. II, 19 ff.

[2]) Torches possessed, as we have seen, a certain power over the evil spirits.

[3]) Notice the exact directions in Beitr. XXVI Col. II, 21.

[4]) IV R. 55 No. 1, rev. 31; Beitr. XL, 7; IV R. 25 Col. II, 28; cf *Maqlū* IV, 111, and Cun. Texts XVII, 30, 38/39.

[5]) Cf. above, p. 125.

Ašipu-ceremonies could apparently be held at any place. This depended of course upon the purpose for which they were held. Thus, ceremonies for a sick man were usually held at his bed-side. A favorite place for holding these services was on a river-bank, the idea being that the flowing waters would carry away all impurity[1]); would bring the evil spirits back to their home in the *tiâmat*. Sin-offerings were also sacrificed on the river-bank, although they too could be offered almost anywhere, depending greatly upon the purpose of the ceremony. Thus, when a tree was to be cut, in order to make images from its wood, a sin-offering was held before it. Again, when the palace was to be purified, a sin-offering was held in the court, and other ceremonies performed at the outer gate. A favorite place for holding a sin-offering was on the roof of a house, the idea perhaps being that here nothing whatsoever intervened between the sacrifice and the gods to whom it was offered. This seems to have been especially customary with the sin-offerings to Ištar.

In cases where the purification-ceremonies were conducted on a large scale, it seems to have been not uncommon to erect an especial building for this purpose, the *bît rimqi*, the "house of ablution"[2]). This was probably a small, temporary shelter, erected by the *mašmašu* in some out-of-the-way place[3]), where there was no danger of other persons being contaminated by the evils purged from the sick man[4]). Here the gods, to whom these ceremonies were especially directed, were thought to be present[5]). Although not certain, there are indications that the usual ceremonies in the *bît rimqi* were those connected

---

[1]) Cf. II R. 51 b. 5—7; IV R. 59 No. 1, rev. 1/2; No. 2 rev. 13—17; and above p. 60.

[2]) Cf. Beitr. XXVI Col. III, 22 ff., IV, 36; V R. 51, 20/21, 48/49, 54/55 b.; A. S. K. T. XII, 13 ff.; *Šurpu* V, 36—39; K. 168 (Harper's Letters 437), obv. 18. The importance of the ceremonies in the *bît rimqi* may be inferred from the fact that there was a whole series of tablets, called by this name (cf. Cat. V, 2051 b).. Of this series, Beitr. XXVI was the first tablet and K. 3392 and K. 6028 formed part of the third. K. 155 also belonged to this series.

[3]) Beitr. XXVI Col. III, 22—23.

[4]) Cf. above, p. 60; also Numbers 12, 14; 19, 3, 7, 9.

[5]) Beitr. XXVI Col. III, 22 ff.; V R. 51, 20 b ff.

with the *qân urigallû*, the *niknakku*, the *gisillû* and similar objects[1]).

In the sin-offering itself, as we have seen, only lambs were used. Regarding their age or sex, we know nothing. Possibly there were no specifications in this matter. We have also seen how a person could be purified by a young lamb[2]) that had been slaughtered without its apparently at all partaking of the nature of a sin-offering. In this case it had probably a similar effect to that of the symbolic objects used in the services. Other animals, especially birds, were sometimes used in these services, but not as sacrifices. They were either to drive away evil spirits, or else to take the state of uncleanliness upon themselves[3]). Other animals, such as swine, could also be used for the latter purpose[4]). In the sacrifices to the evil spirits, the heart of a young swine, as well as a black dog, was often used.

The lamb was the most important part of the sin-offering to the triad, while bread occupied this position in that to Ištar. They were usually accompanied by a libation of either sesame-wine or sweet and fermented wines. To these last other liquids were often added. Incense, usually of cypress-wood, was also offered, as well as a grain-offering[5]) of dates and A-TER-meal, and a mixture of honey and butter. Some of these could at times be omitted, while other things could be added to suit the occasion. The order of sacrifice was immaterial. In fact the sin-offering could be interrupted by other ceremonies.

The most important part of the general purification-ceremony was the *šiptu*. This was invariably spoken by the priest, often however in the name of the sick man. The latter could

---

[1]) Beitr. XXVI Col. III, 22 ff.; A. S. K. T. XII, 13 ff. Cf. above p. 74 ff.

[2]) The distinction between *urîṣu* and *immêru* or *šu'u* is not clear. Perhaps it is one of age.

[3]) K. 626 (Harper's Letters. 24) obv. 12; U. L. tablet B. 64—67. Cf. Leviticus 14, 53 and Wellhausen: "Reste arabischen Heidentums" 2 nd ed., p. 171.

[4]) K. 626, obv. 12.

[5]) Corresponding to the Bibical מנחה ?

however recite a short prayer to the god, asking for help, but this was not a *šiptu*. Finally the sick man could recite a penitential psalm[1]), apparently unaccompanied by other ceremonies. Often the priest and the sick man would recite alternate portions of the psalm[2]).

The part that the layman took in the ceremonies was merely nominal. Apparently little more was expected of him, than to be present. And, as we have seen, he was not always present during the entire ceremony; he might go away after his presence was no longer needed. At times he was forbidden to look behind him while departing. Sometimes, however, the layman took a more important part in the ceremonies, as was the case in those for the king.

During the ceremonies the priest wore especial garments[3]), usually dark red or purple. If the ceremony was conducted on a large scale he changed these several times. There were also especial garments for the layman, but whether they were worn at all services can not be determined.

The purposes for which the *āšipu*-services were employed were various. They were used to clean the sick, to purify houses, idols and other things. In short, wherever the possibility existed that evil spirits, and therefore ritual uncleanliness and sin, might be present, these services were employed. Thus, when Nabopolassar rebuilt Etemenanki, the terrace-tower of Babylon, he first purified the place[4]):

i-na ši-bi-ir ašip-u-tim
ni-me-ki il Ē-a u il Marduk
pi-ša-ar-ša ul-li-lu-ma
By means of the *āšipu*-service,
the wisdom of Ea and Marduk,
its place he purified.

---

[1]) *Šegū*, cf. B. P. and IV R. 54 No. 2.

[2]) B. P. nos. 1, 3, 6, 7, 8.

[3]) Notice the expression, *kitū ša Eridi*, "the garment of Eridu", in which Ea, as *āšipu ša apsē*, is clad; V R. 51 b, 46/47; IV R. 18 No. 2, additions.

[4]) Meissner: M. V. A. G. 1904, 3, pp. 8/9, 10—12 b. cf. Bruce: A. J. S. L. XVI, 178 ff. No. 1 Col. II, 42—46. Cf. also Cun. texts, XVII pl. 39. 65 ff., where the temple and city are purified.

Finally the language employed in the *āšipu*-texts was very technical. In the *šiptu's* themselves this is not so noticeable as in the directions for ceremonies. Naturally the aim in these was to be as concise as possible.

This completes the study of the *āšipu*-ritual proper. However, as we have seen, it was necessary for all priests, no matter to what class they belonged, to make themselves ritually pure, before performing their holy duties. It remains now to learn the nature of these purification-ceremonies.

Chap. IX.

Purification-ceremonies in the Bārū-Ritual.

We have seen how, before a sin-offering was sacrificed, the place where it was to be offered was first swept clean and holy water sprinkled. This was, that no uncleanliness might come upon it. For the same reason, before beginning a ceremony, the *āšipu* had to bathe in holy water. It made no difference if, since he had last bathed, no uncleanliness had come upon him. He could not be sure of this. And if a layman took part in the services, he too had to first be purified. We have seen how, during the course of the ceremonies for the king, the latter bathed in holy water, not once, but several times.

The question naturally arises: if this was the case with the *āšipu*, was it not also so with all other priests as well? Did not they also have to be ritually pure? The answer is, as we expect, a decided affirmative. All priests had to be ritually clean, or else their worship received no response. Thus we read of the *bārū*-priest[1]): "On a favorable day shalt thou purify thyself and put on a clean garment". This was preparatory to the regular *bārū*-services. And again we read[2]): "When the *bārū's* signs are incomplete and obscure, he has approached (to perform his official duties) in an unclean state. When he speaks in the holy place, but receives no answer

---

[1]) Beitr. 1—XX, 29—30.

[2]) Beitr. C. 8—11.

from the god, then he shall perform the ceremonies of washing and opening the mouth, and shall wash himself in a bowl of holy water. After this he may perform the ceremonies"[1]). These passages show that the *bārū* had to be ritually pure before entering upon his holy duties; and if, by chance, his ceremonies remained unanswered, it signified that he was still in a state of impurity.

Luckily we have three texts[2]) in which the purification-ceremonies for the *bārū* are described. The first two of these are practically identical. The first reads as follows: "When the *bārū* is about to practice divination for the king, he shall, in the morning twilight, before sunrise, wash himself in the holy-water-bowl; shall put ŠI-ŠI-plant into sweet-smelling oil and anoint himself with this; shall then put on a clean garment and purify himself with tamarisk and TÚL-LAL-plant; shall gargle (?) with the sap (?) of cedar-wood, and shall chew (?) some grain. He shall then make a necklace of precious stones, strung on a blood red, woolen cord, and put it on his neck. He shall then purify the river-bank with fire and offer a sacrifice[3]). Then he will see visions[4]), and his decision will

---

[1]) This is a paraphrase, rather than a literal translation of the passage

[2]) Beitr. XI Rov. etc. LXXV—LXXVIII, 13—19 and LXXIX—LXXXI. St. I and II.

[3]) This can be nothing else than a sin-offering, because the text proceeds to say that, before the priest really begins to perform the *bārū*-ceremonies proper, he shall remove all these purifying preparations. Besides these seem to be purification-ceremonies for all classes of *bārū's*, and not merely those who practiced divination by observing the liver and entrails of slaughtered animals.

[4]) Zimmern seems to think that this sacrifice was for the purpose of divination. He translates: "He shall offer a sacrifice and prophesy". The text reads *niqā ukān birā ibarrēma ina dīnišu il Šamaš u il Adad kēniš izzazušu.* But the purification-services are not completed until l. 14. This line says that the priest (after performing the above-mentioned ceremonies) shall proceed to prophesy. Line 16, the last of this section of the text, contains the title of the passage: "Purification-services to observe the majesty of the *bārū*-cult, etc." This shows that this passage treats only of the purification-services preparatory to the *bārū*-services, and stops with the conclusion of these preparations. This agrees with our interpretation of the text. Ll. 10—11 are then to be translated 'He shall offer a sacrifice. He will see a vision and Šamaš and Adwill stand supportingly

be supported by Šamaš and Adad. He shall then remove all the purification-preparations and the sacrifice, shall take off the precious stones from his neck, and the grain that he has been chewing, he shall tread under foot, and stand upon it, and then proceed with the real *bārū*-ceremonies". The second text is the same as the first, except that instead of putting a necklace on his neck and offering a sacrifice, the *bārū*, after chewing grain, washes his mouth and hands. The text here becomes fragmentary, but seems to show that the bank of the river was purified just as above, and that the priest poured *upuntu* into the fire there. What other ceremonies accompanied these can not be learned. When these purification-services were completed, the priest proceeded to carry out the *bārū*-services proper.

These were purification-services for the *bārū* preparatory to prophesying for the king. They seem to have been conducted on a rather grand scale. When, however, the *bārū* was to prophesy for a man of minor rank, the purification-ceremonies were correspondingly simpler. Thus before prophesying for an *abkallu*[1]), he purifies himself with different plants, and again makes a necklace of precious stones, but apparently places it this time on the neck of the *abkallu*[2]), who is of course present. He then proceeds with the services proper.

We have also, in this text, directions for two other purification-ceremonies, the meaning of which is very obscure. The first[3]) of these is as follows: "When the *bārū* prophesies, he shall wash himself in the holy-water-bowl. The sinner[4]) shall

---

(literally, 'properly') by his decision". The idea was, that now that he had properly purified himself, his ceremonies would be answered. This agrees exactly with the idea of Beitr. C, 8—11, above.

[1]) Beitr. XI Rev. etc. 25—29.

[2]) This is Zimmern's rendering, based upon words he supplies in a break in the line. However, he does not state upon what grounds he bases this emendation. By analogy with the ceremony with the king we would expect the *bārū* to put the necklace upon his own neck. But since, as we shall see, the person consulting the *bārū* takes part in the purification-ceremonies, Zimmern's reading is highly probable.

[3]) Beitr. XI Rev. etc. 16—24.

[4]) *Bēl arni*.

put sap of cedar-wood upon his mouth and garments, and shall prostrate himself at the right side of the priest and pray: "O Šamaš, decide my cause". While (?) the *bārū* prophesies, the oppressor[1]) of the sinner leaves him. The *bārū* shall anoint his eyes with oil before the vessel used for prophesying, shall put (?) cedar-wood in a SU-KAK[2]), and put it on his neck; he shall put tamarisk-wood on his side[3]) and ears". Then apparently he offers a sacrifice, although this is not sure, and then repeats three times above the sinner the prayer, "Observe this sin," to Šamaš. He then prostrates himself. It is difficult to explain this ceremony; the only apparent solution being that a sinner, perhaps a sick man[4]), had consulted the *bārū* to learn whether he would be freed from his sin; whether his sickness would be removed. Whatever its real meaning, we learn from it that the person for whom the *bārū*-services were conducted, participated in the purification-ceremonies.

The other ceremony[5]) is even more obscure, due in great part to the fragmentary condition of the text. All we can learn from it is that it concerns a sick man who, as above, probably consulted the *bārū* to learn if he would recover. The bank of the river is purified with a fire of thorns in order, as it expressly states, that nothing evil might approach. The *bārū* seems to speak a *šiptu* in the name of Ea and Marduk[6]) over the sick man and thus purify him. He then performs the ceremonies of washing and opening the mouth, washes himself in the holy-water-bowl, and then apparently proceeds with the regular *bārū*-services.

We now turn to the last text[7]) in which we find prescriptions for the purification-rites of the *bārū*. This text too is rather fragmentary, but the following ceremonies are clear:

---

[1]) This must be an evil spirit.

[2]) Something apparently made of leather.

[3]) Or "back". Cf. K. B. VI, I, 464.

[4]) Cf. the next ceremony.

[5]) Beitr. XI Col. IV.

[6]) Here written *il* SILIG-MULU-SAR, as is usual in the *āšipu*-ritual.

[7]) Beitr. LXXIX—LXXXII St. I and II.

"When a *bārū*, of perfect bodily growth,[1]) is about to prophesy, he shall on a favorable day wash himself in the holy-water-bowl". Then comes a break in the text. Then he performs the ceremony of washing his mouth, and puts tamarisk and cedar-wood on his ears. Then comes another break. Then when "the step ceases"[2]), he shall sweep the ground clean and sprinkle holy water. Here the text breaks off again, but possibly at this time a sin-offering was sacrificed. When the text begins again, we find the *bārū* reciting *šiptu*'s in the names of Ea and Marduk[3]), and seemingly Ninaḫakuddu also, over the different utensils of the *bārū*-ritual, in order, as it expressly states, to free them from all uncleanliness. The *šiptu* is, as usual, recited three times into the vessel. He then uses different plants, woods and other objects, "so that no evil might approach". The text once more breaks off, and when it begins again the priest has entered upon the *bārū*-ritual proper.

One more text[4]) must now be discussed. This is clearly a regular sin-offering, consisting of the mixture of honey and butter, of dates and A-TER-meal, and of a lamb, of which the three meats are offered as usual. It seems to be directed against witches, but as it is a mere fragment, its real nature can not be determined. It seems to be offered to Ea, Šamaš, Marduk[5]) and Adad[6]). This last, as well as the fact that the obverse forms part of a *bārū*-text, proves that it is closely related to the *bārū*-ritual, but in just what way is not clear, and therefore no inferences can be drawn from it concerning the use of the sin-offering in the *bārū*-ritual.

These texts bring to light many interesting facts. They show in the first place the great importance attached to ritual cleanliness. Unless the priest was pure, his ceremonies

---

[1]) Cf. above, p. 2. This was the first requisite for the priesthood, which no purification-ceremonies could give.

[2]) = "at night" (?). Cf. Zimmern's note, and above, p. 110, note 1.

[3]) Again written *il* SILIG-MULU-SAR.

[4]) Beitr. XVI. Rev.

[5]) Again written *il* SILIG-MULU-SAR.

[6]) Cf. above, p. 114, note 1.

were unacceptable to the gods. These ceremonies were not different from the purification-services as we have learned them. The same plants and other objects were used as in the regular *āšipu*-services, while the use of fire and water was especially noteworthy in these services. Whether an actual sin-offering was sacrificed is not absolutely certain, yet in the first and last texts discussed it is extremely probable. These ceremonies too, just as those of the *āšipu*-ritual, varied according to the rank of the person for whom they were performed.

Whether the use of cedar-wood, which played such a prominent part in these services, was peculiar to them, or not, is impossible to tell. It seems very probable though, since in no *āšipu*-text as yet published was it used as here. However, each *āšipu*-text contains so many new features, that this practice too may any day be found in that ritual.

The most significant feature about these services, however, is that the *bārū* performed his own purification-ceremonies, unaided by an *āšipu* or *mašmašu*, and especially that the *šiptu* was not confined to the *āšipu*, but could be spoken by the *bārū* in connection with his own services as well. Does this perhaps indicate that originally all priests could exorcise evil spirits, and that only in course of time did this practice come to be peculiar to one special class?

Conclusion.

Such was the doctrine of sin and its removal in the Babylonian religion; both purely ritual matters, for sin meant merely ritual uncleanliness, and its removal was by means of ritualistic ceremonies.

And two great questions arise from these and other investigations of the Babylonian religion: the first: in how far are the Jewish and Christian religions related to it, either through direct influence, or because of race-resemblances and similar developments of religious thought? For no one, not blinded by belief in divine revelation, will deny that startling resemblances and a close relationship existed between the Babylonian religion on the one side, and the Jewish and Christian religions on the other. And this must be the task of the Assyriologist, to determine, scientifically and without prejudice, the true nature of this relationship.

And the second question, perhaps more important and far-reaching in its consequences than the first: how far have we advanced in our religious ideals, during the last twenty-five centuries, beyond the standard of the Babylonian religion? How much of what is generally regarded as fundamental to religion, when viewed in the light of this and other primitive religions, turns out to be merely superstition, the result of contact with an idolatrous faith? And, on the other hand, how much of the Babylonian religion is universal; constitutes religion now and throughout all time? This is a question for the theologian, the philosopher and the historian.

Both these questions can be finally answered only when our knowledge of the Babylonian religion shall have become complete. And this can be only when all religious texts are published and their contents thoroughly understood. However, a great amount of material lies already before us, and this is being constantly increased. Therefore it is possible even now to make investigations in this great subject, and thus gradually advance towards the desired goal. The author hopes that this work will prove one step in that direction.

General Index.

Abkallu, 72 note 5, 135 note 5, 148.
Adad, 95 note 3, 106, 114 note 1, 150.
Adagur-vessel, 104 ff. passim.
Adapa, 72 note 5, 89, 90, 94.
A(e)gubbū, 119 note 2, and passim.
Ahhazu, 16 f.
Altar, (GI-GAB), 103 ff. passim.
Alū, 11, **13** f.
Amulets, 80, **81** f.
Animal, 71 ff. Cf. also under Dog, Kid, Lamb, Swine.
Anu, 7, 10, 87, 94.
Anunnaki, 48, 49, 53, 72 note 5, **87** ff., 116, 130.
Apsū, 8, 31 f., 44 f., 48, 61, 88.
Ardat lilē, 16 ff.
Asakku, 16, **19** f.
Ašāpu, 32, 38 note 9.
Āšiptu, 33 note 2, 73 note 1.
Āšipu, **38** ff., 73, 126 note 9.
Āšipūtu, 33 note 2.
Ašru ellu, 60.
A-TER-meal, 104 ff.
Atonement, 63, note 15.
Azag-šud, 94, 109, 129.
Bābu kamū, 68 note 6, 1.
Balāṭu, 47 and note 1.
Bārū, 2 f., 95 note 3, 105 note 2, 113 note 3, 114 note 1, **146** ff.
Bēl. 7, 51 note 3, 84, 98.
Bīt rimqi, 129, note 4, 143 note 2.
Blood, 63 note 15, 71 f.
Bread, 107 ff. passim, 111 note 5, **112**.
Bulluṭu, 45.
Bunnū, 45.
Cedar-wood, 151.
Censer, 67, **103** note **2**, and passim, **119** ff. passim.
Class-distinctions, 53, 130, 146, 148.
Colophon. 56 note 3
Daily-offering, 121 note 3, **124** f.
Damkina, 7, 47, 84, 88, 90, 125 note 3.
Damqu, 45.
Dates, 130 ff. passim, **103** ff.
Damu, 86 note 5, 100.
Dinānu, 70 f.
Dog, 59, **118**, 144.
Dualism, 22.
Dummuqu, 45.
Dunānu, cf. *salam an dunānu*.
Ea. 7, 31, 47, 51 note 3, 71, 83 ff., 87 ff., 94, 149.
Ebbu, 45.
Eighteen benedictions, 52 note 5.
Ekimmu, 11, **12**, 78 note 2.
Ellu, 44.
Epēšu, 133 note 4.
Ereškigal, 7, 19, 51, 88 note 8.
iṣ Eru, 74 note 5.
Eššepū, 33 note 2.
Eššepūtu, 33 note 2.
Euphrates, 30, 88 note 8, **89** f., 116.
Evil Spirits, 3, **6** ff., 118, 149 note 3. Cf. under separate evil spirits.
Fire, 28 f., **64** ff., 131, 150.
Food of life, 53.
Future life, **47** ff.
Gallū, 11, **13**.
Gamlu, 41, 130 note 4.
Garments, 127, 129, 145, 146.
Genetive, 57 note 1, 103 note 3.
Ghosts, 8 ff., 12, 107 f., **115** ff.
Gibil, 29, 67, 72 note 5, **97** f.
Gilgameš, 98.
Gods of the night, 100, 125, 142.
Gods of water and light, 28 f., **64** f., **95** ff.
Good spirits, 20 ff., 100, Cf. under separate good spirits.
Gula, 52 note 5, 100.
Gumahhu, 78 note 2.
Holy objecs, **74** ff.
iṣ Hulduppū, 74 and note **5**, 121, 127, 130

ᶦˡ ID, 94.
Idlu lilē, 18, note 3.
Igigi, 72 note 5, 84.
'*Iltu*, 43.
Ilu ali, **24.**
Ilu amēli, **23** f.
Ilu biti, **24.**
Ilu limnu, **11** f.
Images, 40, **54** ff., 63 note 15, **65** ff., **69** ff., 74, **80** f., 99, 107, **112** ff., 121.
Incense, **103** ff. passim, 107 note 7, 109.
Išid šamē, 15 note 1.
Išippūtu, 33 note 2.
Ištar, 29, 50, **100, 109** ff.
ᶦˡ *Ištar ali*, **24.**
ᶦˡ *Ištar amēli*, **23** f.
Išum, 24, 29, 99 and note 7.
Jahwe, 52 note 5.
Kasāpu, 115 ff.
Kid, 72.
Kispu, **115** ff.
Kuppuru, 44, 123 note 1, 124 note 1.
Labartu, **15** f.
Labaṣu, **15** f.
Lamassu, **25** ff.
Lamb, 71, 74 note 5, **102** ff., passim, 127, 144.
Language of *āšipu*-texts. 146.
Latarak, 99.
Law of opposites, **73** f. Cf. also under Dualism.
Layman, 54 ff., 128 f., 145, 148.
Libation, 103 ff. passim, **104.**
Li'bu, 16, 19 note 1.
Lilītu, **16** ff.
Lilû, **16** ff.
Lugal-edinna, 99.
Lugal-Ûra, 98, 120.
Luḫḫušu, 63 note 15.
Lumnu ša zumri, 3 note 1.
LU-TI-LA, 77 and note **2,** 121, 127, 130.
Maḫar ᶦˡ *Šamaš*, 107 note 9.
Mamītu, 43.
Mammītum, 48, 53, 87.
Marduk, 30, 31, 46, 47, 51, 71, 83 ff., 90, 94 f., 115, 149.
Mašā'u 43 note 7.
MÀŠ-*gisillû*, 74 and note 5.
MÀŠ-*ḫulduppû*, 74 and note 5.
Mašmašu, **38** ff., 53, 67, 126 note 3.
Mašû, 38, 43.
Meats, 103 and note 3.
Minûtu, 109 note 3.
Mirsu, 103 note 1, 103 note 2.
Mīs pī, **54,** 124, **147** ff.
Mīs qātā, **54,** 59 f., 148.
Mīs zumri, **54,** 59f.
Mû, cf. under Water
mē balāṭi, 48, 53.
mû ellu, 44, 51 and passim.
mē limnūti, 32, 53.
mē mûti, 53.
mē ṭābūti, 31, 53, 47.
Muballiṭ mītu, 47, 52.
Mukīl rēš limutti, 14 note 4.
Mullilu, 41.
Muššipu, 41.
NAM-BUR-BI, 106, 112, 115, 130, **137** ff.
Names of gods, **35** ff., 83 ff.
Namru, 45.
Namtāru, 15, **19.**
Narudu, 91, 99.
Nērgal, 7, 19, 29, **98** f., 109, 167.
Ninaḫakuddu, **94,** 109, 125.
Nin-Âzu, 51.
Nin-girsu, 100.
Nin-giš-zida, 100.
Ninib, 52 note 5, 100.
Nīš, 35 f., 83.
nīš ili, 36.
Nubattu, 115 ff.
Nûḫ, 45.
NUN̂ (-NA), 87 ff.
Nuzku, 29, **97** ff.
Oil, 43, note 7, 53, **61** ff., 103 ff., passim, 126, 134.
Papsukal, 27.
Parsu, 46 note 3.
Pašāḫu, 45, 74 note 5.
Pašāšu, 43 note 7, 61.
Pašīšu, 42, 61.
pašīš-apsē, 43 note 7.
Penitential psalm, 1 note 2, 145.
Personal deities, **23** ff., 101.
Place of holding ceremonies, 60, 68, 103, 107 f., 125, 129, **143** f., 147.
Plants, **82,** 133 ff.
Plant of life, 53.
Priests, 2, 47 note 1, 59, 128, 144.
Prostration, 103, 106, 130.
Pûḫu, 70.
Qibleh, 120, 124, 125, **142.**
Quddušu, 44, 45.
Rabiṣu, **11** f., 13.
Rainbow, 88 note 8.
Ramāqu, 43, 129 note 4.
Ramqu, 42.

Resurrection, 52 note 5, **117**.
Riksu rakāsu, 106 note 3.
River, 60 f., 116, 143.
River-god, 94.
Rubū, **87** ff.
Šabātu, 43.
Sacrifice, 69 ff., 101 ff., 127, 147 ff.
Šaḫātu, 43.
Šakānu, 103 note 2, 133 note 1.
Sakū, 43 note 7.
Salāḫu, 43.
salaman dunānu, 70.
Šalāmu, 40 note 6, 45.
Saliva, 74 and note 1.
Šamaš, 30, 51 note 3, 69, **95** ff., 101, 107, 113, **114**, 131 note 2.
Sap of cedar-wood, 55, 63 note 15.
Šēdu, (good spirits), **25** ff., 80.
Šēdu, (evil spirit), **13** ff.
Šērtu, 3 note 2.
Seven, 11 note 2, 90, 128.
„Seven", the (gods), **91** ff., 99.
„Seven", the (evil spirits), **11** ff.
Šibziana, 100.
Sickness, 3, **5**, **21**, and passim.
Sickness (evil spirits), 18, **21**.
Šiddu šadādu, 105 note 2.
Šīmtu, 48, 51.
Sin, 1, 28, 66 note 12.
il Sin, 100, 117.
Sin-offering, **101** ff., 120, 122, note 2, 127 note 6, 131, 147 note 4.
Šiptu, 52 ff., 44, 46 notes 2 and 3, 47, 54, 59, 73 note 3, 80, 131, 141, 141, 151 f.
Siris, 66, 100.
Ṣirtu, 94.
Šitlamtaēa, 98, 120.
Smoke, 67, 119.
Substitution, **69** ff., 74 note 5.
Sugugallū, 78 note 2, 121, 127 f.
Šullumu, 45, 134 note 2, 136 note 5.
Šūlūm, 12 note 2.
Šumu našū, 35.
Šupuk šamē, 14 note 3.
Swine, 70 note 1, **71** f., 116.
Sympathetic magic, **65** f., **73** f.
Tablet, 129.
Takpirtu, 44, 127.
Tammā'u, 42 43, note 7.
Tammuz, 30.
Third commandment, 36.
Tiāmat, 32, 47 f., 53, 61.
Tigris, 30, 116, 123.
Time of ceremonies, 67, 80, 124, 131, **141** f., 147.
Ti'u, 16 note 2, 19 note 1.
Torch, 67, 73 note 4, **119** ff., 142 note 4.
Touching, 59, 63 note 15, **67** ff., 121, 131.
Triad of *āšipu*-ritual, **101**, 108 f., **112**, 126 note 4.
Ṭubbu, 45.
Ṭuḫḫū, 106 note 4, 133 note 1.
Ullulu, 45.
Uncleanliness, 2, 3, **5**.
Upuntu, 105, 109 note 8, 130, 148.
Ura, 99.
qān Urigallū, **77**, 124 note 3, 129 note 5, 138.
Urīṣu, 111, 129 note 2, 178 note 7.
URUDU-ŠA-DAN-GA, 77, 121, 127.
Uṣurtu, 43, 48 note 5.
Utukku, (evil spirits), 11, **12**, 120.
Utukku (good spirits), **26 note 6.**
Water, 28 ff., 30 f., 37, 43 note 7, 44, 47 f., 51, 53, 59 f., 102 ff., passim, 116.
Witches, **10** f., 65, 73 f.
Zakar šumi, 9 note 1.
Zakū, 45.
Zammāru, 102 note 1.
Zarāqu, 43.
Zuqqurūtu, 70.
מעעת, 25 note 2.
מנחה, 144 note 5.
תנן פה, 131 note 1.
תרן מה, 131 note 1.
ظرف, 56 note 3.

Index to Biblical Passages.

Genesis,	4, 7,	11 note 6.	
	7, 11,	88 " 8.	
	9, 12–16,	88 " 8.	
Exodus,	15, 23,	32 " 3.	
	20, 7,	36 " 3.	
	29, 22,	103 " 3.	
Leviticus,	1, 3—4,	104 " 9.	
	2, 2,	105 " 3.	
	4, 12,	60 " 5.	
	5,	111 " 2.	128 note 2.
	7, 25—26,	103 " 3.	
	9, 21,	103 " 3.	
	11, 31—40,	67 " 3.	
	11, 32–38,	67 " 5.	
	14,	126 " 8.	
	14, 4—7,	60 " 3.	
	14, 50,	60 " 7.	
	14, 53,	144 " 3.	
	15,	67 " 4.	
	21, 1—11,	67 " 3.	
	22, 1—16,	67 " 4.	
	24, 10ff.,	36 " 3.	
Numbers,	5. 17,	37 " 9.	44 note 11.
	5, 18,	32 " 3.	
	12, 14,	143 " 4.	
	19, 3. 7, 9,	143 " 4.	
	19, 11ff.,	67 " 3.	
	19, 24,	32 " 3.	
Deuteronomy,	21, 6,	59 " 6.	
I Samuel,	21, 6,	45 " 2.	
	28, 11ff.,	12 " 2.	
I Kings,	7, 23–26,	43 " 7.	

II Kings,	41, 34,	74 note 5.	
	4, 34—35,	68 „ 3.	
	5, 10,	31 „ 2.	44 note 10.
Jeremiah,	6, 29,	28 „ 3.	
	19, 13,	111 „ 5.	
	41, 12,	88 „ 6.	
	44, 15—19,	111 „ 5.	
Ezechiel,	16, 4,	38 „ 8.	
	27, 26,	88 „ 6.	
	47, 8—11,	47 „ 9.	
Amos,	7, 4,	88 „ 6.	
Malachi,	3, 2,	28 „ 3.	
Psalms,	1, 4,	58 note 1.	
	36, 7,	88 „ 8.	
Job.	8, 3—4,	1 „ 2.	
Matthew,	9, 2,	5 „ 4.	
Mark,	1, 31, 41,	68 „ 3.	
	2, 5,	5 „ 4.	
	3, 10,	68 „ 3.	
	5, 23, 28, 41,	68 „ 3.	
	7, 33,	74 „ 1.	
	8, 22, 25,	68 „ 3.	
	8, 23,	74 „ 1.	
	9, 27,	68 „ 3.	
Luke,	4, 40,	68 „ 3.	
	5, 13,	68 „ 3.	
	5, 20,	5 „ 4.	
	7, 14,	68 „ 3.	
	8, 54,	68 „ 3.	
	9, 13,	68 „ 6.	
John,	2, 6,	74 „ 1.	
	9, 2,	1 „ 2.	5 note 4.
	11, 24,	52 „ 5.	

RDER FROM YOUR FAVORITE BOOKSELLER OR CALL FOR OUR FREE CATALOG

bylonian Influence on the Bible and Popular liefs: A Comparative Study of Genesis I.2, by A. ythe Palmer. ISBN 1-58509-000-X • 124 pages • 6 • trade paper • $12.95

graphy of Satan: Exposing the Origins of the vil, by Kersey Graves. ISBN 1-885395-11-6 • 168 ges • 5 1/2 x 8 1/2 • trade paper • $13.95

e Malleus Maleficarum: The Notorious ndbook Once Used to Condemn and Punish Vitches", by Heinrich Kramer and James Sprenger. BN 1-58509-098-0 • 332 pages • 6 x 9 • trade paper 25.95

ux Ansata: An Indictment of the Roman tholic Church, by H. G. Wells. ISBN 1-58509-210- • 160 pages • 6 x 9 • trade paper • $14.95

nanuel Swedenborg: The Spiritual Columbus, by S.E. (William Spear). ISBN 1-58509-096-4 • 208 ges • 6 x 9 • trade paper • $17.95

ragons and Dragon Lore, by Ernest Ingersoll. BN 1-58509-021-2 • 228 pages • 6 x 9 • trade paper llustrated • $17.95

e Vision of God, by Nicholas of Cusa. ISBN 1-509-004-2 • 160 pages • 5 x 8 • trade paper • $13.95

e Historical Jesus and the Mythical Christ: eparating Fact From Fiction, by Gerald Massey. BN 1-58509-073-5 • 244 pages • 6 x 9 • trade paper 518.95

og and Magog: The Giants in Guildhall; Their eal and Legendary History, with an Account of ther Giants at Home and Abroad, by F.W. airholt. ISBN 1-58509-084-0 • 172 pages • 6 x 9 • ade paper • $16.95

he Origin and Evolution of Religion, by Albert hurchward. ISBN 1-58509-078-6 • 504 pages • 6 x 9 rade paper • $39.95

he Origin of Biblical Traditions, by Albert T. Clay. BN 1-58509-065-4 • 220 pages • 5 1/2 x 8 1/2 • trade aper • $17.95

ryan Sun Myths, by Sarah Elizabeth Titcomb, ntroduction by Charles Morris. ISBN 1-58509-069-7 192 pages • 6 x 9 • trade paper • $15.95

he Social Record of Christianity, by Joseph IcCabe. Includes ***The Lies and Fallacies of the ncyclopedia Britannica,*** ISBN 1-58509-215-0 • 04 pages • 6 x 9 • trade paper • $17.95

he History of the Christian Religion and Church During the First Three Centuries, by Dr. Augustus Neander. ISBN 1-58509-077-8 • 112 pages • 6 x 9 • rade paper • $12.95

Ancient Symbol Worship: Influence of the Phallic Idea in the Religions of Antiquity, by Hodder M. Westropp and C. Staniland Wake. ISBN 1-58509-048- • 120 pages • 6 x 9 • trade paper • illustrated • $12.95

The Gnosis: Or Ancient Wisdom in the Christian Scriptures, by William Kingsland. ISBN 1-58509-047-6 • 232 pages • 6 x 9 • trade paper • $18.95

The Evolution of the Idea of God: An Inquiry into the Origin of Religions, by Grant Allen. ISBN 1-58509-074-3 • 160 pages • 6 x 9 • trade paper • $14.95

Sun Lore of All Ages: A Survey of Solar Mythology, Folklore, Customs, Worship, Festivals, and Superstition, by William Tyler Olcott. ISBN 1-58509-044-1 • 316 pages • 6 x 9 • trade paper • $24.95

Nature Worship: An Account of Phallic Faiths and Practices Ancient and Modern, by the Author of Phallicism with an Introduction by Tedd St. Rain. ISBN 1-58509-049-2 • 112 pages • 6 x 9 • trade paper • illustrated • $12.95

Life and Religion, by Max Muller. ISBN 1-885395-10-8 • 237 pages • 5 1/2 x 8 1/2 • trade paper • $14.95

Jesus: God, Man, or Myth? An Examination of the Evidence, by Herbert Cutner. ISBN 1-58509-072-7 • 304 pages • 6 x 9 • trade paper • $23.95

Pagan and Christian Creeds: Their Origin and Meaning, by Edward Carpenter. ISBN 1-58509-024-7 • 316 pages • 5 1/2 x 8 1/2 • trade paper • $24.95

The Christ Myth: A Study, by Elizabeth Evans. ISBN 1-58509-037-9 • 136 pages • 6 x 9 • trade paper • $13.95

Popery: Foe of the Church and the Republic, by Joseph F. Van Dyke. ISBN 1-58509-058-1 • 336 pages • 6 x 9 • trade paper • illustrated • $25.95

Career of Religious Ideas, by Hudson Tuttle. ISBN 1-58509-066-2 • 172 pages • 5 x 8 • trade paper • $15.95

Buddhist Suttas: Major Scriptural Writings from Early Buddhism, by T.W. Rhys Davids. ISBN 1-58509-079-4 • 376 pages • 6 x 9 • trade paper • $27.95

Early Buddhism, by T. W. Rhys Davids. Includes ***Buddhist Ethics: The Way to Salvation?,*** by Paul Tice. ISBN 1-58509-076-X • 112 pages • 6 x 9 • trade paper • $12.95

The Fountain-Head of Religion: A Comparative Study of the Principal Religions of the World and a Manifestation of their Common Origin from the Vedas, by Ganga Prasad. ISBN 1-58509-054-9 • 276 pages • 6 x 9 • trade paper • $22.95

India: What Can It Teach Us?, by Max Muller. ISBN 1-58509-064-6 • 284 pages • 5 1/2 x 8 1/2 • trade paper • $22.95

Matrix of Power: How the World has Been Controlled by Powerful People Without Your Knowledge, by Jordan Maxwell. ISBN 1-58509-120-0 • 104 pages • 6 x 9 • trade paper • $12.95

Cyberculture Counterconspiracy: A Steamshovel Web Reader, Volume One, edited by Kenn Thomas. ISBN 1-58509-125-1 • 180 pages • 6 x 9 • trade paper • illustrated • $16.95

Cyberculture Counterconspiracy: A Steamshovel Web Reader, Volume Two, edited by Kenn Thomas. ISBN 1-58509-126-X • 132 pages • 6 x 9 • trade paper • illustrated • $13.95

Oklahoma City Bombing: The Suppressed Truth, by Jon Rappoport. ISBN 1-885395-22-1 • 112 pages • 5 1/2 x 8 1/2 • trade paper • $12.95

The Protocols of the Learned Elders of Zion, by Victor Marsden. ISBN 1-58509-015-8 • 312 pages • 6 x 9 • trade paper • $24.95

Secret Societies and Subversive Movements, by Nesta H. Webster. ISBN 1-58509-092-1 • 432 pages • 6 x 9 • trade paper • $29.95

The Secret Doctrine of the Rosicrucians, by Magus Incognito. ISBN 1-58509-091-3 • 256 pages • 6 x 9 • trade paper • $20.95

The Origin and Evolution of Freemasonry: Connected with the Origin and Evolution of the Human Race, by Albert Churchward. ISBN 1-58509-029-8 • 240 pages • 6 x 9 • trade paper • $18.95

The Lost Key: An Explanation and Application of Masonic Symbols, by Prentiss Tucker. ISBN 1-58509-050-6 • 192 pages • 6 x 9 • trade paper • illustrated • $15.95

The Character, Claims, and Practical Workings of Freemasonry, by Rev. C.G. Finney. ISBN 1-58509-094-8 • 288 pages • 6 x 9 • trade paper • $22.95

The Secret World Government or "The Hidden Hand": The Unrevealed in History, by Maj.-Gen., Count Cherep-Spiridovich. ISBN 1-58509-093-X • 270 pages • 6 x 9 • trade paper • $21.95

The Magus, Book One: A Complete System of Occult Philosophy, by Francis Barrett. ISBN 1-58509-031-X • 200 pages • 6 x 9 • trade paper • illustrated • $16.95

The Magus, Book Two: A Complete System of Occult Philosophy, by Francis Barrett. ISBN 1-58509-032-8 • 220 pages • 6 x 9 • trade paper • illustrated • $17.95

The Magus, Book One and Two: A Complete System of Occult Philosophy, by Francis Barrett. ISBN 1-58509-033-6 • 420 pages • 6 x 9 • trade paper • illustrated • $34.90

The Key of Solomon The King, by S. Liddell MacGregor Mathers. ISBN 1-58509-022-0 • 152 pages • 6 x 9 • trade paper • illustrated • $12.95

Magic and Mystery in Tibet, by Alexandra David-Neel. ISBN 1-58509-097-2 • 352 pages • 6 x 9 • trade paper • $26.95

The Comte de St. Germain, by I. Cooper Oakley. ISBN 1-58509-068-9 • 280 pages • 6 x 9 • trade paper • illustrated • $22.95

Alchemy Rediscovered and Restored, by A. Cockren. ISBN 1-58509-028-X • 156 pages • 5 1/2 x 8 1/2 • trade paper • $13.95

The 6th and 7th Books of Moses, with an Introduction by Paul Tice. ISBN 1-58509-045-X • 188 pages • 6 x 9 • trade paper • illustrated • $16.95

Of Heaven and Earth: Essays Presented at the First Sitchin Studies Day, edited by Zecharia Sitchin. ISBN 1-885395-17-5 • 164 pages • 5 1/2 x 8 1/2 • trade paper • illustrated • $14.95

God Games: What Do You Do Forever?, by Neil Freer. ISBN 1-885395-39-6 • 312 pages • 6 x 9 • trade paper • $19.95

Space Travelers and the Genesis of the Human Form: Evidence of Intelligent Contact in the Solar System, by Joan d'Arc. ISBN 1-58509-127-8 • 208 pages • 6 x 9 • trade paper • illustrated • $18.95

Humanity's Extraterrestrial Origins: ET Influences on Humankind's Biological and Cultural Evolution, by Dr. Arthur David Horn with Lynette Mallory-Horn. ISBN 3-931652-31-9 • 373 pages • 6 x 9 • trade paper • $17.00

Past Shock: The Origin of Religion and Its Impact on the Human Soul, by Jack Barranger. ISBN 1-885395-08-6 • 126 pages • 6 x 9 • trade paper • illustrated • $12.95

Flying Serpents and Dragons: The Story of Mankind's Reptilian Past, by R.A. Boulay. ISBN 1-885395-38-8 • 276 pages • 6 x 9 • trade paper • illustrated • $19.95

Triumph of the Human Spirit: The Greatest Achievements of the Human Soul and How Its Power Can Change Your Life, by Paul Tice. ISBN 1-885395-57-4 • 295 pages • 6 x 9 • trade paper • illustrated • $19.95

Mysteries Explored: The Search for Human Origins, UFOs, and Religious Beginnings, by Jack Barranger and Paul Tice. ISBN 1-58509-101-4 • 104 pages • 6 x 9 • trade paper • $12.95

Mushrooms and Mankind: The Impact of Mushrooms on Human Consciousness and Religion, by James Arthur. ISBN 1-58509-151-0 • 180 pages • 6 x 9 • trade paper • $16.95

Vril or Vital Magnetism, with an Introduction by Paul Tice. ISBN 1-58509-030-1 • 124 pages • 5 1/2 x 8 1/2 • trade paper • $12.95

The Odic Force: Letters on Od and Magnetism, by Karl von Reichenbach. ISBN 1-58509-001-8 • 192 pages • 6 x 9 • trade paper • $15.95

The New Revelation: The Coming of a New Spiritual Paradigm, by Arthur Conan Doyle. ISBN 1-58509-220-7 • 124 pages • 6 x 9 • trade paper • $12.95

The Astral World: Its Scenes, Dwellers, and Phenomena, by Swami Panchadasi. ISBN 1-58509-071-9 • 104 pages • 6 x 9 • trade paper • $11.95

Reason and Belief: The Impact of Scientific Discovery on Religious and Spiritual Faith, by Sir Oliver Lodge. ISBN 1-58509-226-6 • 180 pages • 6 x 9 • trade paper • $17.95

William Blake: A Biography, by Basil De Selincourt. ISBN 1-58509-225-8 • 384 pages • 6 x 9 • trade paper • $28.95

The Divine Pymander: And Other Writings of Hermes Trismegistus, translated by John D. Chambers. ISBN 1-58509-046-8 • 196 pages • 6 x 9 • trade paper • $16.95

Theosophy and The Secret Doctrine, by Harriet L. Henderson. Includes ***H.P. Blavatsky: An Outline of Her Life,*** by Herbert Whyte, ISBN 1-58509-075-1 • 132 pages • 6 x 9 • trade paper • $13.95

The Light of Egypt, Volume One: The Science of the Soul and the Stars, by Thomas H. Burgoyne. ISBN 1-58509-051-4 • 320 pages • 6 x 9 • trade paper • illustrated • $24.95

The Light of Egypt, Volume Two: The Science of the Soul and the Stars, by Thomas H. Burgoyne. ISBN 1-58509-052-2 • 224 pages • 6 x 9 • trade paper • illustrated • $17.95

The Jumping Frog and 18 Other Stories: 19 Unforgettable Mark Twain Stories, by Mark Twain. ISBN 1-58509-200-2 • 128 pages • 6 x 9 • trade paper • $12.95

The Devil's Dictionary: A Guidebook for Cynics, by Ambrose Bierce. ISBN 1-58509-016-6 • 144 pages • 6 x 9 • trade paper • $12.95

The Smoky God: Or The Voyage to the Inner World, by Willis George Emerson. ISBN 1-58509-067-0 • 184 pages • 6 x 9 • trade paper • illustrated • $15.95

A Short History of the World, by H.G. Wells. ISB 1-58509-211-8 • 320 pages • 6 x 9 • trade paper $24.95

The Voyages and Discoveries of the Companions Columbus, by Washington Irving. ISBN 1-58509-50 1 • 352 pages • 6 x 9 • hard cover • $39.95

History of Baalbek, by Michel Alouf. ISBN 1-5850 063-8 • 196 pages • 5 x 8 • trade paper • illustrated $15.95

Ancient Egyptian Masonry: The Building Craft, Sommers Clarke and R. Engelback. ISBN 1-5850 059-X • 350 pages • 6 x 9 • trade paper • illustrated $26.95

That Old Time Religion: The Story of Religio Foundations, by Jordan Maxwell and Paul Tice. ISB 1-58509-100-6 • 220 pages • 6 x 9 • trade paper $19.95

Jumpin' Jehovah: Exposing the Atrocities of th Old Testament God, by Paul Tice. ISBN 1-5850 102-2 • 104 pages • 6 x 9 • trade paper • $12.95

The Book of Enoch: A Work of Visionar Revelation and Prophecy, Revealing Divin Secrets and Fantastic Information about Creatio Salvation, Heaven and Hell, translated by R. Charles. ISBN 1-58509-019-0 • 152 pages • 5 1/2 x 1/2 • trade paper • $13.95

The Book of Enoch: Translated from the Editor Ethiopic Text and Edited with an Enlarge Introduction, Notes and Indexes, Together with Reprint of the Greek Fragments, edited by R. Charles. ISBN 1-58509-080-8 • 448 pages • 6 x 9 trade paper • $34.95

The Book of the Secrets of Enoch, translated fro the Slavonic by W. R. Morfill. Edited, wit Introduction and Notes by R. H. Charles. ISBN 1 58509-020-4 • 148 pages • 5 1/2 x 8 1/2 • trade paper $13.95

Enuma Elish: The Seven Tablets of Creation Volume One, by L. W. King. ISBN 1-58509-041-7 236 pages • 6 x 9 • trade paper • illustrated • $18.95

Enuma Elish: The Seven Tablets of Creation Volume Two, by L. W. King. ISBN 1-58509-042-5 260 pages • 6 x 9 • trade paper • illustrated • $19.95

Enuma Elish, Volumes One and Two: The Seve Tablets of Creation, by L. W. King. Two volume from above bound as one. ISBN 1-58509-043-3 • 49 pages • 6 x 9 • trade paper • illustrated • $38.90

The Archko Volume: Documents that Claim Proo to the Life, Death, and Resurrection of Christ, b Drs. McIntosh and Twyman. ISBN 1-58509-082-4 248 pages • 6 x 9 • trade paper • $20.95

The Lost Language of Symbolism: An Inquiry int the Origin of Certain Letters, Words, Names Fairy-Tales, Folklore, and Mythologies, by Harol Bayley. ISBN 1-58509-070-0 • 384 pages • 6 x 9 • trade paper • $27.95

The Book of Jasher: A Suppressed Book that wa Removed from the Bible, Referred to in Joshu and Second Samuel, translated by Albinus Alcui (800 AD). ISBN 1-58509-081-6 • 304 pages • 6 x 9 trade paper • $24.95

The Bible's Most Embarrassing Moments, with a Introduction by Paul Tice. ISBN 1-58509-025-5 • 172 pages • 5 x 8 • trade paper • $14.95

History of the Cross: The Pagan Origin and Idolatrous Adoption and Worship of the Image, by Henry Dana Ward. ISBN 1-58509-056-5 • 104 pages • 6 x 9 • trade paper • illustrated • $11.95

Was Jesus Influenced by Buddhism? A Comparative Study of the Lives and Thoughts o Gautama and Jesus, by Dwight Goddard. ISBN 1-58509-027-1 • 252 pages • 6 x 9 • trade paper • $19.95

History of the Christian Religion to the Year Two Hundred, by Charles B. Waite. ISBN 1-885395-15-9 • 556 pages. • 6 x 9 • hard cover • $25.00

Symbols, Sex, and the Stars, by Ernest Busenbark. ISBN 1-885395-19-1 • 396 pages • 5 1/2 x 8 1/2 • trade paper • $22.95

History of the First Council of Nice: A World's Christian Convention, A.D. 325, by Dean Dudley. ISBN 1-58509-023-9 • 132 pages • 5 1/2 x 8 1/2 • trade paper • $12.95

The World's Sixteen Crucified Saviors, by Kersey Graves. ISBN 1-58509-018-2 • 436 pages • 5 1/2 x 8 1/2 • trade paper • $29.95

www.ingramcontent.com/pod-product-compliance
Lightning Source LLC
Chambersburg PA
CBHW031847090426
42741CB00005B/389
9781585092048